Grant MacEwan's West

Other books by Grant MacEwan:

... and Mighty Women Too: Stories of Notable Western Canadian Women

Charles Noble: Guardian of the Soil

Colonel James Walker: Man of the Western Frontier

Fifty Mighty Men

Frederick Haultain: Frontier Statesman of the Canadian Northwest

He Left Them Laughing When He Said Good-bye: The Life and Times of Frontier Lawyer Paddy Nolan

John Ware's Cow Country

Marie Anne: The Frontier Spirit of Marie Anne Lagimodière

Memory Meadows: Horse Stories from Canada's Past

Métis Makers of History

Pat Burns: Cattle King

Grant MacEwan's West

Sketches from the Past

Grant MacEwan

Western Producer Prairie Books
Saskatoon, Saskatchewan

Western Producer Prairie Books
Saskatoon, Saskatchewan

Jacket design by John Luckhurst/GDL
Jacket Illustrations:

Background: Sketch by Henri Julien in *Canadian Illustrated News*, September 6, 1874. Public Archives of Canada, print courtesy Glenbow Institute-Alberta Archives (NA–361–18).
Inset, top: detail, sketch by Frederic Remington in *Harper's New Weekly*, March, 1892. Courtesy Glenbow Institute-Alberta Archives (NA–1406–55).
Inset, bottom left: detail, engraving in *Harper's Monthly*, August, 1860, 307. Courtesy Glenbow Institute-Alberta Archives (NA–1406–9).
Inset, bottom right: detail, engraving in *Harper's Monthly*, January, 1859, 175. Courtesy Glenbow Institute-Alberta Archives (NA–1406-28).

Printed and bound in Canada
96 95 94 93 92 91 90 89   8 7 6 5 4 3 2 1

The publisher acknowledges the support received for this publication from the Canada Council.

Western Producer Prairie Books is a unique publishing venture located in the middle of western Canada and owned by a group of prairie farmers who are members of the Saskatchewan Wheat Pool. From the first book in 1954, a reprint of a serial originally carried in the weekly newspaper *The Western Producer*, to the book before you now, the tradition of providing enjoyable and informative reading for all Canadians is continued.

Canadian Cataloguing in Publication Data

MacEwan, Grant, 1902–

Grant MacEwan's West

Includes bibliographical references.
ISBN 0–88833–320–X

1. Canada, Western – History. I. Title.

FC3206.M34 1990   971.2   C90–097011–1
F1060.M34 1990

To all Canadians who find their history
more fascinating than hockey.

Contents

Illustrations

All illustrations courtesy Glenbow Institute-Alberta Archives unless otherwise noted.

Preface

Western Canadian history was slow in capturing both academic and public attention until 1967, when Canadians were engaged in celebrating the centennial of Confederation. Almost at once they seemed to recognize, first, the supreme charm of their own story, and then the fact that their history—and all history, which is essentially a record of human experience—holds critical lessons and warnings.

The more one reads from the history of Babylon, Greece, Rome, and Egypt, the more he or she will be convinced that the people of ancient times can tell us something about the results of their prodigality and other errors. It is time that elected representatives in legislative halls took note of the high cost of ignoring the messages of history.

Canadian history—especially western Canadian history—was neglected too long. The new enthusiasm should be encouraged. Canada's history should prove to be a source of pleasure, inspiration, and guidance for the future. Popular interest will help to ensure that it will not fall into neglect.

In the preparation of this book, there was never any thought of designing it to serve the academics or historians, who would require—quite properly—more detail and more documentation. Moreover, the idea of tailoring a broad sweep of history to short and uniform chapters would not appeal to them. But a sampling of senior readers and that ever-growing number of busy citizens with an enthusiastic interest in Canadian history indicated strong support for a handy and convenient form of presentation. History is for everybody who desires it, and this book is presented with the hope that it will prove helpful, especially to busy people, young and old, in towns, cities, and farming communities, those for whom history can be a hobby, a pastime, a companion, or a serious study as useful as it is enjoyable.

Chapter 1

Exploration and the Fur Trade

Henry Hudson and the Mutiny on the Bay

Henry Hudson was the old English sea dog who gave his name to the Hudson River, Hudson Strait, Hudson Bay, Hudson House, and the Hudson's Bay Company, but before he could be honoured for his discoveries in Canada's northern reaches, he vanished in the mists of the subarctic unknown, never to be seen or heard from again. Although unsuccessful, his courageous and stubborn search for the mysterious Northwest Passage merits at least the distinction of being first among the explorers and pioneers presented here.

With agreement at last that the world was round rather than flat, all of Europe's trading countries were keenly interested in the possibility of finding shorter travelling distances to the rich markets of the Far East; they needed a watercourse connecting the Atlantic and Pacific oceans that would allow them to sail west to China instead of east by the old and longer route.

The early French explorers had hoped that by paddling west on the St. Lawrence they would come to a continental height of land and then to another river flowing to the Western Sea, or Pacific Ocean. Hudson, in 1608 and 1609, while sailing for the Dutch East India Company, tested another North American river flowing eastward to the Atlantic, the one that skirts the site on which the city of New York was to be built and that bears Hudson's name. The aging seaman sailed upstream as far as the river offered navigation. To his hopeful Dutch employers, he reported that his only success was in mapping another river route for possible use in the fur trade.

He returned to England, but soon proposed probing for a more northerly passage through the polar seas. He was no stranger to northern sailing, having traded previously between England and Russia's northern ports. Hudson received an offer of financial backing from the Muscovy Company. The good ship *Discovery* was fitted out for him, and he sailed away in April, 1610. Passing near the south end of Greenland, he entered what was later known as Hudson Strait, probably hugging the north shore of Labrador, then entering the Great Bay and sailing south along its Labrador side until reaching the south end of James Bay and dropping anchor at the mouth of the river later known as the Rupert. There, he and his men prepared to winter, and there they suffered in succeeding months from cold, hunger, and scurvy.

The winter passed, and with the approach of spring, Hudson divided the remaining food evenly between the men. But there was trouble ahead: The crewmen were anxious to be on their way back to England, while Hudson was just as determined to continue the search for the Northwest Passage. He was in command, and he ordered further exploration. Hostility grew. The men were more interested in going home than in finding the Northwest Passage. They mutinied. They seized the ship and placed the sixty-one-year-old Hudson, his son, John, the ship's carpenter, and six others who were still loyal to Hudson in a dinghy or rowboat. It was tied behind the big ship, which they turned toward London. Hudson and his friends were given another chance to change their minds, but they were adamant, and the crew's leader reached out and cut the towline to the rowboat, and they sailed away. Neither Hudson nor any of his little party was ever seen again.

For the mutineers, their first problem was in finding food. They stopped at Digges Island in the Bay, hoping to obtain meat from the Eskimos. But the natives attacked the Englishmen with bows and arrows. Many of the men were wounded, and some died. For the balance of the journey, the crew was reduced to eating sea gulls.

Back in England, the men were questioned about Hudson and the other missing crew members. Two of the mutineers, Abacuk Pricket and Robert Bylot, told the truth. Most of the others were convicted and jailed. Pricket and Bylot, truly repentant, volunteered to return to the Bay and search for Hudson. In consequence, an expedition under Captain Thomas Button with two ships, *Discovery* and *Resolution*, left Gravesend on the Thames in April, 1612, and followed the original Hudson course to the bottom of the Bay. No trace of Hudson and his friends was found, but Button, carrying out his instructions, pressed forward in search of the passage to China. They reached the mouth of the Nelson River—the first Europeans to see it—and prepared to winter there. In 1613, they returned to England without anything favourable to report, but their discovery of the Nelson River, the great drainage outlet of the prairies, was to prove far more important than they realized.

Jens Munck: "My Great Distress and Miserable Death"

Western Canadians have discovered—perhaps to their surprise—that most of their early history centres around the North, not the East.

The Great Bay of the North, Hudson Bay, offered a natural if not ideal approach to the fur country of Rupert's Land. Henry Hudson had penetrated as far as the mouth of the Rupert River, and Thomas Button had advanced to the mouth of the Nelson River, or Port Nelson, but the Northwest Passage was still shrouded in mystery. The challenge was as clear as ever.

The next exploratory thrust into Canada's polar waters was made under the leadership of Jens Munck of Denmark seven years after

Button's effort. Denmark was another ambitious trading nation keenly interested in finding the shorter shipping route to the Orient. Munck, with two ships, *Unicorn* and *Lamprey*, and a total combined crew of sixty-four, sailed away on the course tested by Hudson and Button, but he hoped to go much farther than they had. Instead of staying close to the east side of the Bay, Munck crossed in a southwesterly direction and came to the mouth of a big river with a huge harbour at its entrance that would someday be known as the Churchill.

Munck decided to winter in the harbour. The site of his choosing was an inlet known as Sloop's Cove on the west side of the harbour, a couple of miles from the future site of Fort Prince of Wales, which is still standing. Munck's men raised one of the ships to use as living quarters during the winter. It was better than nothing, but hardly adequate against the Arctic cold.

As A. S. Morton tells us in his monumental book, *A History of the Canadian West*, Munck had observed before leaving home that Hudson Strait was at the same line of latitude as the north side of Denmark and that thus winter weather in the region shouldn't be more severe than in parts of Denmark. On this point, Munck was in for a shock. The clothing he and his men brought was quite inadequate, and they suffered.

Worse than that, the winter rations they had brought with them offered no safeguard against deficiency diseases like scurvy. Had Indians been wintering nearby, they might have furnished lifesaving foods or instructed the Danes on where to find them; they would have advised a preventive or curative tea made from spruce needles. It would have been horrible to take, but it would have been effective in the fight against scurvy, and the lives of many brave Danes would have been saved.

Munck and his friends may have had some experience with scurvy in their travels, but they had no knowledge of Indian skills in preventing it. By the beginning of the new year of 1620, everybody in the camp was sick, and the death list was growing. By February 25, deaths had risen to twenty-two, and by May 28, only seven men remained alive. On June 4, only Munck and two others were left. Munck believed that he would be next. On that date he made an entry in his journal, pleading with any person coming that way to "bury my poor body" and forward "this my journal" to the King of Denmark "in order that my poor wife and children may obtain some benefit from my great distress and miserable death."

But Munck didn't die. When spring burst upon the North a short time later, the three men mustered enough strength to take some fresh fish and sprigs of green vegetation. The nutritional benefits were sufficient to produce a minor miracle, and the three men managed to raise one of the ships, the *Lamprey*, and get it afloat. Then, by themselves, they took the big ship home to Denmark. It seems unbelievable, but they did it.

Joy and sadness mingled at their arrival. Munck lived for eight more years and finally met his death in the course of active military service as a naval commander. His famous journal with the entries made at Sloop's Cove, within sight of today's terminal grain elevator and Fort Prince of Wales, found a place of highest honour in the national library in Copenhagen.

"True and Absolute Lordes and Proprietors": The Hudson's Bay Company

The Hudson's Bay Company's official date of birth was May 2, 1670—over 300 years ago. Its purpose was to trade in furs in Rupert's Land, the huge expanse of land from which drainage water flowed to Hudson Bay. The area, for which King Charles II conferred perpetual trading and territorial rights to the company, included all of today's Manitoba and Saskatchewan, most of southern and central Alberta, a corner of the Northwest Territories, portions of Ontario and Quebec, and parts of North Dakota and Minnesota.

The original name as set down in the charter was the "Company of Adventurers of England Tradeing into Hudsons Bay." The fancy name, however, was no more distinctive than the circumstances of its birth, which began with two Frenchmen, Médard Chouart des Groseilliers and Pierre-Esprit Radisson, both born in France, both immigrants to the St. Lawrence region. They were impulsive fellows and aggressive and must have tested the patience of both the English and French with whom they worked.

According to A. S. Morton, Radisson was the better man at self-promotion, but Groseilliers was the mastermind.[1] Radisson came to New France in 1651 at the age of fifteen and rather promptly became engaged in a war with the Mohawk Indians. He was taken prisoner, but, on his second attempt, managed to escape. When he returned to the St. Lawrence, he found that his sister had married during his absence. His new brother-in-law was Groseilliers, who was engaged in trading with the Huron Indians back near Lake Superior.

Radisson and his brother-in-law decided in 1661 to work together in the trade. When the French governor refused to give them permission to trade on their own account, they went without his permission. They loved adventure and remained away for more than a year. Nobody is sure how far they travelled, but it is thought that they saw the headwaters of the Mississippi River and Lake Winnipeg. Almost certainly, they then saw James Bay and camped where Henry Hudson had wintered almost exactly fifty years earlier. Although not the first to see the Bay, they were the first to reach it from the land side.

They were much impressed. The furs they acquired were the finest they had ever seen, and they sensed the possibility of loading furs on ocean-going vessels right there at the mouth of the Rupert River and shipping directly to France and other world markets. They were eager to get back to Trois-Rivières to display their furs, share their idea of shipping direct to world markets, and, they hoped, recover the governor's favour.

But their homecoming was disappointing; instead of being received as heroes, the two men were faced with seizure of their furs, arrest, and a fine for being absent without the governor's permission. The impetuous fellows were angry and took their appeal to the King of France. They expected the king to be enthusiastic about the proposed shipping plan; he was not, and the partners returned to New France in frustration. Their thoughts then turned to the English at Boston, and they travelled there. In Boston they met George Cartwright, who was a sort of envoy of the English King, and were immediately encouraged. Cartwright proposed that the Frenchmen go to London; he would accompany them and arrange a meeting with the king.

Cartwright's plan worked well. The king liked the idea of dealing in furs and sent the visitors to see his cousin, Prince Rupert, a robust entrepreneur. The prince called a meeting of leading Londoners to get their reaction, and from that meeting came a proposal to send a ship to the Bay for furs as an experiment. A single ship, the *Nonsuch*, would be fitted for the journey, but to show the king's interest, a second boat, the *Eaglet*, was loaned from the Royal Navy for the enterprise. With Groseilliers on the *Nonsuch* and Radisson on the *Eaglet*, on June 3, 1668, the two ships left the Thames River on their way to Hudson Bay.

The *Eaglet* was forced to turn back for repairs, but the *Nonsuch* experienced no difficulty. They wintered at the mouth of the Rupert River and returned to England in 1669 loaded to the gunwhales with fine furs. In the meantime, the *Eaglet* was replaced by the *Wivenhoe*, which made the two-way trip in '69 and added to the supply of furs. With the furs from both ships, London staged record fur sales. Prince Rupert's friends responded at once by organizing to prosecute the trade. King Charles granted them the famous royal charter that made the members of the new company the "True and Absolute Lordes and Proprietors" of almost half of what ultimately became Canada.

Where did this leave Groseilliers and Radisson? They expected more than they got, and they left the company to rejoin the French and proclaim that the English had no claim to the Bay. But Radisson again left the French and returned to the company. He finally settled in

England and died there in 1710. The Great Bay, however, was caught up in intermittent war between the two countries, a war that ended with the Treaty of Utrecht in 1713, which restored the Bay and the forts around it to the Hudson's Bay Company.

York Factory

Most Canadians, sad to say, are more familiar with California, Mexico, and Hawaii than with their own North. Many have never discovered the real magic of the midnight sun, northern lights, Arctic raspberries, friendly Eskimos, tundra flowers, and polar bears.

It is a mighty misfortune. Inaccessibility is, of course, a substantial reason for it, but there is no excuse for failure to gain an understanding of great northern landmarks like Dawson City, Whitehorse, Inuvik, Aklavik, Churchill, and especially York Factory, which is the oldest in terms of western history and may have more to tell us than any Canadian community west of Montreal.

York Factory wasn't the first post to be built on the chilly shores of Hudson Bay. Fort Charles, named to honour the English king at the time, was constructed by the crew of the *Wivenhoe* during their short stop in 1669. The location is now in the province of Quebec. The building of Forts Moose and Albany, at the mouths of the Moose and Albany rivers respectively and now in Ontario, followed in 1673 and 1675.

York Factory was next to be built, but it proceeded with some indecision because of increasing strife with the French. The Hudson's Bay Company, anxious to expand along the coast of the Bay, planned to build at the mouth of the Nelson River because they believed that the Indian canoe traffic at that point would bring the maximum in trade. But when a company boat loaded with building material was sent there in 1682, its captain was confronted by two other parties with building schemes, both already laying logs. With one of these were the familiar figures of Radisson and Groseilliers, who had so recently deserted the Hudson's Bay Company and who now told their former fellow-workers that the Great Bay belonged to France and that they should clear out. The other party engaged in building a post was Benjamin Guillam, who had sailed in from Boston with his ship, *Bachelor's Delight*.

Building by all three groups proceeded uneasily, but in the next year, 1683, the French seized Guillam and his ship, seized the Hudson's Bay Company's furs, and sailed away to Montreal. Groseilliers's nephew was left to protect French interests.

Back in New France, Radisson again disagreed with the local rulers and went to France to try to resolve the differences. The unreliable fellow was soon thereafter back in England, yielding to an English proposal that he return to the Hudson's Bay Company and take an English ship to the Bay. By this time—1684—the company was building a new trading post on the west side of the Hayes River, close to the mouth, that would become York Factory.

Still there was no peace on Hudson Bay. In 1686, Pierre de Troyes, with a hundred soldiers and volunteers, marched about six hundred miles overland from Quebec to seize the English holdings on Hudson Bay. Nobody at the trading posts was ready for warfare, and the soldiers didn't really need their battering ram; the marchers captured the Moose River post, then Rupert and Albany, leaving only York Factory in the hands of the company.

It was the beginning of a war that would not end until the Treaty of Utrecht in 1713, when the Hudson's Bay Company got back all its Hudson Bay assets. York Factory, which had been the principal attraction during the fighting, had changed hands six times; each time one flag had been taken down and its counterpart raised over the fort.

After the Treaty of Utrecht, York Factory had an important peacetime role. It became the undisputed capital of the Hudson's Bay Company's trading empire; it was the point at which all cargoes of furs were loaded onto the big ocean-going ships for London or other overseas destinations and the point at which all incoming cargo was unloaded for reshipment by canoe or York boat to company posts across the West. It was the halfway station for settlers, including the Selkirk settlers, who began arriving in 1811. In other words, it was the end of the long and trying sea journey from Britain, a journey that often lasted sixty days. It was the beginning of the equally trying journey by canoe—750 miles to the Red River settlement—that was practically guaranteed to take at least a month and perhaps two or three months. Some of those who came as settlers and stopped to stretch their legs at York Factory were slightly more than twelve months in travelling all the way.

With the passing years and York Factory's advancing age, some of its many buildings were lost to decay, fire, or erosion. Fortunately, the big central building still stands and is being maintained as a great Canadian showpiece.

Henry Kelsey, the Boy Explorer

Three hundredth anniversaries are, so far, rare occasions in western Canada, making it especially important that the 1990 anniversary of Henry Kelsey's historic expedition from York Factory to the heart of the western prairie receive appropriate attention.

When Kelsey, just emerging from his teens, made the expedition in 1690, he became the first European to see the Prairies, the first to meet the western Indians on their own ground, and the first on record to see the prairie bison. On his earlier travels in the North, he had already been the first newcomer to see the muskox, the "ill-shaped beasts" he took to be "Buffillo," although he was puzzled about the horns that "joyn together upon their forehead and so come down on ye side of their head and turn up till ye Tips be Even with ye Buts. . . . Their hair," he added, "is near a foot long."

Kelsey's expeditions, writing style, and infusions of doggerel poetry make him a good and entertaining subject for study. Not much is known about his boyhood years except that he was a Cockney chap whose birth in East London probably coincided with that of the Hudson's Bay Company in 1670. Fourteen years later he was apprenticed to that company and sailed to York Factory to become a clerk in the trade.

Nor was much known about Kelsey's later life until 1926, when his long-lost papers and journal came to light unexpectedly. The material was found in an unsorted pile of papers at Castle Dobbs in Carrickfergus, Northern Ireland, once the residence of Arthur Dobbs, who distinguished himself as a critic of Hudson's Bay Company operations. His descendant, Archibald Dobbs, presented the old records, including the journal, to the Public Records Office in Belfast. Shortly thereafter, the Kelsey papers were published as a joint effort by the Public Archives of Canada and the Public Records Office of Northern Ireland. At once, historians and writers renewed their interest in Kelsey.

If the fourteen-year-old boy was ever lonely or homesick in untamed Rupert's Land, he never admitted it. He was as fearless as a bird dog and ready for any assignment. It was a company rule that its servants were not to socialize with the natives, but Kelsey liked Indian company. He drew reprimands at times, but the governor soon discovered that young Kelsey possessed natural talents for negotiating with the Indians, and while he was still a teenager, the lad was entrusted with missions to the native people. One of these was westward on the Churchill River, where he saw his first muskox.

But these were like outings preceding the main event, the long journey inland that brought him the greatest notoriety. The trip south, from which he returned two years later, was important to the company, which wanted to persuade more Indians to bring their furs down to the Bay. The governor needed a resourceful and courageous man, and the nineteen-year-old Kelsey agreed to go. With several canoes and a small group of Assiniboine Indians, he paddled upstream on the Hayes River in June, 1690. The Indians knew the water courses, and after weeks of paddling, the party was moving westward on the Saskatchewan River. They stopped to consider a winter site at what Kelsey called "Deering Point." Was this key point in Kelsey's travels at or near the present Manitoba town of The Pas, or was it beside Cedar Lake? Nobody is sure.

In reporting his progress, Kelsey wrote:

> In sixteen hundred & ninety'th year
> I set forth as plainly may appear
> Through Gods assistance for to understand
> The natives language & to see their land
> And for my masters interest I did soon
> Set + from ye house ye twealth of June
> Then up ye River I with heavy heart
> Did take my way & from all English part.[2]

Instead of wintering at Deering Point, he joined the Indians on the plains, and in the spring of '91, he and his friends continued west on foot, passing, presumably, the places at which Humboldt, Saskatoon, and Kindersley would later be built. Along the way, he met with Indians, and he proved to be an excellent ambassador for his company. He had much to report when he arrived back at York Factory in June, 1692.

During the next few years, he witnessed the worst of the English-French struggle for the Bay, and especially for York Factory. Twice he was captured by the French, and twice he saw the French flag raised over the fort and Admiral d'Iberville take possession.

But Kelsey's usefulness wasn't overlooked. He rose to be governor of the company's posts on the Bay and died in England in 1724. On the western plains, he was a clear leader.

La Vérendrye's Heroic Search for the Western Sea

As the fur resources of the East were depleted at a shameful rate, the competition for the rich fur country of the West became more intense. The fur-trade war between the British and the French in Hudson Bay had been waged intermittently for twenty-seven years when it was ended by the Treaty of Utrecht in 1713. But the treaty didn't resolve everything: still in dispute was the vast inland territory known as Rupert's Land, over which the Hudson's Bay Company, by virtue of the Royal Proclamation of 1670, claimed trading and territorial rights forever. The English company was content to sit patiently on the northern coastline and wait for the Indians to come to them, but the French and Highland Scots on the St. Lawrence were not ready to let the Hudson's Bay Company have the fur business in the interior by default. The chance to trade in the unoccupied and unexplored Northwest seemed too good to be rejected, notwithstanding the royal charter, the validity of which they questioned.

Among those who were undaunted by the charter was Pierre Gaultier de Varennes Sieur de la Vérendrye, soldier, patriot, trader, explorer, and hero of New France, especially of his birthplace, Trois-Rivières. He had been a dedicated servant of both the colony and France and had seen years of active service with the French forces in Europe. After retiring from the army, he was a ready candidate for duty in some other area of public activity.

He was eager to see an extension of French sovereignty westward; he wanted to discover the elusive water route to the Western Sea, but when he was refused funds for exploration, he asked for permission to extend the fur trade with backing from private sources and use the profits for exploration. That was acceptable, and in 1731, the forty-six-year-old La Vérendrye, three of his four sons, and a nephew, de la Jemerais, were ready for an exploratory invasion westward. A secondary hope was to forge a chain of fortified trading posts all the way to the Western Sea and extend and consolidate French territorial claims. They departed, with a crew of almost fifty voyageurs, in June. They would start in the St. Lawrence, paddle upstream on the Ottawa River, cross westward on Lakes Huron and Superior, and then, by way of Rainy Lake and Lake of the Woods, enter strange country.

After seventy-eight days of paddling, the party was at the west side of Lake Superior and was revising its plans. It was decided that the main body of men would winter there, while a small group under la Jemerais would press on to Rainy Lake, where a post would be built, a post that would ultimately be called Fort Pierre in honour of the expedition's leader.

In the spring, the united party moved on to build Fort St. Charles at Lake of the Woods. Then, during the winter of 1732–33, one of the leader's sons, Jean Baptiste, and his nephew, la Jemerais, went over the snow to build Fort Maurepas near the mouth of Red River, while the elder La Vérendrye made an unscheduled trip back to Montreal to appease his impatient creditors and backers, who thought they were being forgotten.

Returning west with all possible speed, the leader received the sad news that his dedicated nephew had suddenly become ill and died. That was not all: his oldest son, Jean Baptiste, had been killed in an encounter with Sioux Indians. It was a stunning double blow, but the project could not be delayed, and the party moved on to the confluence of the Red and Assiniboine rivers, where, within the limits of the future city of Winnipeg, Fort Rouge was erected. Another fifty miles up the Assiniboine, the men built Fort la Reine where Portage la Prairie flourished later. Then, with a minimum of delay, La Vérendrye, two of his sons, and twenty workers veered to the southwest, hoping to reach the Mandan Indians, who were thought to hold secrets about a water route to the Western Sea.

The Mandans were friendly. The French spent a pleasant winter but obtained no useful information about a water route, and in the spring, the La Vérendrye party started back to Fort la Reine. The fact was that the elder La Vérendrye was sick and believed he should return to Montreal for both business and medical reasons before resuming the search further westward.

But the great leader never saw the West again. While planning to return to the search, he died in Montreal. His two sons were still active but found nothing useful as a feeder to the Western Sea. They thought they would find the passage by following the Saskatchewan, but were disappointed. The great La Vérendrye effort ended with less reward than it deserved. But exploration was often like that.

Anthony Henday: An Old Smuggler Who Made History

If Anthony Henday, raised on the Isle of Wight just off England's south shore, had a profession, it was that of smuggling. When he was caught at it, his punishment was banishment from the island. He went to London, and being a bold and enterprising fellow, he was soon employed again, this time with the Hudson's Bay Company for work at distant York Factory.

There at the fort beside the mouth of the Hayes River, Governor James Isham was worried by reports of French traders from Montreal building on the Saskatchewan River and getting furs from Indians on their way to the Bay. Isham needed the trade and, recalling Henry Kelsey's journey to the interior in 1690, decided to send somebody into the region to persuade the natives to bring their furs all the way to the Bay to trade.

He called for volunteers, and Henday, who had been working as a handyman/labourer said that he would go. By good fortune, a small group of Indians from deep in Blackfoot country was present at the Bay, and its leader, Conawapa, invited Henday to share his canoe. The two men became close friends. The group departed on June 26, 1754. They travelled up the Hayes River and reached the French post, Fort Paskoyac, on the Saskatchewan River twenty-six days later.

Calling at the French post, Henday had an opportunity to test his unpolished diplomacy. He and the French trader viewed each other with mutual distrust. Fortunately, Henday had been instructed to keep a journal:

> "On my arrival, two French men came out, when followed a great deal of Bowing and Scraping between us and then we entered their fort—or more properly a Hogstye for it was no better. They asked me where the Letter was [presumably a letter of authority]. I told them I had no letter, nor did not see any reason for one, but that the country belonged to us as much as to them. He made answer it did not and he would detain me there and send me to France. I said I knew France as well as he did and was not afraid to go. . . ."[3]

Henday's party returned to canoeing, but not for long because the Indians heard that their families were camping in the Carrot River Valley, and, abandoning their boats, the party set off on foot. The park country through which they travelled was rich in wild game, and the trip was made pleasant, according to Henday, by "feasting, smoking, drinking, dancing and conjuring." And if other luxuries were needed, his journal indicates that he had those too: "As I am looked on as a leader, I have ladies of different ranks to attend me."[4]

They moved out onto the prairies and passed, by Morton's estimate, northwest of today's Humboldt, crossed the South Saskatchewan River near Clarkboro, and continued to a point low on the Red Deer River. Then, following that river upstream, Henday and his friends met a band of Blood or Blackfoot Indians east and north of today's city of Red Deer. Henday was the first white man these people had seen. For Henday, it was the best encounter with the native people he was to have. They had two hundred tepees standing in two straight rows and were the first Indians seen riding horses.

The chief was a man of fine bearing and friendly, but he was unenthusiastic about going as far as the Bay to trade. Why? His reasons were clear and almost convincing: they were getting all the guns and beads they needed from the French without going so far. More than that, the chief's people were prairie Indians and were not accustomed to canoe travel; the food upon which they lived was buffalo meat and pemmican, without which they might starve on a long trip. Henday and his friends didn't argue. They moved on toward today's Rocky Mountain House to winter. There the mountains stood gloriously clear, and they were able to gather many furs.

In the spring, they moved toward the North Saskatchewan River and home base. Paddling downstream was faster and easier than paddling up. They made the mistake, however, of stopping at Fort La Corne, where the French brandy proved irresistible, with the result that Henday's stock of furs intended for York Factory was recklessly bartered away to his French hosts. He tried to replenish his supply of furs as he travelled, but at Fort Paskoyac the same mistake was made and the furs were all but lost. On June 20—almost exactly a year after leaving—Henday was back at York Factory. He was forced to explain why he didn't have a full load of furs but was able to report that he had seen mountains with snow on them and Indians riding horses. He hadn't met many Indians who were ready to bring their trade to the Bay, though, so the trip was not instantly rewarding, but the message about taking the trade to the Indians should have been fairly clear.

The Successes and Failures of Samuel Hearne

Samuel Hearne's name is clearly etched on native rock at Sloop's Cove, across the river from Churchill, Manitoba, and dated "July ye 1, 1767." He was born in London in 1745 and was a midshipman in the British Navy when he was only eleven years old. Four years later, the lad signed up for service with the Hudson's Bay Company. At first he was a helper on a company ship sailing between London and York Factory, and then he became a landlubber, based at York Factory. It was quickly evident that his aptitude was for exploration.

The company was anxious to obtain more information about the barren land to the west and the Coppermine River, for according to the Indians, it was easy to find raw copper along its bed. Hearne was instructed to conduct a search and keep in mind the possibility of finding the Northwest Passage.

Hearne made three exploratory trips west and north from Fort Prince of Wales, in 1769, 1770, and 1771. The first two trips were practically failures. On the first, he and the Indians that accompanied him missed the caribou herds and almost starved, and on the second, he had the misfortune to break his sextant and had to return. The third trip, however, was made in the company of the good Chief Matonabbee and some of his Chipewyan followers and was the longest and the nearest to being a success. It wasn't without hardship and tribulation: there was, for example, the terrible spectacle of his Indian crew falling upon a small settlement of Eskimos and killing every one.

Hearne did reach the Coppermine River, and he followed it to the Arctic Ocean, but the recovery of raw copper was restricted to a single chunk—not much of a triumph. Greater was the triumph of being the first European to go overland from the Bay to the Arctic Ocean at Coronation Gulf.

No sooner was he back at York Factory than Hearne began hearing about the growing presence of French and other traders from Montreal on the Saskatchewan River. This was seriously damaging the English company's trade. After many years of stubborn determination on the part of the company men to wait at the Bay for the Indians to bring their furs to them, a complete reversal of policy was gaining support, and Hearne was instructed to travel south, select a likely building location on the Saskatchewan River, and erect the company's first inland trading post.

The first search-and-build crew, under the leadership of Samuel Hearne, left York Factory in June, 1774, well supplied, according to the studies of A. S. Morton, with Indian guides, tobacco, gunpowder, brandy, hatchets, augers, oatmeal, and biscuits. Their destination was for Hearne to determine, although a favoured area would be on the Saskatchewan River, near Fort Paskoyac, and good access by canoe was essential. The ultimate choice was a piece of ground at the south side of Pine Lake, later called Cumberland Lake. It was practically an island, formed in part by the lake and in part by the Saskatchewan River.

Hearne was praised for his choice of site: Cumberland House had the best possible access from the north, south, east, and west. Then, in good standing with the company, he was appointed to the foremost position at Fort Prince of Wales two years later. It might have been a reward for faithful service, but in the light of later events, his judgement—or lack of judgement—proved to be his undoing.

The year 1782 was the spoiler. Britain and France were not at war at the time, but apparently, the French admiral Lapérouse was anxious to settle some old accounts. With three warships, he sailed on a straight course to Fort Prince of Wales. The sun was setting when a fort worker drew Hearne's attention to three strange ships on the horizon. The chief gazed in astonishment but was unperturbed. Why should he be worried with so much cannon power on the strongest fort walls in the world? He retired, still undismayed. But when he awakened soon after sunrise, he was horrified to see the three big warships with French flags in the harbour and four hundred French soldiers lined up in battle formation in front of the fort. He had enough cannon power to reduce the ships to firewood, but the great Hearne must have suffered sudden panic: neither he nor any of his men pulled a trigger or fired a shot. Hearne simply raised a white flag. The French admiral attempted to destroy the mighty fort, but it was nigh indestructible, and after doing minor damage, the French sailed away to do more visible damage at York Factory.

A. S. Morton mercifully tried to apologize for Hearne's moment of failure, saying that although he had the guns, he may not have had the men trained to use them.[5] Lapérouse took Hearne back to France as a prisoner, but he was soon released and back in England, where he died 10 years later.

Fort Prince of Wales

It is national misfortune that Canadians find their great and challenging North too remote to be seen and known. It is regrettable that 99 percent of Canadians have never seen and probably never will see old Fort Prince of Wales. The most fabulous treasure of western Canadian history, it is still standing foursquare at the mouth of the Churchill River in northern Manitoba.

The first trading post at the mouth of the Churchill was a log structure, Fort Churchill, built in 1718, the first new post to be authorized by the Hudson's Bay Company after the signing of the Treaty of Utrecht. Its purpose was to catch the Chipewyan Indian trade. Its life, however, was shortened by fire. Being no less eager to hold the Chipewyan Indians as suppliers of furs and guard the company's fur empire, the leaders resolved to replace the lost fort with one that would serve the trade and be seen as an indestructible bulwark in guarding their fur business and frightening their competitors and enemies forever.

The plans were prepared by the Royal Engineers in England, and the best stonemasons were brought from the Old Country. Work began in 1731 and ended about forty years later. The breaking, lifting, hauling, and fitting of massive rocks was a test of muscle and stamina, and the work progressed slowly. On April 15, 1734, when six additional workers were employed, the total work force stood at thirty-six men and two oxen. They had three wagons. One was for use with the oxen; the other two depended upon manpower. Legend has it that some of the men in service were convicts from Old Country jails sent to discharge their sentences of time and hard labour at Churchill.

When completed and furnished with heavy guns, the fort may well have been the strongest in the Western Hemisphere. With imposing bastions at its four corners, the structure measured slightly more than three hundred feet long and three hundred wide. It wasn't high—less than twenty feet—which, when viewed from a distance, made it appear squatty. To fully appreciate its massiveness, a viewer had to stand on the walls and note their thickness, wider at their base than top. Three of the outer walls measured thirty feet thick at their base, and the fourth wall, constructed to carry the greatest weight of the cannons, exceeded forty feet thick at its bottom.

It was this solidity that created problems for the French admiral Lapérouse when he came against it with three warships in 1782. After making a surprisingly easy capture of the fort because of Samuel Hearne's unexpected surrender, the admiral no doubt wondered what he was to do with it. He couldn't take it away, and he didn't have enough cannon power to destroy it. He managed to damage an archway over the gate and dislodge a few big stones in the wall, but that was about all. Instead of wasting more time on the great stone fort, he sailed away to York Factory, which he found was relatively easy to destroy by fire.

After the Hudson Bay Railway was built to Churchill in recent times, the Government of Canada undertook restoration of the fort. A few stones were reset and the cannons—once forty of them—that had fallen from their gun carriages were returned to their correct positions, leaving the ancient fort looking as formidable as ever and ready to fulfil its new role as a tourist attraction. The trouble is not enough tourists get that far.

There is, however, a companion attraction of the comparatively new town of Churchill on the opposite side of the harbour. It inherited much of the character of the northern frontier and became a "coupling link" between the Far North and the not-so-far North. It is midwestern Canada's only seaport, and has much about which to boast: landmarks galore, frontier personalities, beluga whales coming into the harbour and aquatic "cowboys" who are not afraid to test their skill at riding them, the five million bushel terminal elevator at which ocean-going freighters load grain from the prairies for delivery in far parts of the world, tundra flowers, northern lights in all their glory, big mosquitoes with big appetites, and the justifiable claim to being "Polar Bear Capital of the World."

Peter Pond: Wild Man of the West

The Treaty of Utrecht ended the French competition on and around the Bay, but it did not stop the inland threat from Montreal by French and other traders, mainly immigrant Scots and New Englanders who were emboldened by what they heard in Montreal about the trading opportunities in the West, especially on the Saskatchewan River. It was well known that the Hudson's Bay Company held a royal charter that was supposed to confer exclusive trading privileges, but the Montrealers scoffed, saying the English company could never enforce it, even if it were legal.

French traders like Chevalier de La Corne, Bartholemi Blondeau, and Francois le Blanc followed the La Vérendryes and prospered until the French defeat on the Plains of Abraham, when they withdrew. Then, without so much as an intermission, adventuresome Anglo-Saxons, of whom the Frobisher brothers, Benjamin, Joseph, and Thomas, were leaders, moved in and took the furs that under different circumstances would have gone to the Hudson's Bay Company at York Factory. It was then that the rulers at York Factory decided, for reasons of survival, to break with their century-old policy and send Samuel

Hearne to the interior, where he built Cumberland House on the Saskatchewan River.

Cumberland House was a success from the beginning, and after being in operation for about a year, several eastern independents happened to be at that point on the river at about the same time and saw how the company's new policy could hurt or destroy their trade. The men concerned were to become well known: Peter Pond and Alexander Henry the elder—both New Englanders—Charles Paterson, representing James McGill of Montreal, Thomas and Joseph Frobisher, and others. The surprised group of free traders, clearly dismayed, turned to a discussion about co-operation among themselves. As a result, at least one group decided to work as a team, dividing up trading regions and even accepting the principle of pooling their trade goods.

They called the pooling arrangement their "Common Concern." It was probably a Frobisher suggestion; the three brothers had already been practising planned co-operation. It proved to be a good exercise, and when these traders and others met in 1779 at Grand Portage on the west side of Lake Superior—about halfway between the fur country and Montreal—Simon McTavish, a Montreal Scot who knew more about business administration than about furs, presented a proposal for a proper organization. His idea was accepted. The North West Company was set up with sixteen shares and McTavish as the Montreal ruler.

Of the original partners, Peter Pond was the most aggressive—sometimes too aggressive. He was called "The Wild Man of the West" and was no stranger to fighting. A journal hints of him fighting duels on two occasions in his home community of Milford, Connecticut, when still in his youth. He then marched with the British troops in campaigns that preceded the climactic battle on the Plains of Abraham. It seems that he was not with General Wolfe on the day of battle in 1759, but he followed General Amherst in taking Montreal the next year. Nor did his fighting experiences end when he came to the West: When wintering at Lac La Ronge in 1781, his fellow trader, Etienne Waden, was shot and killed, and Pond was accused but never convicted. Six years later in the Athabasca region, there was another altercation; Pond's neighbour, John Ross, was shot, and Pond was suspected.

The great Peter Pond was the first of the traders to see what is now Alberta. In 1778, he and a few Indians with a flotilla of canoes were paddling up the Churchill River to Île-à-la-Crosse and Buffalo Lakes, then over the twelve-mile Methy Portage to a river that, to Pond's surprise, flowed west rather than east. It was the Clearwater, and it took him to the Athabasca River, where Fort McMurray arose later. Going north on the Athabasca, he built what became known as Pond's House about thirty or forty miles south of Lake Athabasca, where he wintered and collected unbelievable quantities of prime furs, so many that he failed to find enough canoes to take them all out in the spring.

Before long, Pond had a competitor, Alexander Mackenzie, but both men were interested in exploration and got along well, and there was no shooting. Both were pioneers in the rich Athabasca fur country over which the Hudson's Bay Company and North West Company quarreled and fought until the two big concerns finally entered into union in 1821. Pond didn't live to see the union; he had retired and gone back to Connecticut, where he died in 1807 at the age of sixty-seven.

War in the Athabasca

The early fur trade was not only cruel and bloody but wasteful. Scarcely a thought was given to conservation. Hunters reasoned that if they did not take all the beavers in their streams, the next trappers would do it. As the two big trading companies battled bitterly for skins and profits, fur-bearing animal populations—especially the beaver, which has been called "the gold coin of the trade"—dwindled, and participants in the operation simply moved on to find virgin areas.

Trading posts on the lower Saskatchewan River were among the first to be established, and the area was naturally the first to be depleted. For those who could benefit, Peter Pond's Athabasca was completely tantalizing. Pond, the discoverer of the treasure-trove, probably wished he could keep the secret strictly to himself, but he was obliged to share it with his partners in the Common Concern and, in due course, with the North West Company.

The Montreal crowd was determined to keep the Hudson's Bay Company out, completely out. But the English company heard about it and needed a part of it to bolster its sagging business. Peter Fidler went over the Methy Portage and down the Athabasca to build Nottingham post on an island near Fort Chipewyan in 1802 for the Bay, but the Nor'Westers made life so miserable for him that he left after three years.

The English company's fortunes were deteriorating; no dividends were paid in the first decade of the century. In 1810, the company men felt compelled to reorganize to bring fresh vigour to the business. Andrew Wedderburn, of whom more will be heard, became a member of the ruling committee and was probably responsible for the changes that were to make company servants in Rupert's Land more aggressive.

The Nor'Westers were increasingly determined to keep their rivals out, reasoning that if the other company could claim monopoly rights in Rupert's Land, the Montreal men, as discoverers, could claim exclusive rights in the country beyond, where drainage water flowed to the Arctic. The Hudson's Bay Company men were forced to admit that the Athabasca was not in Rupert's Land but argued that as British subjects, they had rights to trade in any part. They prepared to return to Athabasca with the firmness needed to get their share.

The Bay rulers knew there could be trouble and took precautions. They instructed Colin Robertson, a former Nor'Wester, to visit Montreal and there hire a hundred men who would travel together like a small army to Athabasca and there protect the company's servants and interests. John Clarke was hired to take command. It was a long trip to Lake Athabasca, but by carrying some food and buying more from the Indians, they thought they'd make out.

Contrary to expectations, the travellers saw neither Indians nor wild game near Athabasca; the Nor'Westers had convinced the Indians to drive the game deep into the forests and refuse to sell meat to Clarke's men. The idea was to starve the newcomers out. Clarke and his men started to build Fort Wedderburn on Potato Island in the lake but had to stop to search for food. He took half of his men to the Peace River, hoping to find plenty of game, but it seemed that the Indians working for the North West Company were always ahead of them. Some of Clarke's men died of starvation; some obtained food from the Nor'Westers in return for a promise to refrain from working for the English company. Clarke, with his greatly reduced following, returned to the lake but was arrested soon thereafter on instructions from Archibald Norman McLeod, described by A. S. Morton as "that embodiment of violence," and released only when he agreed that he would not take any part in trading for a year.

The time-tested Colin Robertson was then sent in to resolve the conflict, but it didn't work; the Nor'Westers picked a quarrel with him and made him a prisoner.

McLeod's henchmen continued to murder, starve, and kidnap their competitor's men and burn competing posts, but in 1819, the Hudson's Bay Company's local governor, the tough William Williams, took it upon himself to apply some of the same violence to his enemies. Knowing that the Nor'Westers had to take their furs down the Saskatchewan on their way to Grand Portage, he set up a blockade at the mouth of that river and supported it with armed men, a cannon or two on the shore, and a gunboat on Lake Winnipeg. The governor was replying with tactics the Montreal men knew something about. But change was on the way: the Hudson's Bay Company had a new boss at Athabasca, Scottish George Simpson, who was short, stubborn, and good at outguessing his opponents. Even more sweeping was the fact that the leaders of the two great companies were admitting that they had had enough of trade warfare and were actually signing in favour of union. The war was over, and the new united body would carry the old name, the Hudson's Bay Company.

George Simpson, the "Little Emperor of Rupert's Land"

It would be easy to imagine one of George Simpson's fellow Scots saying of him: "He's na big, but he's built like a Kyloe bull and just as stubborn." Nobody loved him, but everybody who knew him admired his drive and tirelessness. He governed Rupert's Land for more than thirty-five years. Some observers pronounced him a dictator; some called him the "Caesar of Rupert's Land." Doubtless, he was a hard master. When travelling between trading posts, as he often did, he expected his voyageurs to adopt his own hours, meaning paddling for at least fifteen hours a day, yet every canoeman in the country wanted the honour of being a member of Governor Simpson's crack canoe team.

Simpson's fur empire extended from Hudson Bay to the Pacific coast, and he insisted upon making personal inspections as often as possible. Although he hated wasting time, he approved of periodic displays of pomp and show to make his arrival at a trading post a spectacle to be remembered. Before rounding the last bend in a river and coming into view at the post, he would call for a brief halt to allow himself time to don a swallow-tailed coat and top hat of the best beaver felt and his paddlers to button into their brightest shirts. Then, for the final dash to the point of landing, the governor would stand erect like a diplomat from the King's court; his paddlers would bend every muscle for a fine display of speed, and the governor's private musician, present for just such moments as this, would fill the air with some glorious Highland melody.

The presence of that private musician demands explanation. In 1826, at the end of Simpson's first six years in the country, he had made out a requisition for supplies to be sent from London for the next year's needs—guns, buckshot, beads, knives, rum, and "one Highland piper, the best available in Scotland." Surprisingly, the company filled the order to the last item. About the middle of 1827, the brigade from York Factory brought the supplies inland, everything Simpson had requested including Colin Fraser, hired at £30 per year. From that time, Fraser piped George Simpson up and down every navigable stream in Rupert's Land, inspiring some listeners and frightening others half to death.

Simpson's birthplace was Loch Broom on the coast of Ross-shire. He was born under a cloud of illegitimacy in "about" 1787. As a boy, he was adopted by his grandfather, Rev. Thomas Simpson, and raised in the atmosphere of the Scottish Kirk. For ten years he worked as a clerk in the London office of Andrew Wedderburn, who was later prominent in the Hudson's Bay Company. When he accepted a position with the Hudson's Bay Company in far-away Athabasca, he was probably quite aware of the dangers of the mission to a place where the traders were in a mood to cut each other's throats at the least provocation.

He arrived in the North with fifteen canoes loaded to the waterline with trade goods. He entered at once into the trade, and his first year there was the first successful year for the Company in its Athabasca history. He ruled with a brand of firmness and justice that won respect, and when the two old companies entered into union in 1821, he was seen as the only person who had a hope of welding men with deep and long-standing hatreds into a single and efficient organization.

Most early traders were bitterly opposed to settlement, and as the head man in the fur trade, he may have had difficulties in supporting the Selkirk Settlement. He did support it, though, however perfunctorily: He aided the settlers by starting an experimental farm in 1831 and another in 1838. Similarly, he helped with the introduction of cattle and sheep. He aided greatly in the importation of the first purebred farm animals in the country, the noted Norfolk Trotter stallion Fireaway in 1833 and the Thoroughbred stallion Melbourne in 1848.

Simpson liked to travel and had no fear of long journeys. A tour of inspection beginning at York Factory and ending at Fort Langley, near the Pacific, in 1828 was not unusual; they didn't even detour for the Fraser Canyon, and the trip took exactly ninety days. He was in England and Scotland occasionally, and while there in 1830, he married his cousin, Francis Simpson. In 1838, in the company of the governor of the Hudson's Bay Company, he travelled to St. Petersburg in Russia and signed the first international agreement affecting the western part of British North America, an agreement dealing mainly with furs. He then travelled around the world; at least part of the trip was by canoe and part by horse-drawn carts. When he visited Russia a second time, the Russians treated him royally.

He was knighted in 1841, but Sir George had no thought of retiring or quitting. He took to spending part of his time at Lachine, above Montreal, and died there in 1860 after almost forty years as the virtual ruler of two-fifths of the North American continent.

"Mackenzie from Canada, by Land"

There were at least three Alexander Mackenzies of prominence in Canadian history. One of the three became a prime minister, and two were knighted. The one presently under examination was a giant in the fur trade, but it was for his explorations that he was honoured and knighted. For many Canadians, he was a school-days hero; they met him for the first time on the pages of their school readers in stories of his quest for the Northwest Passage by inland waterways to the Pacific Ocean. This Mackenzie was not a Canadian by birth and did not die here, but he gave the best of his life to Canada.

Mackenzie was born in Stornoway, a seaport town on the Island of Lewis, in 1764. While still a small child, his mother died, and the family migrated to New York. The outbreak of the Revolutionary War led to the family's move to Montreal, where Alexander completed his schooling. At the age of fifteen, he engaged with the fur traders Finlay, Gregory and Co. and was promptly sent to the trade at Detroit. But in 1787, the firm was taken over by Simon McTavish's North West Company, and Mackenzie was sent to Lake Athabasca, where the notorious Peter Pond was still the dominant figure. Roderick Mackenzie—Alexander's cousin—was about to build Fort Chipewyan on the south shore. The new man met Pond, and instead of quarreling, as people expected of the latter, the two discussed exploration, their common interest, and relaxed.

Pond believed he was too busy and too old for exploration but encouraged the young man to trace the big river he believed flowed west out of the lake known later as Great Slave. That river, he believed from talks with the Indians, would lead to the Western Sea. Mackenzie was keen to go and arranged with his cousin Roderick to manage the post in his absence. On June 3, 1789, the party of thirteen, including himself and his Indians, and three or four canoes left Fort Chipewyan full of hope that they would see the Pacific. Their course took them across Lake Athabasca, down the ever-angry Slave River, across the south end of Great Slave Lake, and into the big river flowing to the west. After a few days of paddling, however, the river began to flow north more than west, but they still hoped that the stream would turn west and they could penetrate the Rocky Mountains.

But both Pond and Mackenzie were wrong in their calculations; when the party came to salt water at the river's mouth, Mackenzie knew he had reached an ocean, but it was the Arctic, not the Pacific. Without needless pause, he reversed directions and began the upstream journey on what he called the "River of Disappointment"; Canadians would come to know it as the mighty Mackenzie. The party returned to Chipewyan on September 12; they had been gone for 101 days. But

Mackenzie had no intention of quitting. Having heard Indians talk of another big river, the Peace, flowing from the west, he announced that he was going home to the Old Country to study mathematics and astronomy to ensure that he would not repeat some of his earlier mistakes.

Late in the summer of 1792, he was ready to start again. He and his party ascended the Peace and built winter quarters, Fort Fork, near today's town of Peace River. On the following May 9, the party of nine started again, struggled through the Peace River Canyon, and on May 31 reached the junction of the Finlay and Parsnip rivers, where the huge Bennett Dam would later be built. Two weeks later, the Continental Divide was cleared, but there were difficult times ahead on the Fraser and Blackwater rivers. With the guidance of a friendly Indian, however, the travellers again enjoyed good paddling, this time on the Bella Coola River. When they reached its mouth, Mackenzie stood triumphantly on the shore of the Pacific and wrote on a big rock: "MACKENZIE FROM CANADA, BY LAND, 22nd July, 1793."

Mackenzie did not find a practical trade route to the Pacific, but his journey was still a triumph: he was the first to see all three Canadian oceans from the land side and the first to cross the continent from Atlantic to Pacific at any latitude north of Mexico.

He returned to Fort Chipewyan and then to Montreal, bringing his four-year canoe travels to an estimated total of ten thousand miles. After a disagreement with Simon McTavish, he went to Scotland to attend to his journals and see them edited and published as *Voyages from Montreal*. The book was well received, and in 1802, the author was knighted.

He went again to Canada and joined the XY Trading Company, which following the death of Simon McTavish soon after, was absorbed by the North West Company; Sir Alexander was back with his old friends. He died in Scotland in 1820.

David Thompson, Mapmaker

Leaders in both trading companies knew that the lack of reliable maps caused delays and losses in productivity. The Hudson's Bay Company was the first to employ a specialist. Philip Turnor, an experienced surveyor, was hired in 1778 and sent to Rupert's Land. He trained Peter Fidler, who in turn surveyed the river-lot farms for the Selkirk settlers. David Thompson, however, was Turnor's prize pupil and was so clever that he was soon surpassing his teacher.

Born in London, David gave no early signs of escaping obscurity. When two years old, his father died, and the family seemed destined to live in poverty. By good fortune, David was admitted to Grey Coat School, where he distinguished himself in mathematics and so won the attention of the Hudson's Bay Company. He accepted the offer of an apprenticeship in the fur trade in Rupert's Land.

He was still only fourteen years old when he landed at Fort Churchill after the voyage of four months. He took instinctively to exploring regions where no company servants had been before. In 1788 he was travelling fearlessly in the Southwest and may have been the first white man to see where the Bow and Elbow rivers came together, the future site of Calgary.

While travelling, the young fellow suffered a painful injury when a falling tree broke and crushed his leg. He was forced to accept the merciful care of Peigan Indians. Recovery was slow, and Thompson was glad to be moved to Cumberland House where he could benefit from the attention of the only doctor in the country. Another benefit was his meeting there with Philip Turnor and a chance to gain some basic instruction in surveying from him. He loved the new work and the challenges it offered. As soon as he was well enough, he set out to discover a new and shorter route between York Factory and Cumberland House and then explore the wild country between York Factory and the Athabasca.

When the Hudson's Bay Company announced a new policy demanding that servants abandon sideline occupations like mapping and give all their time to trading, he was unhappy. In May, 1797, he walked away from his post at Reindeer Lake and tramped seventy-five miles to the nearest North West Company post, where he enquired about work in making maps.[6] Thompson's skill was becoming known, and the Nor'Westers welcomed him with open arms, assuring him of work for the rest of his life.

His most productive—and happiest—days were ahead. When paddling on Lac Île-à-la-Crosse in 1799, he paused at the North West Company post, where Patrick Small lived with his native wife and children, among them some pretty daughters. There was an immediate attraction between Thompson and one of the daughters, fourteen-year-old Charlotte, and Thompson, well aware that he might never be back that way, proposed to the parents that she should become his wife from that day forward. Her parents agreed, and Charlotte moved her belongings to David's canoe, and the newlyweds paddled happily away into the sunset to spend the next fifty-eight years together.

Unlike many of those attracted by the fur trade, Thompson had high ideals: he was opposed to the use of liquor in trading and believed that marriage should be for life. Ultimately, the Thompsons had thirteen children and needed a big canoe. If they had a real home, it was at Rocky Mountain House, from whence Thompson conducted most of his searches for mountain passes suitable for travel and intermountain rivers offering transportation outlets to the Pacific.

In 1811, he followed the Columbia along its great length, mapping every mile and arriving at its mouth near today's city of Portland on July 15, a few days too late to be the first white man to reach that point from the land side and make fair claim to the location. Although he lost that claim to the mouth of the river to John Jacob Astor's fur interests, the river itself seemed to belong to him.

In the next year, 1812, David and Charlotte, with six canoes, departed for Montreal and at least partial retirement from the West. David's mapping travels, mainly by canoe, were estimated to have totaled fifty thousand miles. One of his remaining tasks was to complete the "Great Map" of what is now western Canada—one inch to represent fifteen miles—which would become the prized property of the North West Company.

David accepted other surveying and mapping assignments in the East. Some were very important, but they did not pay well, and Thompson was not a success in saving and managing his own money. Canada's greatest contributor to maps and mapping was reduced to pawning his coat to buy bread for Charlotte and himself.

He died in February, 1857, in Montreal, and Charlotte followed him to the grave three months later. In preserving his memory, Canadians failed rather shockingly.

Chapter 2

Red River

The Fifth Earl of Selkirk

Born at beautiful St. Mary's Isle in southwestern Scotland on June 20, 1771, Thomas Douglas was the seventh son of the fourth earl of Selkirk. Strange to say, he went on to inherit both the title and the fortune and to author the first plan to introduce agriculture to what is now western Canada. With neither assistance nor encouragement from any government, he spent his family fortune and the best part of his life establishing a pioneer farm colony in the West and virtually stood alone when greedy fur-trade interests fought bitterly to destroy the agricultural scheme.

After succeeding to his father's estate and seat in the House of Lords, the fifth earl of Selkirk might have lived in comfortable seclusion in Scotland, but being a man of feeling, he grieved for the Highland crofters who were being evicted from their farms and had no place to go. He conferred with the government, offering to settle many of these people in Rupert's Land if granted a proper location. He was told to see the Hudson's Bay Company because the land had been given to it by royal charter, but the company was horrified at the suggestion of a farm colony in the fur country.

Going back to the government, he heard about a big tract of available land on Prince Edward Island. Selkirk bought eighty thousand acres on the island and by July of 1803 had three ships—*Dykes*, *Polly*, and *Oughton*—carrying eight hundred men, women, and children, many of them from the Isle of Skye, ready to sail. True to form, the earl accompanied the group; he faced exactly the same hardships as the settlers. Arriving at Prince Edward Island, the earl's tent was pitched among the other canvas shelters, and there the great man remained for a month, until he was satisfied that his people could look after themselves.

The Prince Edward Island venture was a success. Not so successful, however, was the earl's second colony, known as Baldoon, beside Lake St. Clair in Upper Canada. Still, his hope for a big colony at Red River in Rupert's Land was as compelling as ever. The Hudson's Bay Company remained adamant in refusing to allow land for settlement, but Selkirk did not give up.

In 1807 he married Jean Wedderburn, sister of Andrew Wedderburn, a man of influence in the business world. Soon thereafter, Wedderburn joined his brother-in-law in buying Hudson's Bay Company stock. In light of his reputation in the business community, it wasn't surprising that he was induced to accept an appointment to the company's committee of directors.

Then, in what was more than coincidence, the committee, meeting on February 6, 1811, recorded a resolution reflecting a complete reversal of policy, that "Mr. Wedderburn be desired to request Lord Selkirk to lay before the Committee the terms on which he will accept a Grant of Land within the Territories of the Hudson's Bay Company."[1]

Lord Selkirk was received in person at the next meeting of the committee on March 6. His proposal was approved by the committee, but the shareholders' approval was needed. It was given at a meeting on May 30. As expected, there was opposition, but the recommendation was finally passed, and Lord Selkirk found himself the new proprietor of 116,000 square miles of land, most of it in the future province of Manitoba.

So confident was he about the success of the great venture that he made prior arrangements for ships to carry Miles Macdonell—his choice to become the governor of the new colony—and a vanguard party of workmen to Hudson Bay. The real settlers would go later.

The fur trade did all possible to frustrate the arrangements, but Macdonell and his men departed Stornoway on the island of Lewis on July 26, 1811, for the long journey to York Factory. They arrived sixty-one long and monotonous days later only to find that it was too near freeze-up to safely attempt the canoe trip to Red River.

Adam and Eve Travelled by Canoe

Miles Macdonell and his twenty-three workmen were stuck at York Factory for the winter because of their late arrival and the fact that ice was already forming on the Hayes River. With less than sufficient room for the crew at the fort and not enough food, Macdonell decided to take his men upstream on the Nelson, where he hoped to find a location offering enough driftwood to build shelters and enough deer and ptarmigan to feed the men during the winter. About twenty-two miles up the river, they made liveable cabins with mud fireplaces at a place they called Nelson Encampment.

It was not a happy winter. With difficulty, the men snared enough deer and game birds to feed themselves, but scurvy was a constant threat. The men quarrelled: the Scottish and Irish disagreed constantly, Protestants and Catholics fought, and nobody remained friendly with Miles Macdonell.

During the winter, canoes for the trip to Red River were made at York Factory, and the men were eager to start south almost immediately after the breakup of the river ice on June 22. The paddling days were painfully long, but Macdonell promised a day or two of relaxation at Oxford House, roughly halfway to Red River. There, he was able to hire three more men to compensate for defections, bringing his crew back to twenty-three, but better still was the astonishing discovery of two young cattle. Cattle were thought to be completely unknown in the region, yet here they were, a half-grown heifer and a bull, presumably brought in as small calves a year earlier.

Macdonell, who still had sorrowful memories of cattle left on the dock at Stornoway because there was no room for the feed and fresh water the animals would consume during the trip, must have rejoiced. Macdonell now laid claim to these two. He called them Adam and Eve, hoping they would be "fruitful and multiply." These half grown cattle would make the trip by canoe, and would have to be loaded and unloaded daily. But determination, like faith, can move mountains, and Adam and Eve travelled all the way and received loving care.

There was relief from rapids but not from danger when the canoes passed into Lake Winnipeg and then into Red River to halt, finally, on August 30 on the east side of the Red, opposite the mouth of the Assiniboine. Of course, nobody in the party had seen the area before, and it was now for Macdonell, on Selkirk's instructions, to make a final selection of location: "The first and most important point," the Earl had written, "will be the choice of situation . . . near the edge of a woods . . . with fertile soil. . . ."[2]

Macdonell acted promptly and after several days fixed upon a bend in the Red River a mile north of the mouth of the Assiniboine, afterwards known as Point Douglas, as the approximate centre for the settlement. One of his worries was that the first real settlers might be arriving at any time. He was not ready for them. Acting on advice from Hudson's Bay Company officials, he decided to make winter preparations at Pembina River, sixty miles to the south, where the settlers would be nearer buffalo herds and hence nearer winter meat.

As he suspected, the first contingent of settlers—seventy-one men, women, and children—under the jovial Irishman, Owen Keveny, ended their journey on October 27, and joined in the rush to erect log-cabin homes and make them ready for winter. They were thankful for a safe journey without casualties. Actually, they had started with seventy souls but ended the journey with seventy-one because Mrs. McLean had a baby daughter on the way.

The settlers brought twenty-one sheep with them all the way from Scotland. It was Lord Selkirk's idea, of course, that his people should have something to export, and he had decided upon wool. Instead of settling for the lowly Blackface breed of the Highlands, he imported Spanish Merinos, world famous for their fine wool, and sent them along with the settlers. Unfortunately, the Merinos had a bad time due to predators and human error and did not survive long.

The settlers had good luck as well as bad. They were fortunate in securing the services of that great French Canadian Jean-Baptiste Lagimodière to be their full-time buffalo hunter for each of their first two winters and were never really hungry. And in the spring of 1813, when they returned to Point Douglas, Peter Fidler came down from Brandon House and surveyed the land up and down from Point Douglas, laying out long and narrow river-lot farms so that each family could have one.

The big contingent of settlers expected in 1813 suffered hardship and delay and did not arrive until '14. Known as the Kildonans, their story is unique.

The Kildonans

Seven hundred crofters from the parishes of Kildonan and Clyne in Sutherlandshire wanted to travel to Selkirk's colony on the old ship *Prince of Wales*, which left Stromness in the Orkneys on June 28, 1813, but only one hundred could be accommodated. Lord Selkirk was present to wish them well, but the trip seemed to be jinxed from the start, and good wishes were not enough. First, a highly contagious fever, thought to be typhus or "jail fever," appeared, and ironically, the first person to suffer from the illness and die was the ship's doctor, whose presence on the ship was one of Selkirk's thoughtful provisions. Most people on board became sick; seven died and were buried at sea.

The ship's Captain Turner, who should have exercised mercy at such a time, proved totally insensitive. Perhaps he could no longer stand the smell of sick people, and to shorten their presence on his ship, instead of sailing on to York Factory where he had been instructed to deliver the settlers, he turned in at the mouth of the Churchill River and there unloaded and tried to abandon the sick people.

Miles Macdonell made the long trip from Red River to York Factory to meet the newcomers and escort them to the settlement, but missed them. William Auld, the tough old trader at York Factory, received a report of Captain Turner's inhuman conduct and set out for the Churchill in an open boat. He arrived before Turner's departure, and as a senior officer in the Hudson's Bay Company service, he ordered Turner to reload and take the settlers to York Factory, presumably threatening dismissal if he refused.

Angrily, the captain reloaded the freight, taking it bit by bit in a small boat from the shore to the bigger ship anchored out in the harbour, then loading the passengers in the same way. When he carelessly allowed a metal chest containing the settlers' supply of tea—precious tea—to fall into deep water, he was viewed with suspicion. When loaded and ostensibly heading for the deep water, the ship was allowed to run aground on the gravel. The condemnation became loud. It was necessary to again unload to lighten the ship. This further delay gave force to the captain's contention that if he was to clear the ice and take the ship back to London before winter, he could not take the settlers to York Factory. Even William Auld could hardly disagree, and the settlers, almost a hundred men, women, and children, were left stranded in what must have seemed the coldest and most inhospitable place on earth.

Fort Prince of Wales was big by outside dimensions, but its interior was small, and it was quite incapable of accommodating the settlers for the winter. In intense distress, they tramped upstream beside the Churchill River about sixteen miles to the mouth of Colony Creek, where they found enough driftwood to construct rough shelters and supply firewood. For food, they depended upon fish, rabbits, and ptarmigan. Midway through the winter, they estimated they had taken and eaten eight thousand wild birds.

The winter was extremely dismal. There were six more deaths from the fever. No doubt there was general regret at ever leaving the Highlands, but they did not give up. Near the end of winter, while the snow was still deep, fifty-one of the restless people resolved to walk to York Factory. Walking single file through the still-deep snow, the strongest men took the forward positions where they could break a trail. Next came the weaker men, some still feeling the effects of the fever, the stronger women and children, and finally, the ailing women. In the middle of the line was a kilted piper supplying musical encouragement. At the end of each day, they bedded in the snow.

At York Factory, the eager ones still had to wait for their friends to join them and for the Hayes River to become free of ice; only then could they begin the long journey by water, paddling against the current most of the way. It was a happy day, June 21, exactly one year less one week after leaving Stromness, when they received a warm welcome at Point Douglas.

The Kildonans had displayed great patience and courage. Archibald MacDonald, who had become their leader on the journey, reported to Lord Selkirk immediately upon arrival at Point Douglas. After all they had suffered, he said, the new settlers were "never happier and more contented in Kildonan than they are here already."[3]

The Pemmican War

Pemmican was made from dried buffalo meat, melted fat, and berries. High in protein, rich in energy, and convenient, it was a sort of nutritional panacea. It was easy to dispense and store, and with these advantages, it didn't have to be palatable. It was the "staff of life" for prairie

Natives, hunters, traders, and even the early settlers. For voyageurs serving both trading companies, it was essential, and if the supply failed, the canoe brigades would grind to a stop.

The main supply came from the Indians in the good buffalo country drained by the Qu'Appelle and Assiniboine rivers, making the North West Company's Fort Gibraltar at the mouth of the latter the most important pemmican depot in the country. With the coming of the Selkirk settlers, the need grew, and shortages became a threat. Miles Macdonell wondered if the additional settlers expected in 1814 would create famine conditions, and on January 8, 1814, he acted, declaring primary claim to all food resources in the Selkirk territory. No foods of meat or vegetable origin could be removed from his area without his permission.

Copies of his proclamation as governor of Assiniboia were carried to all posts. Pemmican for the voyageurs was the fuel from which "paddle power" was generated, and traders shouted angrily that enforcement of such an order would cripple transportation. They were in no mood to acquiesce, and they prepared to smuggle the crucial supplies from the Assiniboine River to the mouth of the Red.

Macdonell knew he had an enforcement problem. He placed armed men on the Assiniboine. When he received word of a boat load of pemmican coming down river in May in defiance of his order, he prepared to intercept it. Hearing of his actions, the owners placed the cargo in hiding near the river, but Macdonell's men found and confiscated all ninety-six bags of pemmican.

The biggest confiscation came a few days later. Macdonell knew the Nor'Westers had a big cache of pemmican at Fort Souris on the Assiniboine. He sent his sheriff, John Spencer, with canoes and armed men to take it. Spencer pounded on the gate, demanding entrance, and when the demand wasn't met, Spencer's men were ordered to use their axes to cut the gate down. With the gunmen standing by, the canoemen carried out 479 bags of pemmican—each presumably holding 90 pounds—93 kegs of grease, and 865 pounds of dried meat.

The North West Company was furious, but lacking the armed might to force recovery, they could only plead with Macdonell to return sufficient pemmican to meet the immediate needs of the company's canoe brigades. There was much haggling and some compromise. When the company partners gathered for summer meetings at Fort William, all discussion was about the high-handed seizures and the need to destroy the settlement at Red River. One proposal was to inspire the Métis to attack, but before going to that length, they decided to get Duncan Cameron of Fort Gibraltar to attempt to win the settlers' confidence with food, whiskey, and bagpipe music and then destroy their loyalty to Macdonell and the settlement.[4]

Cameron succeeded. At an opportune moment, he told his friendly listeners that they had no hope of surviving and prospering at Red River, but that the North West Company had so much concern for their future, it would furnish free transportation to Upper Canada with all the food supplied. The canoes would leave the following day.

So convincing were Cameron's words that 134 men, women, and children presented themselves at Fort Gibraltar the next day prepared to accept the offer and bid farewell to Red River forever. It was a sad day for the colony; only about sixty people remained. And no sooner had the deserters departed than a mounted troop of Métis galloped in shooting guns in the air, killing a few horses, and firing some buildings. The frightened settlers still in the colony sent word to the Nor'Westers that they were ready to quit the settlement. They paddled north to Jack River, near the north end of Lake Winnipeg. The enemy traders rejoiced at what they believed was the end of the experiment in farming.

But the end was not yet. The settlers were persuaded by Colin Robertson, the former North West Company man who became Selkirk's useful and loyal worker, to return to their river, and before long there was a new body of immigrants with a new governor, Robert Semple. The outlook brightened, but only briefly; the enemies of the settlement were not finished with their evil work. For the settlers, the worst was yet to come.

A Home in the West: Jean-Baptiste and Marie-Anne Lagimodière

Jean-Baptiste Lagimodière, the frontier fur trader, died at St. Boniface on September 7, 1855, at the age of seventy-eight years. He had seen the Manitoba area sixty-nine years before there was a Manitoba and was the perfect portrayal of the spirit of western adventure.

Leaving his village birthplace of Maskinongé on the north side of the St. Lawrence River in 1801, he took his place as a voyageur in one of the North West Company's canoe brigades going west. From Montreal, the brigade followed the popular fur-trade route upstream on the St. Lawrence, then upstream on the Ottawa River, where paddling was made difficult by thirty portages. The old hands in the crew knew the point at which to leave the Ottawa and portage and paddle to Lake Huron, then navigated Lake Superior and took Grand Portage, Rainy Lake, Lake of the Woods, the Winnipeg River, Lake Winnipeg, and the Red River in stride. When they entered the Red River, the canoemen knew they were about one hundred miles from Pembina, the prescribed destination for some of them, including Jean-Baptiste.

Pembina, he figured, would become his base for hunting, canoeing, and pursuing the free life of which he had dreamed. But after four years without any communication from home, he decided to go back for a visit. When he arrived, there was a party for him—dancing, wine, and girls in pretty clothes. Marie-Anne Gaboury, the little girl he once saved from drowning but to whom, in his boyhood bashfulness, he had never spoken, was there. Now there was instant infatuation. Before many weeks, they asked their priest to marry them.

The idea was that they would build a log house on a small farm and raise a big family and be very happy, but there were problems ahead. Still in their first weeks of married life, Jean-Baptiste announced his urge to return to the West. He told his new wife that he would make things comfortable for her at Maskinongé and that he would return before long and then they could settle down. Naturally, she was horrified. If he was going, she was going too.

She went. Marie-Anne Lagimodière became the first white woman ever to go to the untamed West to stay.

For Marie-Anne, Pembina was frightening, and the hardships were terrible. Her first baby, a girl given the name Reine, was born there on January 6, 1807, the first white child born in what became the province of Manitoba. As Jean-Baptiste travelled the water courses and trails, his wife accompanied him, and she added to the Lagimodière record by giving birth in the next year to the first white baby born in what became the province of Saskatchewan and then, after another year, the first in what was to be Alberta.

They were far west at Fort Edmonton when they heard the news about a Scottish earl, Lord Selkirk, who was about to bring settlers to a new farm colony beside the Red River. Not wanting to miss anything of importance, they paddled back to Pembina, where they saw the first of the settlers arriving—seventy of them—in 1812. These newcomers needed help. When famine threatened, Jean-Baptiste spent two long winters far back on the buffalo range as the hunter for the settlers, adding to the supplies of buffalo meat with such regularity that the threat of starvation vanished.

When the settlers returned to Point Douglas to stay, Jean-Baptiste and his family went too, and when the North West Company seemed determined to destroy the settlement in order to safeguard their fur interests, Jean-Baptiste stood with the settlers. There was an attack in June, 1815, and the settlers fled, but Colin Robertson persuaded them to return.

There were rumours of a more savage attack being planned for 1816, and Robertson was anxious to get a message to Lord Selkirk in Montreal, an appeal for help. Getting the message to Montreal in winter would be a task for a hardy man travelling on snowshoes. Robertson asked the only possible man: Jean-Baptiste said he would go "as soon as I can get my blankets and snowshoes and gun and say goodbye to my wife and children."

Jean-Baptiste set out across the snow on October 17. On the following March 10, he delivered the message to Selkirk, who invited him to stop and rest for a few weeks. But he was in a hurry to get home, and he started back the way he had come, on foot. Luck was not with him this time: he was arrested by agents of the North West Company and made a prisoner in the company's jail at Fort William, where he was held until Selkirk was able to get him released. Again he set out on foot, and he arrived back with his family the day before Christmas, 1816.

Lord Selkirk later presented Jean-Baptiste with a grant of land on which the city of St. Boniface would later grow, and there he lived until his death.

The Battle of Seven Oaks

The Pemmican War started on January 8, 1814, when Miles Macdonell posted his inflammatory proclamation prohibiting the removal of all pemmican and other foods from the territory under his jurisdiction. To define its end would be difficult—it dragged on and fizzled out without a formal conclusion—but the obvious date is June 19, 1816, when the conflict reached its brief but tragic climax in the Battle of Seven Oaks. The site of the battle is today marked by a commemorative stone close to Winnipeg's Main Street a couple of miles north of the Assiniboine River Bridge.

The memory of the warlike tactics of the Métis, who as servants of the North West Company had descended upon the settlement in June of the previous year, remained clear and frightening. The settlers were worried—with good reason—by rumours of another attack, this time to demolish the settlement. The new governor, Robert Semple, a former army man, appeared confident that his people could repulse any native attackers, but Semple's courage was better than his judgement.

Late in the afternoon on that day of tragedy, a boy in the Fort Douglas watchtower noticed mounted horsemen approaching from the west by the river road and called down to the settlers idling on the main level: "The halfbreeds are coming."

Governor Semple promptly climbed the tower, placed the telescope to his eye, and nodded. Back with the settlers, he called for twenty men to follow him; twenty-six stepped forward. "All right, get your guns and fall in," Semple said.

"Will we take the cannon?" someone asked.

"No," Semple replied. "We won't need it."

In the interval, the Métis had changed direction, veering to the northeast as if to bypass the fort. But Semple was undeterred and marched away northward with his small force as if to intercept the mounted men.

Following their respective courses, it seemed inevitable that the two parties would come together. It soon became apparent that there were at least sixty mounted men, more than Semple had anticipated. They were predominantly Métis, with a few Indians in feathers.

As the two groups were about to meet, Semple's people recognized Cuthbert Grant as the leader of the Métis. Grant halted, and one of his men, Boucher by name, rode toward Semple. "What do you want?" he asked.

The governor replied with the same question: "What do you want?"

"We want our fort," Boucher answered, referring to Fort Gibraltar, which Semple's men had dismantled to get the logs with which to reinforce their own fort.

It is said that the governor unwisely reached forward and seized Boucher's gun. A burst of gunfire followed, and one of the first to fall wounded was Governor Semple, his hip shattered by a charge thought to have been from Cuthbert Grant's gun. After a few seconds, Semple raised his head and spoke to the Métis leader: "Are you Mr. Grant?" When Grant nodded, Semple said: "I'm badly wounded, but if you would have me conveyed to the fort, I think I would live." Grant turned his horse as if to comply, but before he could reach the wounded Semple, one of his followers shot Semple in the head.

In a matter of minutes, the shooting stopped. The battle was over. Of the twenty-two men lying on the field, twenty-one were from the fort. One was Métis. Excluding the two men who went back for a cannon and two or three who may have fled when they saw the hopelessness of their position, John Pritchard was the sole survivor from Semple's followers.[5] When the fighting ended, Pritchard at once approached Cuthbert Grant and offered himself as a prisoner. He then added that if Grant had any messages for the sad people at the fort, he would be willing to carry them, hoping, of course, that Grant would offer assurance that there would be no more attacks. Grant agreed; Pritchard could convey the promise that there would be no more slaughter, provided the settlers would abandon the settlement at once. After taking the message, Pritchard was to return to become Grant's prisoner of war.

The distraught settlers, including twenty new widows and many more fatherless children, agreed to leave as quickly as they could load their canoes. They went again to Jack River, promising themselves they would never return to this heartbreaking land. But less than a year later, when these sad people heard that Lord Selkirk was on his way with a hundred hired soldiers, they had a change of heart, and the settlers returned.

Next Year Country

One of the handicaps in farming in a totally new area was the complete absence of past experience; there was no one to warn: "Don't do that; it was tried and it didn't work." The frontier had no agricultural history, none of the wisdom born of mistakes. Hence, the first generation of Red River farmers made costly errors from which experience might have spared them. Their efforts in wheat growing are examples.

Miles Macdonell, on his first trip to Red River in 1812, carried a bushel and a half of seed wheat and planted it dutifully. Unfortunately it was winter wheat that could not survive the Manitoba brand of winter, and the precious seed was wasted. The new farmers planted spring wheat in 1814, but they planted too late, and the crop was lost due to fall frost. The next two crop years were disrupted by human enemies, and 1817 brought a repetition of loss by fall frost.

Years of destruction by grasshoppers followed; the insects appeared without warning in 1818 and ate voraciously, but the Red River women gathered enough heads of wheat missed by the hoppers to furnish seed for 1819. When the new generation of grasshoppers began to hatch that year, however, it was soon evident that they had doubled their numbers. They ate everything the settlers had planted, leaving nothing for the good women to glean.

The pioneer farmers still wanted to plant wheat, but they had to travel far into the United States to find seed. The grasshoppers were still present in 1820 but were in decline, and the growers got a partial return. There is only scanty information about wheat returns in the next three years, but then the unpredictable new land did what it has done periodically ever since: it yielded a bumper crop, the first really good harvest in twelve years of trying. They got forty-four bushels of wheat per acre from land that had been ploughed and sixty-four bushels per acre from land cultivated with hand tools.[6] Nature had not exhausted all her tricks, though, and 1825 went into the record books as a year of crop failure, failure caused by the invasion of mice. Some people wondered if the rodents came down in the rain, but whatever the explanation, the year of the mice was not to be forgotten.

Looking back upon fourteen crop years, the settlers may have thought they had experienced every form of crop failure. They hadn't. One of the most destructive natural forces of all—flood—made 1826 a year of almost total loss. The river-lot survey, which gave every farm a water frontage of 220 yards—one-eighth of a mile—and a depth of two miles, had several advantages: the river became the common "highway," and farmers were assured of water and the benefit of close neighbours in case of attack. But the plan had one serious disadvantage, as people discovered in this year of flood: loss of buildings.

The Red River rose nine feet in one day, May 2, and continued to rise. Overflowing its banks, the water flooded homes, driving occupants to higher ground. They could only watch as their humble homes and every wooden structure built near the river was carried away. (That river level is now known to have risen six feet higher than the highly destructive flood on the same river in 1950.[7]) Nobody escaped without heavy loss, even the ingenious settler who took his bed and a big supply of food to the top of his haystack, where he proposed to relax until the water subsided. He didn't relax for long: when he awakened in the middle of the night, he and his hay were rafting toward Lake Winnipeg.

Forty-seven houses were known to have floated away on May 5. George Simpson believed that this would be the death blow to the settlement. It was not, but it was another cruel test of perseverance. Only at the end of May did the river water show signs of receding. It was the middle of June before the land was dry enough for cultivating, and then it was too late for planting most crops.

By the time the snow fell in the year of the flood, almost every farm along the river had a new house and the amazing settlers were making ready for "next year's crop."

Significantly, the cropping record improved. The most difficult of the experimental years had passed, and for the next fifty years, or until 1876, the Red River farming community had enough wheat and other foods for all local needs and some left over to sell to the Hudson's Bay Company.

Milk, Butter, and Cheese

"Wha's a farm wi'out coos?" early settlers of Scottish origin were known to ask. There were children of seven and eight years of age in the pioneer farming community at Red River who had never tasted cows' milk, but it was almost impossible to obtain breeding stock.

When Miles Macdonell discovered cattle at Oxford House, he could hardly believe his eyes. When he took them to Red River by canoe, he firmly believed he had the only representatives of their species in the British Northwest. He was wrong: there were at least three others at

Souris House, a bull, a cow, and a calf, the property of the North West Company. In 1813 these were bought by Peter Fidler for £100 and taken to the settlement at Red River. With five head, the Selkirk farmers now had all the cattle in the West.

But cattle raising is never without reverses. The bull bought from the North West Company turned ugly, and because they already had one bull, he was slaughtered for beef. Then Adam, exercising a bull's prerogative to explore, strayed away and became lost. The settlers hunted but did not see Adam again until the next spring, when his dead body was seen floating down the river on a slab of ice. It left the settlement with three cows but no bull, a most unsatisfactory situation.

Until 1817, there were no further additions to the settlement's herd. In that year, however, Selkirk's soldiers, coming from Fort William to recover Fort Douglas, brought with them five head—one bull, one ox, and three other cattle—that they had seized at the North West Company post at Lac la Pluie. But these, in the next year, were repossessed by the company and shot. In 1819, four heifers were bought on Selkirk's instructions in the Orkney Islands and sent to York Factory. They arrived at York too late in the season to be taken directly to Red River. Two of the four died during the winter, so only two were delivered in 1820.

Lord Selkirk, when at Red River in 1817, had vowed that he would not rest until a big and worthwhile herd was delivered at Red River. On his return to the East, he paused at Prairie du Chien, high on the Mississippi, and tried to find a frontiersman who would accept an order for fifty to one hundred cows, travel far enough south—into former Spanish territory if necessary—to find them, and then drive them back. He didn't have much success, but the interest he had shown led to correspondence with Michael Dousman of Michilimackinac. He eventually signed a contract to find and deliver seventy-six good milk cows, twenty oxen, and four bulls, a total of one hundred head, to be driven north and turned over to representatives from the Red River settlement at Big Stone Lake, in present-day South Dakota. The price for cows was not to exceed eighty dollars a head, and for bulls and oxen, not more than one hundred dollars. Robert Dickson, as Selkirk's agent, signed the agreement and made a payment.

Before there was time to act, Dousman sold his contract to Adam Stewart, also of Michilimackinac, who travelled south to St. Louis and beyond to obtain the needed cattle. His intention was to drive the herd as far as Prairie du Chien, winter there, and drive on to Big Stone Lake in the early spring.

Unfortunately, Stewart miscalculated the amount of hay available at Prairie du Chien, and his cattle starved to death during the winter. He was no quitter, however, and in the spring of 1821, he was on his way back to the south country for another herd. Still pursued by bad luck, his misfortune this time was to encounter Sioux Indians who were both angry and hungry, and they cleaned him out.

After trying unsuccessfully for two years to fill the contract, what could a man do next? With a double measure of determination, Stewart went south again in the early spring of 1822. It is unfortunate that nobody knows exactly where he went to obtain these herds or the terms, if any, by which he got them. St. Louis was a thousand miles from Fort Douglas, and the most likely cattle country at that time would have been far south or southwest of St. Louis. Did Stewart's cattle have long horns or show Spanish breeding? Nobody knows.

In any case, the drive of 1822 ended at Point Douglas on August 28. It was one of the happiest days in the life of the settlement. Stewart arrived with 170 head of cattle, enough to meet the terms of his contract with some left over for private sale. The settlers danced and sang, and the West's first farmers were never again without cattle, oxen, beef, milk, butter, or cheese.

Buffalo Wool

The Red River settlement was eight years old in 1820, and the many spinning wheels that had been carried tenderly from Scotland or Ireland were still idle, like mere ornaments, for lack of sheep. But John Pritchard, the former North West Company partner who chose to retire at the settlement and who was one of the volunteers who followed Governor Robert Semple on the dreadful day of Seven Oaks, had an idea. His proposed Buffalo Wool Company would, he believed, bring prosperity to Red River.

"Why wait any longer for a proper stock of sheep," he asked, "when there is buffalo wool right here, the very stuff that gives the prairie buffalo one of the warmest winter coats?" He demonstrated how to pull the wool from the hides and then separate the fine undercoat from the long-haired and coarse outercoat for processing.

Pritchard had, however, overlooked the characteristic that makes sheep's wool unique. Hair fibres, as seen under magnification, are straight, making it difficult to twist them into a strong yarn or thread. Wool fibres, because of their crimps or serrations, can be twisted to make a yarn that is both fine and strong. The finest wool has the most crimps per inch. The practical fact was that the buffalo's undercoat was fine in texture, but it was still hair, with all the limitations of hair.

Nevertheless, Pritchard's letters to Andrew Wedderburn and leaders in the British woolen industry aroused interest. They were willing to put the buffalo wool to the test in their mills. In a letter written in June of 1821, he reported his wool recovery at Pembina to be "300 pounds of fine wool and 1,000 pounds of coarse wool." He expected to double these amounts before the last canoe brigade for the season departed for York Factory.

To be a successful salesman, a man must be an ardent optimist; Pritchard would certainly qualify. He expressed the opinion in a letter that the sample of buffalo wool he was sending to England was "equal to the finest [wool] that has ever been seen on the London market. . . ." In the same letter, he offered some general information about his operation. "A good skin," he wrote, "will yield six or seven pounds of wool, from which two or three pounds will be of the finest quality, suitable for export to England. The rest is principally fit for coarse cloth, blanket stuff and mattresses. Besides, there is a low quality hair from which we intend to make rope."[8]

His optimism must have reached dizzying heights. He believed he could win the favour of Andrew Wedderburn, with whom he was negotiating Buffalo Wool Company business, by sending a gift of two young buffalo, a bull and a heifer, to his London address. There is no record of Wedderburn's words when he tried to take delivery of the dubious gifts.

In spite of the gifts, Pritchard did get Wedderburn's approval for the project. As Lord Selkirk's brother-in-law and administrator of the earl's estate, Wedderburn granted Pritchard one hundred acres of Red River land for the company's headquarters and warehouse. But Pritchard didn't fool anybody in the British woolen trade. The British manufacturers were doubters from the beginning, but were kind enough to put the buffalo wool to an honest test. A few simple garments like shawls were made from the product, but they didn't win much approval. The millers reported that they saw no future for buffalo wool: their mills couldn't handle the coarse fibres, and yarns made from the short, fine hair lacked strength and quality.

Pritchard was not ready to give up, however, and neither was Lady Selkirk, the late earl's widow. She persuaded the woolen manufacturers to try again in the hope that she could make the coarse shawls, stockings, and sweaters popular in high society. Out of respect for Jean Selkirk, the manufacturers agreed. Courageously, the lady wore the hairy stockings and other items of apparel, but the London socialites were unimpressed. The effort did nothing for Pritchard's wool sales and nothing for Lady Selkirk's prestige.

As he passed the unfavourable report to Pritchard, it may not have escaped Wedderburn's thoughts that anybody who would send him two untamed buffalo as a gift deserved no better. In any case, he reasoned that the only hope for the project's success would be in making coarse cloth for sale and use in the settlement.

The practical lesson should have been clear: buffalo hair *should* have a use, but it is not wool and could never be a proper substitute for it.

Kentucky Sheep

Selkirk's first group of real settlers came to Red River with their leader, Owen Keveny, in 1812. Before their arrival, there were no sheep in Red River, but, thanks to Lord Selkirk, they brought with them twenty-one head of the aristocratic Merino breed. Sad to say, predators and other forces of destruction combined to obliterate them, and the country was again without sheep.

The good earl, when visiting the settlement in 1817, announced his intention to repeat the Merino experiment and in due course ordered twenty head—fifteen ewes and five rams—from Saxony. The imported stock was delivered safely at York Factory, but before the animals could be carried by canoe to Red River, they suffered a new misfortune.

As a precaution against some tragedy that might wipe out the entire flock, half the sheep were moved to a small island that was believed to be predator-free, but the danger of a sudden rise in river water was overlooked. Five ewes and all five rams had been placed on the island, and almost at once heavy rains inland caused a sudden flood, and the ten sheep, including all the rams, were drowned.

The ten surviving ewes were taken to Red River, and an appeal was made to the Hudson's Bay Company for a ram. The company agreed to find one, but it didn't arrive until 1824, when the ewes were either dead or in decline.

The successful cattle drive from somewhere a thousand miles to the south in 1822 brought local people to talk hopefully about attempting a sheep drive of similar proportions. A total of £475 was subscribed for the purchase of stock, and late in 1832, ten men were chosen for a purchasing expedition. William Rae, a Hudson's Bay Company clerk, was named leader; Robert Campbell, recently arrived from Scotland and familiar with sheep, was to be the deputy leader. Fortunately, Campbell kept a journal in which he recorded the departure of the ten men, two carts, and several saddle horses on November 8, 1832.[9]

At Pembina, the party heard disturbing reports about Sioux Indian aggressions; they changed travel hours to make themselves less conspicuous, but kept on. When they reached the Mississippi, they abandoned their horses and carts and took to canoes. When ice formed on the river, they were forced to walk, but arrived at St. Louis on January 3.

The men were then fifty-six travelling days from home, but their journey was just beginning. They searched far around St. Louis and found no sheep. "No sheep nearer than Kentucky," they were told. When Campbell enquired about where they'd find Kentucky, he was told, with a swoop of the hand, "Over that way." Rae went ahead to Kentucky, and by the time his friends joined him, he had purchased 1100 sheep and lambs. Soon, 270 more were added, making a total of 1370. The mature sheep were sheared at once to make for easier travel, and on May 2, the big and noisy flock started in a northwesterly direction.

If the men were fortunate enough to have a sheep dog, there is nothing about it in the diary. They covered eleven miles a day at first, which was regarded as good progress. Their troubles, however, started when it was time for the native speargrass to lose its barbed spears or seeds. The sharp spears have always caused trouble for sheepmen, especially when they penetrate the sheeps' skin, causing suffering and sometimes death. Campbell reported three or four deaths per day, and there was nothing he could do except halt the drive and wait until the spears dropped to the ground.

After leaving the speargrass menace behind, the herders drove innocently into rattlesnake country. More sheep were lost when they accidently stepped on rattlesnake tails. After the rattlesnake trouble, there were some encounters with Sioux Indians, and what was a big flock at the beginning of the drive was down to 670 sheep and lambs by July 7.

Settlers from Fort Douglas came to meet them, bringing fresh food for the men and a wagon with which to pick up ailing sheep and lambs. Both men and sheep seemed to take encouragement, and at noon on September 16, 1833, the great drive ended. There was joy at the conclusion of one of the longest sheep drives in history, but disappointment that the 1370 sheep and lambs that left Versailles, Kentucky, on May 2 had dwindled to 251 head at their destination. Even that reduced number, however, furnished a foundation that served the settlement well and put scores of spinning wheels back to service.

The Pioneer Ordeals of Laidlaw's Pigs

William Laidlaw brought the first pigs to the first farm community in the West. The small herd of the world's most obstinate domestic animal suffered a 750-mile journey by canoe and toboggan, but they survived, and they deserve better than to be forgotten.

Pigs were often carried on sailing ships because they would consume food waste, serving as porcine garbage disposals while converting the waste to fresh pork, which was sure to be wanted on long voyages. Some of these pigs may have been taken ashore at points like York

Factory and used for breeding. It is doubtful, however, if pigs were ever taken inland from York until Laidlaw's historic delivery late in 1817 of a few specimens to Red River, where they were placed on the new experimental farm.

Lord Selkirk, when at the settlement earlier that year, had recognized the testing and demonstration value of an experimental farm and promised that there was one in his plans. He added that he had already hired a progressive young Scottish farmer to direct it. It was logical that the man who was coming to fill the new post should bring something needed and useful with him—like pigs.

During the ocean voyage, Laidlaw's seven pigs were penned on the deck and well fed. We can only speculate about their size. They would have been small pigs, probably two months old when bought for the journey, but with lots to eat, they would have grown rapidly and might have weighed a hundred pounds each when removed from the ship at York Factory. At that age and weight, the problems of transportation would have been growing too.

At York Factory, late in the season, Laidlaw was warned of the danger of being frozen in on the icy rivers. He was advised to wait until spring, but he knew that as the new man responsible for the experimental farm, it was important that he be at Red River as quickly as possible. He elected to start and hope for the best. The seven pigs were enclosed in a boxlike compartment at the back of his canoe and travelled easily as long as the rolled oats brought from Scotland lasted. But just as he was warned, the weather turned wintry, and before he was quite halfway to the settlement, frozen rivers forced him to abandon travel by canoe.

What then? What was he to do with the pigs, probably the only ones within a radius of a thousand miles? He could slaughter them and present the carcasses to the native families along the way, but the settlers at Red River would never forgive him if he didn't make delivery. Searching for alternative transportation, Laidlaw traded his canoe for an Indian-made toboggan and a team of dogs.

He was practical enough to know that unless he could restrain his pigs, there'd be no chance of keeping the unco-operative critters on the toboggan, but if restrained by ropes, they'd be in danger of freezing. After a day or two of experimentation, he adopted a plan: After feeding them in the morning, he "dressed" each pig by wrapping it in a buffalo robe and tied them to the floor of the toboggan. Needless to say, the fiendish squeals of protest that echoed through the frosty air startled the Indians and no doubt led to some unflattering remarks about "crazy white men." Another part of Laidlaw's routine consisted of muzzling his sled dogs, which displayed a constant urge to attack the pigs and sample fresh pork.

The next calamity was the depletion of the grain feed carried for the pigs. It was impossible to replace along this route, and Laidlaw resorted to the only alternative: feeding the pigs raw or cooked fish. There was no shortage of fish in Lake Winnipeg, but three pigs got fish bones stuck in their throats and died.

Four pigs did survive the hazardous winter trip from Hudson Bay and were received at Point Douglas with admiration usually reserved for conquering heros. The local Indians, who had never seen pigs before, were captivated and did not hide their ambition to compare boiled pork with boiled buffalo hump. As for the settlers, their highest hope was that Laidlaw's pigs would multiply, which pigs do so well and, for the farm community, did again.[10]

A Wonder of the New World

Fireaway, the most admired horse of his time, earned greatest acclaim for improving the common horse stock of the West. His record as a sire should have given him a rating like that of Baron's Pride in the Clydesdale breed, Justin Morgan in the Morgan breed, and Man O' War in American Thoroughbreds.

The great horse's story begins with ancestors of small size and unattractive form hiding in the swamps. As revealed by the fossilized "pages of the rocks," the North American horse gained size, speed, and prominence, but it then disappeared completely. The reasons for its extinction have never been confirmed, but by good fortune, some of the North American horses had escaped earlier over a land bridge connecting Alaska and Siberia and became well-established in the other hemisphere. Some were taken to North Africa and Arabia and then to Spain. Spain, it was said, became a "nation of horsemen," and their conquistadors took some of the best horses to the New World in the years after Columbus.

Thus the horse species was back on native soil. The principal beneficiaries were the Indians, whose lives were completely changed. Through the popular pastime of horse stealing, horses moved from one tribe to another and appeared as mounts of the attacking Snake Indians in the Bow River region about 1730. Soon Blackfoot, Cree, and Assiniboine Indians had horses.

The first farm settlers, of necessity, came to the West without horses and were pleased to discover that the Indians had them—such as they were. Although the Spanish horses brought to the continent possessed quality, lack of selective breeding under Indian ownership led to deterioration, and the settlers, while admitting that a small horse of low quality was better than nothing, looked upon the native ponies with scorn. Again and again they wished aloud for a stallion of an improved breed, Shire, Clydesdale, or Thoroughbred.

It came as a pleasant surprise when Nicholas Garry of the Hudson's Bay Company reported to George Simpson that: "We shall send a stallion of a proper breed by the ship to York Factory. We think the Experimental Farm at Red River the best place to commence raising horses."[11]

The settlers at Red River were delighted but somewhat skeptical. "What do those people in London know about a proper breed?" they asked. "And if they do choose a good horse, how do they think they'll carry a grown horse in a canoe from York to here?"

The stallion was delivered at York Factory without mishap and, however it was achieved, with either canoe or York boat, the tall horse was taken the rest of the way to Point Douglas precisely as hoped for. Citizens from far and near came to see for themselves. The horse stood like a monument, his head held high, and a score of questions were answered. His registered name was Fireaway, and he was of the Norfolk Trotter breed, a general-purpose breed developed in Norfolk. He was a bright bay in colour, stood sixteen hands high, was well muscled, and was said to be able to trot fifteen miles an hour. The settlers were more than pleased and agreed that he was a sensible choice in light of their varied needs, which ranged from plough horse to buffalo runner.

George Simpson reported to the governor and committee in London that Fireaway was looked upon as "one of the wonders of the world, and many natives had travelled far just to see him." The best mares in the country were being assembled for breeding, and after the first Fireaway foals were born, the sire's popularity soared higher than ever.

There were problems, of course, just in keeping a superior horse at Red River, where some believed that superior horses were for stealing. Thefts were attempted until an armed guard was stationed with him day and night. He was indeed the horse sensation of his time.

The rest of the Fireaway story is unknown. Did he die at Red River? Was he sold to the United States? Was he finally lost through theft, or was he shipped back to England when his breeders concluded that they had made a mistake in letting him leave? It seems strange, but these questions go unanswered. The Indians may have had what may be a satisfactory explanation: Fireaway was so good that he was whisked away to the spirit world, where the Great Spirit kept him for his own enjoyment.

The Annual Buffalo Hunt

The Red River Métis and halfbreeds sang, danced, and laughed and were more interested in fun and contentment than in wealth. Some farmed indifferently, some accepted work as voyageurs, and many wished they could be buffalo hunters full time.

There were two extensive buffalo hunts per year—spring and fall—that might take a total of three months; much of the remaining months were spent talking about the last hunt and preparing for the next. The buffalo hunt was for everybody; it furnished food and fellowship.

The buffalo hunt came to be seen as a Métis institution; it was a carnival, a war exercise, and a holiday all rolled into one. It was a family outing, and all family members except small children found some useful role. Military discipline was accepted and did not discourage anybody.

Time changes many things. By 1820, four years after the Battle of Seven Oaks, the settlers were trying to forget the animosities born in that awful hour of slaughter. The Métis, they discovered, were not altogether bad. The Selkirk settlers sought permission to go along on the hunt under Métis leadership. They too needed the food the hunts supplied. They were glad to join the march to the favourite hunting ground southwest of Pembina.

According to Alexander Ross, Red River historian of that period and author of *The Red River Settlement*, 540 Red River carts belonging to the Métis and settlers went out for the 1820 hunt, 820 in 1830, and 1,210 in 1840.[12] Ross was an eyewitness to the 1840 hunt and reported fully. The point of assembly was a grassy place in the Pembina River valley, just south of the international border. There, on June 15, all participants gathered for the organization meeting. The count made at that time showed 1210 Red River carts, 620 hunters, 650 women, 360 children, 403 horses good enough to classify as buffalo runners, 655 cart horses, 566 oxen, and 542 dogs.[13]

Ross called it the biggest hunting expedition in the world. The first order of business was organization and delegation of authority. The supreme command would, as always, rest with the chief captain or president, who in 1840 was Jean Baptiste Wilkie, "an English halfbreed brought up among French." Immediately under him were ten elected captains, and under each captain were ten soldiers, all chosen by vote.

The next business was the acceptance of rules, which in the year in question were as follows:

> No buffalo to be run on the Sabbath day.
> No party to fork off or go ahead without permission.
> No person or party to run buffalo before the general order.

Every Captain with his men, in turn, to patrol the camp and keep guard.
For the first trespass against these laws, the offender to have his saddle cut up.
For the second offence, the offender's coat to be taken and cut up.
For the third offence, the offender to be flogged.
Any person convicted of theft, even to the value of a sinew, to be brought to the middle of the camp and the crier to call out his or her name three times, adding the word "thief" at each time.

Twenty days and 250 miles from the settlement, the hunters found themselves within two miles of a big herd and prepared at once for attack early the next morning. Soon after daylight, the mounted hunters took their places to form a straight front line. Captain Wilkie, with spy glass in hand, studied the herd from his saddle and gave the order to advance, first at a slow trot and then at a gallop. The orderly line came as quietly as possible to about 450 yards from the herd, and when the bulls were seen to curl their tails and paw the ground, the order was given to charge at top speed. "Shots were heard and all was smoke, dust and hurry," Ross wrote. "In less time than we have occupied with the description, a thousand carcasses strew the plains."

By this time, the carts driven by the women and old men had arrived. They skinned and dressed the carcasses and prepared the red meat for drying and the making of pemmican.

There was a second run at another big herd, and when it was concluded, there was enough carcass meat to make a moderate load of dried meat, tallow, and pemmican for all the carts. The chief captain then ordered preparation for return to the settlement. Alexander Ross estimated the kill at 2,500 buffalo and that 1,089,000 pounds of meat were recovered, enough to furnish 200 pounds for every man, woman, and child in the region. The big party, tired out and talked out, was back home two months and two days after leaving.

It was the opinion of Henry Youle Hind that the total buffalo kill by the Red River hunters in those pristine years was not less than 652,000 head.

The Red River Cart

The royal charter of 1670 that conveyed monopoly trading rights in Rupert's Land to the Hudson's Bay Company proved difficult to enforce. The first challenge was from the French, who tried to drive the English company from Hudson Bay and almost succeeded. The Montreal-based North West Company also refused to recognize the validity of the charter—until the union of the two old companies placed the former Nor'Westers in the position of being beneficiaries of the charter; they at once became supporters rather than opponents.

By 1849, the militarily powerful Métis were becoming highly critical of the injustice of a major monopoly being left in the hands of a private company. At the same time, they were attracted by new trading posts built on the Pembina side of the boundary by Canadian-born Norman Kittson on behalf of the American Fur Company. With strong convictions about their inherited rights, they had no compunctions about making bootleg sales across the line. When Guillaume Sayer and friends sneaked their season's furs across the border and were caught, they were ordered to stand trial before Recorder (or Judge) Adam Thom, an unpopular Scot who never outgrew his prejudices.

For the judge, it proved to be a most difficult test. If he ruled in Sayer's favour, he would be repudiating the company's laws he was employed to enforce. If he ruled in favour of the Company, he would enrage the native people, who had military strength on their side and were becoming angry enough to use it.

The Métis assembled on the St. Boniface side of the river early on the day of the trial. Four hundred strong and scowling, they came with their guns to hear the wisdom of Louis Riel, the "Miller of the Seine" and father of the West's leading maker of history by the same name. Riel proposed to have a chat with the magistrate and offer him some advice before the trial, and his followers agreed.

The Métis crossed the Red and were milling about the court when the magistrate appeared and was offered Riel's words of practical wisdom. The jury in the case brought in a verdict of guilty, but the judge declined to impose a sentence. This was interpreted, rightly or not, as an acquittal, and the crowd outside became wild with glee, shouting: "The trade is free! The trade is free!"

The company refused to change its policy, but its control of the trade was weakened, and more furs were going as far south as St. Paul, known widely as "Pig's Eye."

With this shift in trade came the birth of the big business of carting or, in other words, freighting with ox-drawn Red River carts. The trail from Fort Garry—later Winnipeg—to St. Paul was roughly five hundred miles one way and was the first to be developed with heavy cart traffic. Freighting with trains of carts, like the organized buffalo hunts, suited the Métis well and was largely in their hands.

The first Red River carts were probably made and used at Pembina. They were distinct in various ways: They were of all-wood construction with a basket or rack intended to carry up to a thousand pounds of freight, a fair load for a single ox. The two disked wheels were constructed from Red River or burr oak. No axle grease or other lubricant was used on the axles because an accumulation of sand and grease would hasten the wearing of the wood. The turning of the wheels on dry axles produced a screeching sound that could be heard for miles when a train of a hundred or several hundred loaded carts was in motion.

In the absence of metal for wheel hoops, green, wet rawhide was cut in strips and wrapped tightly around the rims. After wet rawhide starts to dry, it shrinks and becomes tight and hard and tough. A supply of wet rawhide, called *babiche*, was always carried on long cart trips in case it was necessary to "change a tire."

Oxen were favoured over horses because they could live off the land. Farmers drove oxen in teams of two or more, but for carting, the animals were driven as singles. With many carts moving in single file, the "train" might well be as long as a modern freight train on rails. Trains of two hundred carts appeared on the five hundred mile trail between Fort Garry and St. Paul and on the thousand mile trail linking Fort Garry and Fort Edmonton. On the latter route, a string of carts made just one round trip in a summer.

Carting had its period of importance, but it ended rather abruptly with the advent of steamboats on the western rivers and rail trains elsewhere. The Métis, deprived first of buffalo hunting and then Red River carting, suffered.

Chapter 3

Opening the West

Agriculture Versus the Fur Trade

It was 1857. For 187 years, the owners of the Hudson's Bay Company had been the "Lordes and Proprietors" of Rupert's Land. Suddenly, all that is now western Canada came under the critical gaze of British parliamentarians as never before. The company had asked for the renewal of its licence, and members of the parliamentary committee, before passing it, had some searching questions to ask.

The probe was prompted by facts in company history. The Hudson's Bay Company and North West Company, after lawless trading conflicts over the years, had concluded a union in 1821. The British government, as an approving gesture, had given the reorganized company a twenty-one-year lease with all trading privileges on that portion of the British Northwest lying beyond Rupert's Land, thereby extending its jurisdiction to half of British North America. In 1838, the lease had been renewed for another period.

In 1857, the company applied again, but this time, members of parliament wanted more information about company affairs. They wondered if there was no better use for the region than raising furs and if the company was doing its duty in furnishing schools for native children. They were also concerned about the charge that liquor was used too freely in getting furs from natives. After some parliamentary debate, it was decided that a select committee be named to enquire into the affairs of the Hudson's Bay Company. The committee included parliamentary "heavyweights" like Lord John Russell, Lord Stanley, William Ewart Gladstone, and Henry Labouchere. The twenty-four witnesses called were well-informed people from both sides of the Atlantic. Of two star performers, one was the seventy-year-old warrior from numerous fur trade engagements, George Simpson, who gave short, crisp answers to questions, always sure of himself and sometimes hostile. The other star performer was the distinguished London journalist and lawyer Alexander Kennedy Isbister, a halfbreed born at Cumberland House on the Saskatchewan River and educated in Britain. Isbister contradicted much of Simpson's testimony.

Sir George Simpson was the first to be called and spent most of two days on the stand. Members of the committee were not readily convinced by his statements but enjoyed him and kept him going. They quizzed him about his administration, his policies with respect to Indians, liquor in the trade, and especially, his views concerning prospects for settlement and the suitability of the soil for agriculture.

"Will you," asked the chairman, "have the goodness to give the Committee your impressions of the character of the territory in point of soil and climate, particularly with reference to its adaptation for the purposes of cultivation and colonization?"

Simpson was a fur trader without much sympathy for agriculture and replied: "I do not think that any part of the Hudson's Bay Company's territory is well adapted for settlement; the crops are very uncertain."

"Would you apply that observation to the district of Red River," he was asked in reference to what was later seen as the richest soil in Canada.

"Yes," Sir George answered.

When asked why he held that opinion, the man who had travelled the country for thirty-seven years gave an astonishing reply: "On account of the poverty of the soil except on the banks of the river. . . ."

"Have you an equally unfavourable opinion of the country on the Saskatchewan River?" he was asked.

"Yes," he replied. "The climate is more vigorous and the crops are even less certain. . . . The scarcity of timber also is a great bar. There is little or no wood in the country."[1]

On the strength of what was later to be demonstrated, Sir George's judgement on the soil was outrageous enough to be laughable. Fortunately, Isbister was yet to be heard. His father was a company trader at Cumberland House, where Alexander was born. He was a bright boy and worked and explored for the Hudson's Bay Company before going overseas to complete his education. There he remained to make a name for himself as a teacher, lawyer, journalist, and historian. He never returned to the Northwest, but retained his loyalty to his race and the scenes of his youth. On the stand, he said convincingly that the soil of Rupert's Land was good and that the company's policies were unfavourable to the country and should be changed.

The testimony produced too many contradictions, and the committee decided to offer the company a one-year lease to allow the committee to send an independent party to Rupert's Land for an unbiased report. Palliser was their man.

Palliser's Triangle

Captain John Palliser, an Irishman by birth, a redhead by luck, a bachelor by choice, and a zestful adventurer by nature, was recommended by the Royal Geographical Society to the British government in 1857 as well qualified to lead an expedition. He was at once engaged to serve the select committee of the House of Commons in exploring "that portion of British North America which lies between the River Saskatchewan and the frontier of the United States, and between the Red River and the Rocky Mountains."

Palliser wasn't a complete stranger to the region; ten years earlier, he had spent almost a year on a protracted buffalo hunt near the Missouri

River, but is not clear if he was on the British side of the border during that outing. From that experience came his book, *Solitary Rambles*.

News of his appointment to lead the new expedition was communicated to Palliser on the last day of March along with detailed instructions. He was to keep a journal and send duplicates of entries to England as often as possible. He was to faithfully record such physical features as "the principal elevations, the nature of the soil, its capabilities for agriculture, the quantity and quality of its timber and any indications of coal or other minerals." The instructions did not fail to mention the importance of economy, and in the event that Palliser wished to return to England by way of Victoria and the long south route, he would be permitted to do so, but he would have to pay the extra costs himself.

Palliser was not one to waste time. He quickly made arrangements with Dr. James Hector, physician, geologist, and naturalist, and Lieutenant Thomas Blakiston, physicist and astronomer, to be his assistants, and they sailed from Liverpool on May 16. After travelling for fifty-seven days, he arrived at Fort Garry. There, he hired extra men at a wage of £40 per year and bought two wagons, five Red River carts, and thirty horses, the latter at an average price of £20. The assembled party then travelled south to Pembina, west to Turtle Mountain, and northwest to Fort Ellice, where Palliser noted some cultivation of potatoes, wheat, barley, vegetables, and feed for a few cattle. Beyond that place, as the party moved toward Moose Jaw Creek, Palliser saw drought conditions so intense that he described what he saw as "an extension of the Great American Desert." On the advice of his Indian guide Nichiwa, he carried wood for campfires from the Qu'Appelle Valley for use with buffalo chips.

Conscious of oncoming winter, the explorers turned toward the elbow of the South Saskatchewan River and Fort Carlton, which would be their winter headquarters. Dr. Hector, using Carlton as a base, would explore through the winter, travelling as far as Fort Edmonton, while Palliser would take leave to travel to Montreal, there to confer with Sir George Simpson. A tireless rider—probably too tireless for the horse he was riding—he left Fort Carlton on October 11 and was at Fort Garry twenty-one days later. Later, on the trail south of Fort Garry, he lost the horse and was forced to continue to St. Paul on foot, but he arrived in Montreal within the allotted time. On June 4, 1858, he was back at Fort Carlton, ready for the next summer. He would work mainly between Fort Edmonton and the Bow River, while Dr. Hector would press the search for Rocky Mountain passes suitable for wagon roads.

Initially, Palliser planned to limit his explorations to two years, but when members of the select committee found that there was no longer a need to hurry, they notified him to take a third year if he thought it would be of benefit. He elected to take the extra year, and after spending the winter of 1858-59 at Fort Edmonton, he and Hector extended their efforts further south and to the Cypress Hills. They then turned west to take different routes to the Pacific, where at Victoria, they hoped to obtain a ship back to England.

They still had their report to prepare, a voluminous thing that was completed in 1862.[2] There was widespread interest in the findings, especially those regarding land use. Palliser was enthusiastic about settlement by farmers in the park belt; both the soil and climate appealed to him, and he was sure the tree growth would be of great benefit. As for the prairies, especially the driest part enclosed by the so-called Palliser Triangle, he was hesitant. It would be suitable for grazing by cattle, sheep, and horses, but as he saw it, as part of the Great American Desert, it would be risky for cropping. He also advised that reservations be established for Indians, and he recommended prohibition for Indians and hence an end to the use of liquor in trading with them. He endorsed schools for young Natives and non-Natives and advocated the formation of a strong force of "military police," presumably patterned after the Irish Constabulary.

Some critics said he was a pessimist. More correctly, he was a realist. His name now honours a mountain, a river, a triangle of dry land, a hotel, and a political constituency.

The Prairie Merchant Marine

It was a bright and peaceful June morning at Old Fort Garry in 1859, John Palliser's third and last year in the country. Two small girls sitting on a stone wall were doing what little girls have always done for enjoyment: braiding each other's hair. One of the girls was Mary Ramsay Wright, a widely known Winnipeg pioneer, and she remembers that their attention was suddenly arrested by a strange noise like that of "somebody blowing in a bottle, only louder."

Local adults, no less inquisitive than the girls, flocked to the Red River to determine what had caused the sound. There they saw a strange structure floating down river that looked much like a farm woodshed mounted on a raft. It was actually a riverboat, and it had a steam whistle and a stern-end paddlewheel to prove it. It was named *Anson Northup* after its owner, who was competing for a cash prize from the St. Paul board of trade. The recent cart deliveries of Rupert's Land furs had awakened interest in St. Paul in generating more trade with the British side of the border, and the board of trade had offered a prize of one thousand dollars for the first owner to take his steamboat all the way.

The forty-two-year-old Northup had been a frontier cattleman, wagon boss, and navigator on the Mississippi before hearing about the prize. He told an officer of the board of trade that if the prize was raised to two thousand dollars, he'd enter a boat in the contest. The prize was raised, and Northup bought an old boat from a Mississippi proprietor, cut it into three pieces, and hauled it overland to Moorhead, where it was reassembled on the Red River. By no stretch of the imagination was the boat beautiful, but it was ninety feet long and had four compartments, called "staterooms," supplied with beds. All other travellers slept in the saloon or on the deck.

The boat made two trips to Fort Garry in that first year and was supposed to make a round trip between Fort Garry and Moorhead every ten days in the second year. The freight rate from Fort Garry to St. Paul was five dollars per hundred pounds; passengers paid thirty-five dollars for a ticket from Fort Garry to Moorhead or Georgetown and stage coach from there to St. Paul, altogether an eight-day trip.[3]

The next steamer on the Red was the *International*, 137 feet long and better looking. It appeared at Fort Garry in 1862 with about two hundred passengers, most "Overlanders" on their way to the B.C. gold rush. The best-known of the early Red River steamships, however, was the *Selkirk*, built in 1871. It made history five years later when it hauled the first wheat out of the West and a year after that when it brought the first railroad locomotive, the Countess Of Dufferin, into the country.

An item appearing in the *Manitoba Free Press* on November 1, 1875, gave an indication of the size of the river business that was destroying the Red River cart traffic: "The steamer *Cheyenne*, with twelve flat boats heavily laden with freight, arrived today." In 1875, the Winnipeg freight handled was said to total seventy-six million pounds. It was big business.

Steamboats moved into the Assiniboine River in 1876; the shallow-draft *Prince Rupert* went as far as Portage la Prairie that year and reached Brandon in '78. But the Assiniboine was shallow at times and always loopy, and steamboats had constant problems.

Shipping seemed to prosper on the Red River, and the steamers were readily induced to extend their routes to the mouth of the river and then north on Lake Winnipeg. After a two-mile tramway was built to transfer freight around the dangerous water at Grand Rapids at the river's mouth, boats had about 1250 miles of moderately good water to Fort Edmonton. It was a climb of 1780 feet, 275 feet of which was at Grand Rapids.

The first steamboat to reach Fort Edmonton was the *Northcote*. Its arrival on July 22, 1875, gave residents of the place good reason to cheer. Thereafter they had boat service all the way to Winnipeg in the summer, and they were thankful. The railroad would reach Calgary some years ahead of Edmonton, but as readers of the Edmonton *Bulletin* were reminded, while trains were faster than riverboats, the latter were more economical and more pleasurable.

The steamboats were quick to bring Red River carting to an end, just as railroads brought to a sudden end the exciting chapter on the prairie merchant marine.

The *Nor'Wester*

The year that brought the first steamboat to the West brought a printing press too. The printing press, just delivered by ox-cart, was a source of wonder and interest to the idlers at Fort Garry. They speculated skeptically about why two young men would haul it to this rump end of civilization where half the population could neither read nor write and the other half couldn't afford the price of a year's subscription to the proposed paper.

According to the story, the only person in the settlement to regularly see a daily paper was an immigrant who subscribed to one published in London, England. Because there was only one delivery per year to Fort Garry at the time, he received all the back copies from a full year together. Still glad to have them, he stacked all the papers in correct chronological order and allowed himself to read one paper each day. He was reported to have said that although each paper was exactly one year old at the time of reading, he enjoyed it as much as if it were hot off the press.

Nonetheless, there they stood in the first snow of winter: William Coldwell, who had gained some brief newspaper experience with the Toronto *Herald*, and William Buckingham, who had worked just as briefly with George Brown's Toronto *Globe*. Looking tired after their month-long trail trip from St. Paul, they set about finding a log cabin big enough to accommodate a couple of beds and the printing press.

Was it the spirit of adventure or miscalculation that brought them there to produce a newspaper where nothing of the kind had been done before and where the Hudson's Bay Company still ruled? They had travelled from Toronto to St. Paul, Minnesota, with moderate ease, but trouble awaited them there. They hadn't realized that they would have so much trouble obtaining printing equipment and transporting it over the five hundred mile trail. The only printing press available for purchase was an old one that had been in a fire and fallen through a burning floor to the basement. There being no other, they bought it. They shopped for paper and other printing supplies and then faced the necessity of buying three Red River carts and the oxen to haul them.

It seemed reasonable to expect that the oxen would be broken and ready for work. They were not broken, and when hitched to the carts, they dashed away wildly, scattering supplies and the old press. Finally, the green critters got the idea and settled down, but it was a trying trip and a trying month. Looking back on the journey, Coldwell wrote on November 1, 1888: "This day 29 years ago, Buckingham and I stood on the bank of the Assiniboine, opposite Fort Garry, with the material for the first newspaper printed in Assiniboia. We had oxen and their hooves were worn through owing to the long tramp and the frozen ground. I will never forget the dreary look of the place. We knew no one, had no letters of introduction, knew little or nothing about the country or people and felt lost."[4]

The new men found living quarters and made plans to produce the first issue of the *Nor'Wester* on New Year's Day, but when they learned that the next mail out would leave on December 28, they knew that if they missed it they would have to wait months for the next one. By a special effort, they managed to meet that deadline. The initial issue was a four-page paper, its pages measuring twelve inches by fourteen inches. It was intended to appear weekly. Single copies were priced at sixpence, and a year's subscription was twelve shillings.

Coldwell and Buckingham were still young men—in their twenties—but they knew the importance of a newspaper backed with convictions. They were convinced that the Hudson's Bay Company, which had ruled for almost two hundred years, had to stand aside to make way for a crown colony or province of Canada if and when it became possible. The company took a dim view of the *Nor'Wester*'s editorial policy, and Coldwell and Buckingham had a fight on their hands.

Buckingham withdrew and went back East after a year and did very well, becoming secretary to Prime Minister Alexander Mackenzie and then deputy minister in the Department of the Interior. Coldwell sold an interest in the paper to his brother-in-law, James Ross, and then to Dr. John Schultz. In 1865 a fire destroyed the printing plant and consumed Coldwell's investment. Leaving the future of the paper to Dr. Schultz, Coldwell took his family to the East, where he worked for the *Globe* for four years. He returned to Fort Garry in the year of the Red River Rebellion. He was not through with journalism, but he was increasingly handicapped by rheumatism or arthritis, and he was more or less crippled for the last twenty-five years of his life. He died in Victoria, B.C., in 1907.

The First Gold Rush

In demonstrating human folly, a gold rush does very well. Dreams of easy wealth breed frenzy that is undeterred by obstacles of distance, hardship, mountains, deserts, and lawlessness. So it was in California in 1849; so it was in the colony of British Columbia in 1858 and '62; and so it was in the Yukon in 1898.

The first strike of importance on the west coast north of the United States was on the Queen Charlotte Islands. It was made in 1850, the year in which Vancouver Island was declared a crown colony and Richard Blanshard was appointed governor. When the gold strike was reported, a rush of aspiring miners from California resulted. Local officials believed that the islands needed a firm administration. Accordingly, James Douglas, the chief officer of the Hudson's Bay Company in the area, was named governor, first for the Queen Charlottes and then, when Richard Blanshard left his post, for Vancouver Island.

The Queen Charlotte Islands gold didn't last long, but a much bigger discovery was made on the lower Fraser River in March, 1858. Hill's Bar, which carries the name of its discoverer, yielded gold worth two million dollars and caught the eye of mining interests everywhere.

A great rush of miners—and those who knew how to "mine the miners"—followed, mainly from California, where there were still romantic memories of the rush of '49. The old hands wanted to try again, and the traffic from San Francisco was all in one direction. The population of Victoria and the river camps soared. James Douglas, as governor of Vancouver Island, was worried about possible trouble, and although he had no jurisdiction on the mainland, he stepped in to maintain order. Soon thereafter, the British secretary for the colonies declared British Columbia a crown colony, with Douglas as its governor.

The search for gold was extended up the river from Hill's Bar. An estimated twenty-five thousand miners were at work, many of them doing very well. With one gravel bar leading to another, the area of intense activity shifted to Cariboo Lake and the wide Cariboo district. Miners began changing their techniques and going to underground deposits. "Dutch" William Steitz dug down on William's Creek and struck it rich. A host of others were soon shovelling gravel on the same and neighbouring creeks; Antler Creek, Lightning Creek, Lowhee Creek, and Grease Creek gained instant fame.

It was also on Williams's Creek that H. F. Davis, of the "Twelve-Foot Davis" legend, was said to have taken twenty-five thousand dollars in gold from a twelve-foot slice of a resurveyed claim. A man with a big and generous heart, he quickly gave his money away and in due course went to Northern Alberta to trade. There, he won greater admiration and fame for his acts of kindness than he could have done with a personal fortune. The epitaph on the Davis gravestone on a high hill overlooking the town of Peace River tells it all: "He was every man's friend and never locked his cabin door."

Billy Barker, a Cornwall Englishman who went to sea, quit his ship at Victoria to follow the lure of gold. He was one of those who sunk a shaft that ultimately converted the shabby shack-town of Barkerville into a historical treasure. In less than a year, five thousand miners were probing the underground gravel and hoping for the kind of luck that made Billy Barker rich and famous.

The miners who flocked to the Cariboo gold fields in 1862 were from many parts of the world. Most were from California, but there were more from Britain and the Canadian East than ever before. The most widely heralded group, about 125 persons comprising several small groups, became known as the Overlanders. They set out from the Canadian East to the B.C. gold fields. They wanted to get there as quickly as possible, and so they travelled the most direct route to the gold.

They started by way of Chicago and St. Paul and reached Fort Garry on the Red River steamboat the *International*, which was making its maiden voyage on that river. It was late in May, 1862, and the Overlanders continued west on the cart trail to Fort Edmonton, where they abandoned their carts and shifted their supplies and belongings to 140 packhorses. They followed the Yellowhead Pass route across the Rockies as far as Tête Jaune Cache on the Fraser River. Some members chose to stay with their horses; others took rafts or canoes. Canoes were a mistake, and there was loss of life, but some reached the gold fields. Others elected to farm and met with the success they so much deserved.

The Republic of Manitobah

Confederation, in 1867, gave the best of reasons for celebration for the leading actors in the show: Ontario, Quebec, Nova Scotia, and New Brunswick.

In the West, still isolated by distance and lack of communication, most residents, except those who were readers of the *Nor'Wester*, didn't hear of the event for weeks or months after the first of July, and when they did, were only slightly impressed. For the most part, Rupert's Land, like a sleeping giant, didn't bestir itself beyond a few yawns. Nevertheless, there were signs of political awareness. The *Nor'Wester*'s editors demanded an early end to Hudson's Bay Company rule and the adoption of some form of democratic government. Nobody bothered to conduct an opinion poll, but if an assessment of public interest had been made, the outcome might well have shown equal support for each of five possible avenues of action:

1. maintaining the status quo, leaving Rupert's Land to be administered like a huge private property by the Hudson's Bay Company;
2. persuading the imperial government to declare the area a crown colony like Vancouver Island and the British Columbia mainland;
3. petitioning for annexation to the province of Canada West (the future province of Ontario), which favoured such a plan;
4. encouraging annexation to the United States, Minnesota in particular. Certainly Minnesota favoured this plan; and
5. petitioning for annexation to the projected Dominion of Canada, with the hope of being admitted as the fifth province.

There were enough servants of the Hudson's Bay Company in the area to keep its case alive and enough infiltration from St. Paul and other parts of the United States to ensure ongoing support for a "marriage" with the southern neighbour. The *Nor'Wester*, which was a forceful influence for the ten years between 1859 and 1869, at first backed the idea of a crown colony; it then switched its support to the goal of provincial status when it became likely that a confederated union would be achieved in the East.

There was yet another possible alternative, although it was regarded by some as more humorous than serious. It arose from the antics of Thomas Spence, a Montreal man with some skill as an organizer and a double share of ambition. After a year at Fort Garry, Spence moved to Portage la Prairie, ostensibly to operate a store. Portage was still a small centre when Rev. William Cochran came and built a church there in 1853, and by his efforts, the settlement had a local council. Almost at once, Spence managed to get elected to the council and then to become its chairman. The taste of authority was addictive.

Fortunately, the events that followed were placed on record by Robert Hill, a Portage la Prairie blacksmith who left a remarkable 764-page book entitled *History of Manitoba*.[5] Portage la Prairie, with "no laws but what [local residents] made themselves and which they chose to observe, was the place for such a man as Spence," said Hill, "and very soon we find a republican monarchy, if such there could be, with Spence as President and Findlay Ray, secretary." The birth of the "Republic" called for a new name, and both the settlement and the surrounding area became known as Caledonia, and later, Manitobah.

A council for the republic was chosen, a courthouse and jail were constructed, and boundaries were fixed. To raise needed funds, a customs tariff was adopted and charged against all goods imported. Local residents, noting the construction of the jail, didn't protest much, and outside authorities didn't know how to stop this frontier vagary. Spence no doubt enjoyed being president, but as often happens, he overstepped the bounds of propriety; he picked a quarrel with one MacPherson, a shoemaker at High Bluff, and charged him with treason against the republic.

There was snow on the ground when the president's two constables drove out to arrest the accused. MacPherson was tough, and there was a tussle, but the accused was soon being driven back to Portage. When the party passed MacPherson's friend John McLean, he demanded to know what was going on. When he heard MacPherson was to be tried for treason against the republic at seven o'clock that evening, he said he would be on hand.

When the case was called in the new courtroom, McLean, accompanied by a couple of muscular friends, entered and, according to Hill, shouted to Spence: "Come oot o' that ye whited sepulchre; ye canna be baith accuser and judge." At this, Spence ordered McLean's arrest too, and at once there was a riot. McLean and his friends inflicted most of the punishment, and in Hill's words, the mêlée "broke the back of the Republic completely."

The short life of the republic made no lasting impression upon the history of government in the West except to generate some laughs and show the sorry state of government in the West in 1867.

Manifest Destiny

American expansionism was a striking success story, though its neighbours didn't always approve. Beginning with the small cluster of thirteen colonies on the Atlantic coast at the end of the Revolutionary War in 1776, it had an amazingly rapid rise to become one of the wealthiest and most powerful nations of our time.

One of America's guiding principles was a tenet known as Manifest Destiny, which made expansion a moral obligation. The name came later, but the idea of Manifest Destiny was expressed in the policies of Thomas Jefferson, the third president of the United States, under whom the Americans bought the huge area known as Louisiana from France for $15 million. The area extended from the Gulf of Mexico to the present boundary of Canada, and from it, fourteen States, in whole or in part, were ultimately carved. Land acquisition in the Southwest was no less significant. For almost three centuries after Spain's Cortez conquered the native people, the land had remained Spanish, but gradually, through war, revolt, or purchase, all but Mexico became part of the United States.

The young nation won most of its boundary and territorial disputes and Manifest Destiny was glorious. The term itself wasn't used until 1845 when a prominent author declared that it was America's manifest destiny to claim "the continent allotted by Providence." Regardless of the origin of the slogan, politicians of all parties fancied its application and continued to voice it.

The policy didn't work for President James Polk when he tried to acquire what is today's British Columbia in 1846, but it did work in 1867 when the United States bought Alaska from Russia, paying $7.2 million for it. Some Americans believed that Secretary of State William Seward, who negotiated the purchase, believed that it was "a prelude to the peaceful annexation of Canada,"[6] and certainly, the American House of Representatives, before the end of the year, received a second bill proposing the United States take over parts of what is now Canada.

The first of the two measures, dated July 2, 1866, was introduced by a Mr. Banks and entitled: "A Bill for the admission of the States of Nova Scotia, New Brunswick, Canada East and Canada West and for the organization of the Territories of Selkirk, Saskatchewan and Columbia."

The wording suggested that such a transfer would be highly acceptable to the British government and the various British North American colonies. It read like an invitation to join the United States rather than a demand. When all had consented or accepted the proposition, the United States would publish by proclamation that "the States of Nova Scotia, New Brunswick, Canada East and Canada West and the Territories of Selkirk, Saskatchewan and Columbia with limits and rights by this Act defined, are constituted and admitted as States and Territories of the United States of America."

The bill was "read twice, referred to the Committee on Foreign Affairs and ordered to be printed," but it must have been withdrawn somewhere along the way. In any case, before the end of 1867—Canada's Confederation year—the House of Representatives placed a similar bill before its members. This one, submitted by Representative Ramsay from Minnesota, asked for the pursuit of a treaty with Canada, one clause of which would read:

> That Canada with the consent of Great Britain, shall cede to the United States the districts of North America west of longitude ninety degrees [the line of longitude running north and south across the west end of Lake Superior], to wit: The United States will pay six million dollars to the Hudson's Bay Company, in full

> discharge of all claims to the territory or jurisdiction in North America, whether founded on the Charter of the Company or any treaty, law or usage. The United States will assume the public debt of British Columbia, not exceeding the sum of two million dollars. . . .

This time, the prime minister was worried, as well he should have been. In haste, he ordered two of his strongest cabinet members, Sir George Cartier and William McDougall, to proceed at once to London and bring the essential representatives of the Hudson's Bay Company and the imperial government to the negotiating table to hammer out a deal by which the West would become part of Canada.

Buying the West

It was November 19 in the 200th year of Hudson's Bay Company rule in Rupert's Land when the company signed away its controversial claims to exclusive trading privileges there and to the land itself. It was a sad day for some, a day of triumph for others, but one of supreme significance for all westerners, whether they realized it or not. From that day forward, Rupert's Land would be part of Canada, with new goals and horizons.

For many of the native people, it was a dubious exchange. For the Honourable George Brown and other easterners who had been consistent supporters of annexation of the fur country, it was a day of jubilation. For those Americans with unwavering trust in Manifest Destiny who believed they were nearing the time when all North Americans would salute the same flag, the flag of the United States, the day was one of setback if not defeat. And for the like of James Wickes Taylor, that congenial American frequenter of Fort Garry and a sort of self-appointed American ambassador to Rupert's Land, it was a day of shock and confusion.

The imperial government in London had anticipated and encouraged the major land transfer. By the time the two Canadian cabinet ministers, Cartier and McDougall, arrived in London for negotiations, the Colonial Office had already opened discussions with the Hudson's Bay Company, and the two were considering terms. British officials conceded that the company should be allowed to retain its trading posts and certain lands around them, as well as a fraction of all other lands when surveyed. Some payment of money as compensation was also advised. Nobody disagreed with the principle, but the company's suggested price—a shilling per acre—brought loud objections. It was too much, the Canadians said. There were offers and counter offers, but not much agreement. Lord Granville of the Colonial Office became fearful that negotiations would break down. But like any good mediator, he convinced the men on both sides that it was to their own advantage as well as a public duty to find a workable compromise.

Ultimately, the accepted compromise was reached. It provided for a cash payment of £300,000, or about $1.5 million, to the company, blocks of land on which the trading posts were located, and a grant of one-twentieth of all land surveyed in the Fertile Belt. After the land survey was made, this "one-twentieth" of all lands translated to one and three-quarter sections in each township. To ensure that land allotted to the company was of average quality, the parcels reserved were all of section eight and three-quarters of section twenty-six in every township. Much of this Hudson's Bay Company land became quite valuable and was easily sold.

The British government had been very eager to see Rupert's Land returned to the Crown and then turned over to Canada, and that same government was ready to loan Canada the needed money.

The deed of surrender was signed on November 19; the company was to receive the cash payment twelve days later, on December 1, when the land would revert to the Crown—the Imperial government—and then be transferred to Canada. But unforeseen complications arose. The company quite understandably assumed that having signed its land away to the Crown, its responsibility for administration ended forthwith. Unfortunately, between November 19 and December 1 the Red River Rebellion took an ugly turn, and on December 1, when £300,000 of good English cash was to be paid, the British government had second thoughts about confirming a deal for a region in a state of rebellion.

The consummation was delayed, but the purchase had been made on November 19, 1869, a date that in light of its significance, should be recognized and marked with a celebration.

Students have been known to quibble about the proper term for the transaction; was it a purchase or a means of making compensation? It is not a question that demands an answer, but when a person or a government accepts a tract of land and simultaneously pays the contributing party a predetermined amount of money, the deal has all the marks of a purchase.

The Red River Rebellion

The negotiations that brought Rupert's Land back to the Crown and then to Canada deserved high praise. Unfortunately, however, the whole programme of land transfers suffered because the Métis, who believed they had some primary claims to the land, were ignored and left without so much as an explanation of what was taking place.

The Métis were worried and angry. They hadn't always agreed with the Hudson's Bay Company, but they had more confidence in the company than in the Dominion government, which was ignoring them. The Métis had hoped to hear that they would be assured of title to the land on which they lived. They didn't hear it. The Toronto *Globe* placed the blame on what is called Sir John A. Macdonald's "contemptuous silence."

It took nothing more than the high-handed actions of a government survey crew undertaking to reshape the traditional river-lot farms along the Red without even permission to be there. On October 11, 1869, a farmer, André Nault, ordered them off his land. He was ignored. He left, but returned with some gun-carrying neighbours, among them their spokesman, Louis Riel, twenty-five years old and only recently back from Montreal, where he was attending college. Needless to say, the survey party left and did not return. It was young Riel's first act of leadership and very much of a success. For the Métis, the victory was sweet.

Days later, when it was known that William McDougall—one of the two cabinet ministers who went to London to negotiate the recent land deal—was on his way west to become lieutenant-governor, Riel and his friends again asserted themselves. They didn't like McDougall anyway; they blamed him for their failure to obtain jobs on the Dawson Road to connect Lake of the Woods and Fort Garry. Moreover, they opposed any appointment about which they had not been consulted. They prevented McDougall's entry at Pembina, leaving him fuming on the south side of the border.

After two convincing demonstrations of what they could do, Riel sent 120 of his men to Fort Garry to seize the big post and its stock of rifles and supplies. He then called a general meeting, inviting English and French as well as his own people, and called for the preparation of a bill of rights to be sent to Ottawa. They produced a list of entirely reasonable demands: a legislature for the territory; the election of magistrates, sheriffs, and constables; that a portion of the public lands be appropriated for schools, roads, and bridges; that lands be set aside for partial payment of railroad construction; that a military force be recruited from residents of the area; that French and English languages be used in the legislature and all acts passed by the legislature be published in both languages; that treaties be concluded with local Indian tribes; that there be full representation from the area in the House of Commons; and finally, that these rights be guaranteed by Mr. McDougall before he was permitted into the territories.[7]

Dr. John Schultz—later the lieutenant-governor of Manitoba—was one of the leaders in an attempt to overthrow Riel's force. The attempt failed. He was taken prisoner, but escaped. Another body of volunteers opposed to Riel gathered at Portage la Prairie and marched from there to the Fort Garry district under Major Boulton but didn't attack. Actually, they were taken prisoner before they saw any action. Boulton was obliged to face a Métis court and was sentenced to die, but Donald Smith, who was there as the prime minister's personal representative, interceded with Riel and obtained a pardon.

Not so fortunate was Thomas Scott, who had been a constant annoyance to Riel's people. As a prisoner at Fort Garry, he was charged with assaulting a guard and was sentenced to be shot. Again, Donald Smith tried to persuade Riel to acquit the prisoner, but with no success. Scott was brought before a firing squad and sent to his death, though sad to say, in a protracted manner.

Scott may have been a chronic troublemaker, but his execution was a colossal mistake. Many people regarded it as murder, but charges were never laid. Meanwhile, a force of twelve hundred soldiers under Col. Garnet Wolseley left Collingwood on May 21 and arrived to restore order at Fort Garry on August 24, 1870. The fort was empty, Riel and his lieutenants having departed hours or minutes earlier, and the soldiers soon returned to the East, but the insurrection had ended. In the interval, the Manitoba Act had been passed in Parliament on May 12, and Manitoba became a province on July 15, 1870.

"Why Don't You Ask for a Railroad?"

Manitoba was the fifth province to join Confederation; British Columbia was next, joining one year and five days later.

Of the two candidates for the rank of province, British Columbia was the much better prepared, having had experiences—good and bad—with a gold rush and the exercises in government that accompanied a few years of crown colony rule. By 1867—Confederation year—the gold rush had ended and the colony could claim a population of roughly fifty thousand, including many who remained behind after the gold rush. There were liabilities too: a debt of about a million dollars and a depression, the usual price of a boom.

Like the people at Red River before the birth of their province, political sentiment was divided to form at least three blocs. Support for a place within the Dominion of Canada was on the ascendancy, but there were many who warned against haste in getting it. There were almost as many who favoured annexation to the United States. The gold rush years had brought hoards of Americans, and their influence was still strong; nobody thought it strange that U.S. stamps were commonly used on outgoing mail. The American purchase of Alaska left residents wondering if this was a forerunner to its acquisition of the rest of the Pacific coastal region. There were also those who opposed both of these options, believing they would be wise to cling to crown colony status and enjoy their lovely isolation.

One of the earliest and most ardent advocates of a province of British Columbia within the Dominion was the black-whiskered and eccentric Amor de Cosmos, who was as unusual as his name. Born at Windsor, Nova Scotia, in 1825 and christened William Alexander Smith, he followed the gold rush trail to California in 1851. As one of the famous forty-niners, he didn't mine much gold, but while in California he obtained the necessary state legislation to allow a change of name; he became Amor de Cosmos, "Lover of the World."

In 1858, he joined the rush to the Fraser River but stopped at Victoria, where he started a newspaper, the *British Colonist*. He gained election to the legislature at a time when the colony's political future was much in debate. From the outset he backed all democratic processes. He submerged himself in politics, often occupying two political seats at the same time: he was a member of the provincial legislature while he held a seat in the House of Commons and was the premier of British Columbia while still a member of the House of Commons.

He became the vocal leader of the faction seeking alignment with Canada West, Canada East, Nova Scotia, and New Brunswick in their entry into Confederation. But the majority of British Columbians were not yet ready, and even the Colonial Office in London appeared to be trying to tell de Cosmos to go slow until more of the intervening country east of the mountains was also ready for Confederation.

At length the B.C. legislative assembly authorized a formal discussion with members of the government of Canada about terms for the entry of British Columbia into Confederation. The governor named three members of his executive council to go to Ottawa in 1870. The committee departed on May 10 on the journey, which required twenty-five days. The members carried a list of concessions they would expect in return for the entry of their province into Confederation, among them a commitment to furnish improved transportation facilities between the East and West, including "a wagon road" across the mountains.

The prime minister was ill, and Hon. George Cartier attended the discussions on behalf of the federal government. The B.C. delegation made their request for a wagon road across the mountains and were quite surprised to hear the minister say, in effect: "Why don't you ask for a railroad?"

After almost two months in Ottawa, the westerners were on their way home with favourable answers to all their requests and more. It was agreed that the Dominion would assume the colony's debt and pay an annual grant of $35,000, plus eighty cents per head on the population; there was also the "surprise package," an undertaking to build a transcontinental railway, to be started within two years and completed within ten. It seemed too good to be true.

It was a bill of goods that was easy to sell at home. The legislative formalities were relatively simple, and British Columbia's entry into Confederation took effect on July 20, 1871.

A Police Force for the Firewater Frontier

Until there was law and order in the West, there could be no hope of attracting settlers and no inducement to build railroads. Captain William Francis Butler would write in his book, *The Great Lone Land*, that "the institutions of law and order, as understood in civilized communities, are unknown" in these regions, and the situation was desperate.

One of the most shocking evils going unchecked was the sale to Indians of an outrageous intoxicant, flatteringly called trade whiskey. The principal traders were from Montana. "Firewater" was the better name for their product, the formula for which might change from day to day, but which was likely to include tea, tobacco, Perry's painkiller, molasses, turpentine, red ink for colour, a little alcohol, and much slough water.

Strange to say, many of the native people were eager to get it and would willingly pay for it with buffalo hides or horses. For the traders, the business was highly profitable; for the Indian consumers, it was demoralizing.

If the notorious trade had a Canadian capital, it had to be Fort Hamilton, built at the junction of the Belly and St. Mary's rivers by Healy and Hamilton of Fort Benton in 1867. When it burned down, it was rebuilt as Fort Whoop-up, to flourish as the most lawless post of all. Lieutenant-Colonel Patrick Robertson-Ross, who was asked to visit the West in 1872 and report back to the prime minister with recommendations, mentioned that eighty-eight Blackfoot Indians were believed to have been "murdered in drunken brawls among themselves" in one year.

Butler, with the Irish Constabulary in mind, had recommended a force of 100 to 150 men, one-third of them mounted. Robertson-Ross saw a need for a military force of five hundred mounted riflemen and estimated the annual cost at $300,000.

Sir John A. Macdonald recognized that the situation was urgent and prepared a bill to establish the North-West Mounted Rifles. But somebody reading the draft mentioned that the name had a military ring to it and might be offensive to the Americans. The story goes that Macdonald crossed out the word "Rifles" and inserted "Police." The bill found ready support in Parliament and received royal assent on May 23, 1873. It provided for a force not to exceed 300 men, "able to ride, of good character, able bodied, between 18 and 40 years of age and able to read and write in either English or French." They would sign for a three-year term, with pay of a dollar a day for constables and seventy-five cents a day for sub-constables.

The government did nothing more until August, when news of the Cypress Hills Massacre was received. It then passed an order-in-council putting the plan in motion. Recruiting began, and before the leaves had fallen, the first small contingent of men, under the command of Major James Morrow Walsh, was on its way to winter at Lower Fort Garry in Manitoba. Colonel George Arthur French, an imperial army man, was appointed commissioner, and Colonel James F. Macleod, assistant commissioner.

The main body of the force left Toronto on June 6, 1874 in two special trains. They travelled by way of Chicago and St. Paul to Fargo, North Dakota, the nearest railroad point to Fort Dufferin in southern Manitoba, where the small group from Fort Garry and the large group from Toronto would meet and prepare for the long trek into parts unknown.

In marching order, they were the most imposing group ever seen in the West. The two commissioners rode at the head of the parade, followed by 318 mounted officers and men, 315 horses, 147 work oxen, 114 loaded Red River carts, 93 wagons, two 9-pound cannons, 21 Métis drivers, and various farm machines like mowers and rakes. What a cavalcade, but there were no cameras and practically no spectators!

The pace, at first, was brisk, but then horses, oxen, and men began to tire. Horses and oxen were beginning to die, and a few men deserted. After two months on the trail and many more deaths among the animals, the party was somewhere in the area of today's Medicine Hat and was quite lost. It was decided that the commissioners would leave the main body of the force near the Sweet Grass Hills and make a side trip into Montana. When they returned, it was with a stock of supplies, fresh horses, and a new hired man, the small, bowlegged halfbreed Jerry Potts. Because of his knowledge and instincts, the force was never lost again. He led them on a direct course to Whoop-Up. To general surprise, only one man was found inside the famous fort. After four more days, Potts brought the force to a favoured place on the Old Man River, almost a thousand miles from Fort Dufferin. There, the men began building Fort Macleod, and from there they would attack the nefarious whiskey trade, earning admiration from generations yet unborn.

The Cypress Hills Massacre

The Cypress Hills Massacre was simply murder on a large scale. Even if the white killers from Fort Benton were intoxicated, their attack upon an inoffensive camp of Assiniboine Indians, predominantly women, children, and old men, was cowardly, senseless, and wicked. Unfortunately, the aggressors were never brought to trial.

If the atrocity achieved anything useful, it may have served to hasten the formation of the North-West Mounted Police and the force's arrival in the lawless Northwest. Some writers have expressed the opinion that it was the shocking news of the massacre that inspired the government to organize the force in the first place. This is doubtful. The prime minister had given notice of his intention to introduce the mounted police bill on April 28, and although the exact date of the massacre is not known, it was in May. Considering the primitive state of communications at the time, it is doubtful if anything, good or bad, that happened in the Cypress Hills in May would have been heard in Ottawa before midsummer. The report of the massacre would have been more likely to accelerate the passing of the August order-in-council that started recruiting for the force than hasten earlier events.

It all started when Montana traders and wolfers working on the southwestern prairies were on their way home with wagons loaded high with buffalo hides, wolf skins, and empty barrels. While still one day's travel from Benton, a group of the men halted to camp beside the Teton River. When they awakened in the morning, their horses were missing, having strayed or been stolen. The traders chose to believe the latter and vowed revenge against the Indians responsible. But before they could indulge in any such "sport," the horseless men had to find a way to deliver the season's harvest of hides. They walked to Benton, borrowed horses, brought the wagons to town, and then prepared for an organized hunt of the horse thieves.

With Thomas Hardwick as leader, the hunting party, augmented with other traders, set out. Well mounted and well armed, they rode back to the camp, where they easily convinced themselves that they had located the tracks of the thieves. They proceeded in a northeasterly direction toward the Cypress Hills. On reaching the hills, they camped at Battle Creek and paid a fraternal visit at a post operated by another Bentonite, Abel Farwell, a man who enjoyed a better reputation than most of those in the business. He had no knowledge of any newly acquired horses in the possession of nearby Indians and mentioned that he had found the band of Assiniboines under Chief Little Chief—about forty lodges—to be good people. They had suffered much from food shortages during the past winter and were obviously weakened.

Farwell wanted to go alone to look at the Indian horses and then report back to the others, but the Hardwick men, who had been consuming some of their own liquid trade goods, didn't think any Indians were "good people," and they insisted on making their own inspection. They went, taking their arrogance and their guns with them. Shots were fired, and shots were returned. Farwell testified later that the traders shot first. The Benton men fell back to sheltered positions and kept shooting. One trader, Ed Grace, was killed. How many Indians died isn't known, but estimates ranged as high as eighty.

When the account of the one-sided slaughter reached Ottawa, there were calls for arrests and punishment, but not much could be done until the mounted police were in the area. Later, a few of the killers made the mistake of wandering back across the border and were arrested, but most of them were careful to stay away. The mounted police were given permission to conduct their investigation in Montana, from where they hoped that the accused men could be extradited for trial in Canada. The suspected men were rounded up and applications were made for extraditions.

The hearings were conducted at Helena. All of Montana was ablaze with excitement. The United States authorities co-operated well, but Montana public opinion was overwhelmingly on the side of the alleged murderers. The evidence was so contradictory that the judge was left with little choice and discharged the men. One of those given discharge promptly obtained a warrant for the arrest of Assistant Commissioner Macleod on a charge of false arrest. Macleod had the experience of sitting in a Montana jail for a few days while he waited to be cleared and was allowed to go home. So ended the unhappy and unsatisfactory story of the massacre in the hills.

Sitting Bull and the Medicine Line

Sitting Bull was the most widely known member of his race in the United States and the most feared. He and his belligerent followers gave Canadians a special reason for interest and fear. For four troubled years after the bloody and tragic Battle of the Little Big Horn in Montana on June 25, 1876, Sitting Bull and his Sioux people were Canada's unwanted and unwelcome guests.

The chief hoped to stay in Canada; while he and five thousand members of his tribe were at what looked like a permanent camp at Wood Mountain in what is now southern Saskatchewan, he pleaded with the Canadian government to give them a reserve and let them stay. In support of the request, he contended that he was really a Canadian Indian, born near Manitoba's section of the Red River. That claim, however, was never verified—he probably didn't know exactly where he was born or when—and there is not much information in the records except that he was born "somewhere in buffalo country about 1834." But Canada didn't want Sitting Bull, and in practically starving him and his followers to force their return to the United States, there wasn't much evidence of mercy.

The chief seemed to be in lifelong conflict with the American authorities, a conflict that reached its climax at Little Big Horn River in southeastern Montana. It had been United States military strategy on this occasion to use three squadrons of cavalry for a three-pronged attack that would deal a knock-out blow to the troublesome tribe. Lieutenant Colonel George Custer was to lead one of the attacking columns, co-ordinating precisely with the other two, but for reasons soon hidden by deaths, Custer seemed to believe he and his men could and should do the job by themselves. Without waiting for the other two columns, he struck a full day ahead of schedule. He and his detachment were exterminated. In what has been called "Custer's Last Stand," he and 225 mounted men went to their deaths.

The Sioux rejoiced, but they knew they would be pursued with a bigger force and more vengeful vigour. For the rest of the year, the Sioux, handicapped by the presence of their families, were engaged in rear-guard fighting, consoling themselves with the thought that if capture appeared imminent, they would retreat across the "Medicine Line" to Canada.

They crossed late in 1876 and early in '77 and set up their camp at Wood Mountain. The few mounted police at Fort Macleod appeared insignificant, but they never waivered. The commissioner sent an urgent message to Major James Morrow Walsh, on sick leave in the East at the time, to return to assume liaison duty with the Sioux. Walsh responded by moving to Wood Mountain and becoming one of Sitting Bull's nearest neighbours.

For the next four years, the Americans tried to persuade the chief to return, and the Canadians tried to persuade him to go. His presence in Canada looked like an invitation to trouble. Five thousand extra Indians looking for food would surely deplete the wildlife and cause more Canadian Indians to go hungry. Worse than that was the danger of Sitting Bull rekindling old hatreds and causing intertribal wars. Still worse was the chance that he might form a powerful Indian alliance of western tribes and, with himself as the supreme leader, make a broad attack upon Canadian authority and Canadian settlements. After destroying Canadian resistance, the triumphant Natives could be expected to cross the boundary and wreak the same vengeance there. That Sitting Bull had made the proposal to Chief Crowfoot at least once and perhaps twice seemed pretty certain.

Keeping the Indians in a state of hunger was an effective instrument in persuading them to return home, where they'd have reserves. Gradually, the Sioux numbers dwindled. The last to surrender to the cruel threat of starvation was Sitting Bull. His only future, it seemed, was at Standing Rock Reservation in North Dakota, where he died as he had lived, in a struggle, on December 5, 1890.

One of the finer aspects of Sitting Bull's stay in Canada was the relationship of respect and trust that grew between him and Major Walsh. They were both strong characters, and many people expected a violent confrontation. It didn't happen. What did happen was a shift from mutual fear and hatred to mutual understanding and admiration. Walsh would have gone to Washington to plead for his friend, but the Government of Canada frowned on the idea. Before they parted, Sitting Bull wanted to give Walsh a present as a token, but the officer didn't need another horse, and Sitting Bull had no money. He presented his friend with what was his dearest possession, his aging feathered war bonnet, relic of a hundred warpaths. It would have been a touching scene.

The old headpiece, shabby and moth-eaten, rests today in the Royal Ontario Museum in Toronto, a symbol of a friendship that could transcend hatreds and war.

Treaty No. 6

Bringing the important Indian treaties to a conclusion—like the Lands Act and the enabling legislation for a western police force—was high on the prime minister's list of priorities after the Rupert's Land takeover. By 1876, five western treaties had been finalized and signed, but they were considered minor ones. Clearly, the Ottawa administration was leaving the more difficult treaties to the last, and there now remained the two big, potentially troublesome, treaties: one with the widely scattered Plains Crees, and the other with the powerful Blackfoot and neighbouring tribes.

The Crees, who were once residents of the low country around James Bay, became the first and best trading customers of the Hudson's Bay Company and hence the first to have guns. With their new wonder-weapons, they advanced onto the prairies and became dedicated buffalo hunters and remained. By 1876, the year chosen for the treaty negotiations, they were spread across the central parts of today's three prairie provinces. Their territory was so big, there was no hope of assembling a proper representation of the tribesmen at one place. It was therefore decided to have two treaty gatherings, one at Fort Carlton and the other at Fort Pitt.

Alexander Morris, lieutenant-governor of Manitoba and the North-West Territories, was appointed chief commissioner. The other commissioners were Chief Factor William Christie of the Hudson's Bay Company and the exceptionally popular halfbreed James McKay, who weighed 350 pounds and was built like a Durham bull. The official escort and best possible guarantee against trouble was Superintendent James Walker of the mounted police.

Fort Carlton was to be the scene of the first meeting, with the eastern Crees. The leading native actors were the good and reliable Chief Mistahwahsis and the tribe's unfailing entertainer, Chief Beardy.

Superintendent James Walker planned to meet the commissioners at the Batoche ferry the day before the discussions would begin. Beardy hoped to reach the officials first to present his demand for a special deal and bigger treaty payments for himself and his friends. If it hadn't been for Walker's unexpected appearance, the commissioners might have had trouble in protecting the treaty cash they were carrying. Beardy was seeing a mounted police uniform for the first time, and he may have been mesmerized. He withdrew, but not for long. He was back well before the treaty money was to be paid and was the first in line to receive the twenty-five dollars to which each chief was entitled. Then, according to legend, he retired briefly and reappeared with a change of warpaint and a different headpiece, looking like a different Indian, and went through the line to collect the fifteen dollars that each of the headmen could claim. Finally, as the story was told, Beardy reappeared wearing only a breechcloth and was able to add the twelve dollars to which all other Indians were entitled.

Perhaps it was an injustice, but his name came up again and again when it was discovered that the government herd of cattle, driven to Fort Carlton for the occasion, had disappeared. It was government practice to supply all Indians attending treaty negotiations with beef, flour, tea, and sugar. There being no cattle in the district and no longer many buffalo, a herd of about two hundred head of cattle was brought from the south. Mysteriously, the whole herd vanished. Searching revealed nothing. A Winnipeg newspaper told that 145 cattle had disappeared.[8] The cattle were never found. Nobody could say that Beardy was guilty, but nobody was sure he was innocent. Beardy could never escape accusing glances.

Fort Pitt was a long drive from Fort Carlton by democrat, and with

James McKay as one of the passengers, it was a test of fitness for horses and vehicle. At Pitt, the party was greeted by Chiefs Pakan and Sweet Grass, pleasant people. Big Bear was there, but he never agreed to reservations or the surrender of any Indian rights.

For Superintendent Walker and the commissioners, the two treaty gatherings turned out to be an opportunity to study contrasts in Indian chiefs: the traditional Chief Mistahwahsis; the troublemaker Beardy; the one with a good heart and frightening face, Big Bear; one of the first friends of the idea of agriculture for Indians, Pakan; and the West's first conservationist, more interested in saving buffalo than collecting treaty money, Sweet Grass.

"The Last to Break the Promise"

"The Blackfoot Indians are a bold and warlike race," said the Minister of the Interior in his annual report for 1877. He might have added that the same tribesmen were the first Canadian Indians to have horses and perhaps the best of the native horsemen.

The powerful and much-feared Indians making up the Blackfoot confederacy—the Blackfoot, Blood, and Peigan tribes—were seen as intractable people resembling the Sioux in the United States. For fully a hundred years, traders and travellers were advised, for reasons of safety, to stay away from Blackfoot country, now southern Alberta. It was a warning that most travellers accepted. Until there was a treaty, homesteaders and ranchers would shun the southwest.

Their sad experiences with the white man's diseases and whiskey had increased Blackfoot hostility. Both evils were at their worst in the few years before the coming of the mounted police. The tribesmen suffered severely from smallpox, of which Father Constantine Scollen, a missionary among them, could speak with authority: "In 1870," he wrote, "came that disease so fatal to Indians, the smallpox, which told upon the Blackfoot with terrible effect, destroying between 600 and 800 of them. Surviving relatives went more and more for the use of alcohol, endeavouring to drown their grief in the poisonous beverage."[9]

Lieutenant-Governor David Laird and N.W.M.P. Commissioner James F. Macleod were appointed to treat with the three Blackfoot tribes and the two smaller ones nearby, the Sarcee and Stoney. Fort Macleod would be the meeting place, but that choice of location was made, unwisely, before consultation with the Indian wiseman Chief Crowfoot, who ruled that the negotiations would be at Blackfoot Crossing on the Bow River, south of present-day Cluny, and nowhere else. The date would be September 17.

Lieutenant-Governor Laird was still in residence at Swan River but was in the midst of preparations for a move to the new territorial capital at Battleford. He left Swan River in a horse-drawn democrat on August 11 and arrived at Battleford thirteen days later and there turned onto the trail to Fort Macleod. The journey from Battleford to Fort Mcleod—"365 miles as measured by Major Irvine's odometer"—took ten days, and there was still the trail trip to Blackfoot Crossing.

The commissioners were ready for the negotiations on the appointed day, but a large number of the Bloods and Peigans, exhibiting typical scorn for the white man's obsession with time, had gone on a buffalo hunt and would be late. The commissioners may have been annoyed, but they agreed to wait, and when the hunters returned, the formal meeting began with nearly five thousand men, women, and children assembled on the grass.

With the help of an interpreter, the lieutenant-governor assured his big audience of their queen's concern for the health and happiness of her Indian children. He then explained what was proposed by way of reservations, help in making starts in farming and stock-raising, schools for Indian children, and the money payments that would be the same as those made to the Crees.

Would the Indians of the five tribes accept? All eyes were turned toward Chief Crowfoot, the acknowledged Man of Wisdom. No Indian would speak before him, but he wasn't ready to speak. He would take a day or two to consider and, presumably, confer with the Great Spirit. He'd let the commissioners know when he was ready.

A day passed. Two days passed. Then the chief sent word that he would speak. Again, the great body of native men, women, and children came together, and the commissioners asked Crowfoot to express his advice. It was a serious moment, and everybody seemed to sense it. The chief stood with dignity and made a short speech, one that might have passed as the oration of a scholar. He concluded by saying: "I am satisfied. I will sign the treaty." He would be the first to sign, he said, and "the last to break the promise."

The signing followed and then the making of treaty payments. The total amount paid to the 4,392 men, women, and children of the five tribes was $52,954. The aging Chief Crowfoot, whose fine sense of honour would not let him accept any of the government's food rations until after the discussions so that there could be no suggestion of bribery, ate freely, while the mounted police cannon boomed a salute and the good news of the Blackfoot treaty success brought joy all the way to Ottawa.

The First Western Railroad and the Countess of Dufferin

The first railroad in Canada was a midget line constructed for hauling coal at a Pictou County, Nova Scotia, mine in 1827. It depended upon a team of strong horses driven beside the track for propelling power. By Confederation year, Canada had twenty-five hundred miles of railway, all in the East. The West would have to wait for another decade before it saw a train in motion.

The Canadian government would not be allowed to forget the promise it made in 1870 to give British Columbia a rail connection with the eastern provinces within ten years. And regardless of that commitment, the conviction was growing that, in the interest of unity, the East and West needed the connecting bond which only a railroad could supply. The only point in doubt was whether a young and sparsely settled country like Canada would be able to pay for it.

Prime Minister John A. Macdonald had a clear vision of a transcontinental railway and some ideas about how the dream could be realized. When he was embarrassed by the Pacific Scandal and obliged to resign, his railroad plans were halted. His successor in office, Alexander Mackenzie, adopted the cautious policy of building railroads one segment at a time. Hence, the first railroad in the West, which ran south from Winnipeg to connect with an American line at the border, was started in 1874 and completed in 1878. It was an exciting development. For Manitobans, three items of railroad news appearing in the *Daily Free Press* were significant:

"On Saturday last [Sept. 19, 1874], the Pembina Railway was actually commenced. The first sod was turned . . . at the present northern terminus of the work, about eight miles from Winnipeg. . . . Work will be continued in earnest this week."[10]

There were annoying delays due to the failure of operating funds expected from Ottawa, but the news of December 5, 1878, was cheering: "The last rail is laid; the last spike is driven. Manitoba, after many vexatious delays . . . is now connected by rail with the outer world."[11]

And the third item spoke triumph: "The first regular train on the Pembina Branch arrived at St. Boniface shortly after 11 o'clock on Saturday night [Dec. 7, 1878] with about 20 passengers. The train consisted of a locomotive, passenger coach, two cabooses and some flat cars. The first regular departure was made next morning at four o'clock."[12]

History's best single relic from those first years of railroading was the small but sturdy locomotive that became known and loved as the Countess of Dufferin. If the name confirmed the gender, she was indeed the railroad's leading lady after her arrival at St. Boniface on October 9, 1877. Accompanying her on a barge lashed to the Red River steamboat *Selkirk* were six flatcars, a caboose, and a quantity of wood ties to carry the rails. Joseph Whitehead had hoped to have the engine in Winnipeg before the departure of Governor General and Lady Dufferin and have the latter christen the locomotive. The steamboat *Selkirk* was running late, but as the viceregal party was travelling upstream on the Red, returning to Ottawa, members of the party requested a stop at Fisher's Landing where the *Selkirk* and barge were temporarily tied. Lady Dufferin boarded the barge and, after some complimentary remarks about the radiantly new locomotive, consented graciously that it carry her name.

Unloaded at St. Boniface, the engine moved under its own steam and went to work on the new line the next day and every day until construction was completed. Then the Countess began hauling trains over the new line. When the main line of the C.P.R. was completed to Winnipeg, she was transferred to the broader service.

In 1884, when Prime Minister and Lady Macdonald visited the West, he was anxious to travel to the end of construction in the mountains, and the Countess of Dufferin was assigned to his train. When Lady Macdonald expressed a wish to see the Rockies from the very front of the train, somebody asked if she would care to ride on the cowcatcher. She nodded, and a strong chair was bolted to the front-end structure, and there she rode, further enriching the story.

When the Countess began showing her age, she was sold to a lumber company at Golden. When retired from there, through the efforts of Mayor Waugh of Winnipeg, she was presented to that city, where she was accorded a royal homecoming and assured a place of honour until the end of time.

Louis Riel's Return

Anybody can make a mistake, but nobody should make the same mistake twice. It is the edict of history and applies to governments as well as individuals.

The Canadian government was already guilty of ignoring the Métis when negotiating the takeover of Rupert's Land, to which the native people believed they had a primary claim. To quell the ensuing insurrection the government sent Colonel Wolseley and a field force of 1200 men over the ninety-five-day land and water route from Collingwood to Red River. It seemed unthinkable that the same government with the same prime minister would repeat the sin of ignoring the deep concerns of about the same people just fifteen years later, and then find it necessary to pay much more dearly in lives and dollars for its mistakes.

The Métis were a proud and independent people wanting most of all to be left alone to their hunting and simple social pleasures on their untitled land. But for those on the South Saskatchewan River there was the ever haunting fear of white men closing in on them. Gabriel Dumont, their robust leader, wrote to the prime minister about it, but apparently received no reply. Fearful of being swamped by a tide of white immigrants, the Métis believed they needed a second leader who was strong where Dumont was weak. In a fight, he would be the best, but Dumont couldn't make a speech, and he was no diplomat. Before the end of summer in 1884, Dumont and three others on good horses were riding away toward Montana, hoping to find Louis Riel and persuade him to return. They found him teaching school in the western part of the state and living fairly quietly with his wife, Marguerite, and family. He hesitated about returning, but yielded to Dumont's pleading, and he and his family accompanied the party back to Batoche.

The reception at Batoche was warm and boisterous. Riel spent most of the first winter trying to improve the public understanding of his people, but on the following March 19, he declared a provisional Métis government, as he had done at Red River. Enthusiasm brought a sense of belligerence, and when there was looting at a Duck Lake store, Major Crozier of the N.W.M.P. with fifty-six of his own men and forty-three volunteers, all mounted, rode to Fort Carlton and, on March 26, toward Duck Lake to suppress further trouble.

They were confronted a few miles west of Duck Lake by a force of mounted Métis led by Dumont. After an exchange of unfriendly words, a shot rang out, followed by more shots from both sides, and the Battle of Duck Lake was aflame. It was short but especially disastrous for Crozier, who had twelve men dead and twenty-five more wounded. In a test of marksmanship, Dumont's men were winners.

The victorious Métis sent messages to their Indian friends to join them in the fight for freedom. Seven days later, Big Bear's Crees went on a massacre spree at Frog Lake, killing nine white citizens, including the Indian agent and two priests, but the Chief himself may not have been present.

The reports reaching Ottawa brought quick government action. A force of almost four thousand men under General Middleton was rushed west on the new C.P.R.

Middleton, a former Imperial army officer and new to the Canadian West, divided his army into three columns: the main body would leave the train at Troy, later called Qu'Appelle, to follow Middleton toward Batoche; the second column would detrain at Swift Current and follow

Colonel W. D. Otter to the relief of Battleford, where Chief Poundmaker's Crees were looting and burning; and the third body would continue to Calgary, there to become part of the Alberta Field Force, to march behind General T. B. Strange to Fort Edmonton and east from there.

After bringing the desired relief to Battleford, Otter set out to "punish" Poundmaker's Indians at Cutknife Hill, but suffered defeat there. General Middleton attacked Riel's men at Fish Creek, near Batoche, and was driven back with heavy losses. After reinforcing, he attacked again on May 9 and, with the advantage of sufficient ammunition, dealt the blow of defeat to the insurgents. Riel, refusing a chance to escape with Dumont, surrendered and was taken to Regina to be jailed and face trial.

One by one, the Indian leaders surrendered and the Rebellion of '85 ended. The Regina trials got underway on July 28. The principal interest was in Louis Riel. In the end the jury decided that he was guilty of treason, but recommended mercy. The judge pronounced the sentence of death by hanging. The appeal court didn't change anything. The prime minister could have invoked the prerogative of clemency. Whatever he did would be popular in one eastern province and unpopular in another, but Ontario had more voters than Quebec, and Louis Riel went to his death on November 16, 1885. The public debate about the justice of it all has never ended.

On the Main Line

Everybody wanted to be close to the new transcontinental railway, and real-estate fortunes were made and lost with changes to the route. The town of Selkirk was on the main line as it was originally drawn; the city of Winnipeg was not. Both wanted to be, of course. Hundreds of small communities were caught up in the uncertainty, and the real estate trade resembled a lottery.

Prime Minister Macdonald's handsome plan for the building of the transcontinental railway by Sir Hugh Allan's group of financiers, a plan to which he committed subsidies of 50 million acres of western land and $50 million of government cash, collapsed like a house of straw in a gale after the revelation of political indiscretions with campaign funds. But the amazing politician led his party back to power in the next election in 1878 and at once set about to revive his railway policy by awarding a contract to another group of Canadian capitalists who would undertake the colossal task. George Stephen of Montreal—cousin of Donald Smith—agreed to head the group and accept the prime minister's revised list of subsidies, which would include 25 million acres of western land, $25 million, and some 700 miles of ready-made railroads already in the possession of the government. The contract was signed in October, 1880, and Parliament ratified it four months later.

The route that would have taken the railroad in a northwesterly direction after crossing the Red River to pass Lake Manitoba at the Narrows and continue by way of the Swan River and Saskatchewan River valleys, Fort Edmonton, and the Yellowhead Pass, had already been abandoned in favour of a direct course across the Prairies to enter the mountains toward the Kicking Horse Pass, thereby inventing places like Brandon, Regina, Calgary, and Banff. It also gave Winnipeg a chance to become a main-line city at the expense of Selkirk. Naturally, Selkirk, Rapid City, and Fort Edmonton didn't like it.

The early indication of losing the advantage of a main-line location was most galling to Winnipeg people, but they never gave up the fight. The city leaders pestered Ottawa for reconsideration of route plans but received no encouragement until the formation of the new syndicate. As they continued their lobby, the total value of their contributions and concessions increased. Their final offer was convincing, and in 1881, the syndicate agreed to reroute the rail line through the city and locate the shops and yards nearby in return for Winnipeg's guarantee of municipal tax exemptions, the gift of a bridge—the Princess Louise Bridge—to span the Red River, and sufficient land to meet the need for a station, shops, yards, and right-of-way.

Winnipeg people were happy and the city's real-estate boom soared to new heights of frenzy. Selkirk's speculators were shocked, and some were ruined. They would now be sidetracked.

While the main line was being built from Port Arthur to Winnipeg, contractor Andrew Onderdonk was engaged with the most forbidding part of the entire route, including the Fraser and Thompson canyons. William Cornelius Van Horne brought his natural forcefulness to the prairie sector. One hundred and sixty miles of construction was built west from Winnipeg in 1881, but Van Horne set five hundred miles as the goal for 1882; he didn't quite achieve it, but the year's performance was a record anyway.

The rails reached Calgary on August 11, 1883, and construction for the season ended at Lake Louise. The momentum was maintained, and Donald Smith drove the last spike at Craigellachie, deep in the mountains, on November 7, 1885.

Landmark dates came thick and fast. The first train of western wheat was shipped from Portage la Prairie to Fort William for trans-shipment to Montreal and Liverpool in 1885. But the most widely acclaimed railroad accomplishment of that year was the delivery of combat troops from the East to the scenes of rebellion around Batoche. The prime minister was reported to have asked Van Horne how fast he could move 3,500 troops from eastern points to Qu'Appelle. The contractor, after considering the four incompleted gaps over which the men would have to pass on foot or by wagon, said ten days. Thinking of the three months taken to move 1,200 men from Collingwood to Fort Garry during the Wolseley Expedition in 1870, Macdonald laughed and said: "You can't do it." Van Horne did it in eight days, and by so doing, he impressed the members of the House of Commons and induced them to give quick approval to a bill for a loan to bring the railroad to completion.

Chapter 4

The Promised Land

The Great Giveaway

Now that Canada had acquired the North West, the prime minister, whose government had invested $1.5 million in it, had to decide what was to be done with it. As a son of Clan Macdonald, he might well have been wondering how the money was going to be recovered. There had been no soil survey except the rough appraisal done by John Palliser, who recognized only two kinds of soil, dry prairie and park belt. Immigrant settlers were ill-qualified to appraise their own land. Circumstances promised the biggest trial-and-error learning experience in the history of land use.

Western lands would serve two main purposes, first to furnish free homesteads with which to attract immigrants and, second, for use as subsidies in paying for railroad construction. There is no evidence that the dominion government was very conscious of quality variations in land. A quarter section was 160 acres, good soil or poor.

In any case, there had to be a land survey and a policy. A survey had been started earlier but ran into trouble from Louis Riel's friends and had to be halted. It was resumed, however, in 1872, the same year the Dominion Lands Act was passed. The earlier survey was based on 800-acre sections that were easily divisible into 100-acre and 200-acre fractions with which settlers from eastern Canada would feel at home. But between 1869 and '72, the 800-acre sections were abandoned in favor of 640-acre units, the size adopted in the western United States.

The new survey began with the international boundary as a base line and meridian lines running at right angles northward. The first or principal meridian began at a point on the boundary about ten miles west of Pembina. A township consisted of thirty-six sections; rows or tiers of townships were numbered from the boundary northward, while the north-south rows called ranges were numbered westward and eastward from the principal meridian and westward only from the more westerly meridians. With sections exactly one mile square and townships exactly six miles square, the western survey served well and will endure in spite of poorly considered ideas about abandoning the mile as a measuring unit.

Homesteaders were the first to benefit from the survey and land act, which read: "Any person who is the head of a family or has attained the age of twenty-one years shall be entitled to be entered for one quarter section or a less quantity of unappropriated Dominion lands for the purpose of securing a homestead right in respect thereof."[1]

The applicant, regardless of his national origin, paid a filing fee of ten dollars and then faced the obligation of complying with three basic requirements before qualifying for the title on his land: he had to live on the property for at least six months per year for three years, acquire or build a livable house or cabin, and cultivate a specified amount of land for cropping. The homesteader could fulfil the requirements in three years and then obtain legal ownership to the farm. If the place had good soil, it was a good deal; if it had poor soil, it could be a waste of time.

The land giveaway began as early as the survey. The Hudson's Bay Company was, by agreement, to get one-twentieth of the lands surveyed in the area designated as the fertile belt and was, accordingly, allotted sections eight and three-quarters of twenty-six in most townships. At the same time, sections eleven and twenty-nine were set apart as an endowment for the purposes of education. The sections became known commonly as "school lands."

To further the distribution of lands, the dominion government sold land to land companies and immigration organizations for settlement or resale. In most cases, the government's price was one dollar an acre.

The biggest land concession of all was to the Canadian Pacific Railway in 1881. As an inducement to build and complete the transcontinental railroad, the government of the day agreed to contribute $25 million in cash and twenty-five million acres of western land in alternate sections within twenty-four miles of the right-of-way. By this time, homestead quarters could be selected from any unappropriated land on even-numbered sections, so the C.P.R. allotments were limited to uneven-numbered sections.

It's easy to criticize now, but still, public lands at the time were being distributed with a laxity that was not flattering to their considered worth.

"You'll Never See Your Cattle Again"

Cattle ranching in British Columbia started with a few unsaleable cattle left over from herds trailed from Oregon to feed miners in the British Columbia gold rush. Branded and turned loose on the good valley grass, they seemed to sense a future in cattle ranching and multiplied.

On the prairie side of the mountains, there was no gold rush and no reason for importing cattle except to get ready for a time when the human population would be high and the buffalo population would be all but wiped out. So it was that John B. Smith of Sun River, Montana, drove a small herd, fourteen cows, one bull, and ten calves—a total of twenty-five head—to Fort Mcleod. There, he planned to sell milk and butter at the police barracks. The mounted police hunters could still get a buffalo when fresh meat was needed, but there was no substitute for the milk and butter from Smith's cows. But early in the autumn, about the time Lieutenant-Governor Morris of the North-West Territories was negotiating Treaty No. 6 with the Crees at Fort Pitt, the little herd of Smith cattle came into the ownership of Constable Robert Whitney of the N.W.M.P.

There was something strange about the transaction because Smith had appeared well satisfied with his milk sales at the barracks and Constable Whitney had neither farm nor ranch and had never shown any interest in starting either. He was at Fort Macleod to help the force stamp out the illegal whiskey trade, which was clearly demoralizing the Indians, and put an end to horse stealing. He had enough to do without becoming involved with a herd of cattle.

Both Whitney and Smith were loathe to explain. The explanation never did get into the police records, but one police pioneer confided that Whitney did not buy the cattle but won them in a poker game.

Having neither land nor shelter for cattle and no feed for winter months just ahead, he had good reason to be apprehensive. He felt the dilemma so strongly that he declared with rancour that he would turn the cattle out to face the winter and suffer the consequences. Friends felt compelled to warn him: "You'll never see hide nor hair of your critters again. Either they'll freeze in this North-West winter or the Indians will shoot them down the way they would take buffalo. And if they should escape the frost and Indians, they'll likely be overtaken by a herd of migrating buffalo and be swept away like sheep in a blizzard. They're liable to end up in Kansas. Any way you take it, you'll never see your cattle again."

Whitney listened and then asked: "What else can I do?" He turned the cattle out to the mercy of the winter range and tried to forget them.

But he didn't forget them. Came spring, and to satisfy a lingering curiosity about what remained of the little herd—maybe nothing more than fresh bones picked clean by coyotes—he saddled up and rode away to learn the worst. He probably didn't realize it at the time but what he was doing in that spring of 1877 was conducting the first and most humble range roundup in the history of prairie ranching. After an absence of a couple of days, he rode back to Fort Macleod in triumph, driving the bull, fourteen cows, ten yearlings and fourteen brand-new calves born on the range that spring.

Nobody was more impressed than Whitney himself, who almost immediately resolved to terminate his police years and go ranching. On the following May 1, he arranged for a substitute to complete his contract term of police service, took his discharge, and began raising cattle in earnest.

Others followed Whitney's example. Fred Kanouse, hearing the mounted police message that it was time for wise men to quit the whiskey business, drove twenty-one cows and a bull from Montana later that year. After branding them, he turned them out to graze where they chose between the Missouri and North Saskatchewan rivers. The next herds to be brought in were big ones. Spectators had witnessed the birth of cattle ranching on the Canadian plains.

Red Fife

Nobody would suggest that the fur trade ended abruptly on a particular day or that the new wheat economy suddenly became a full-fledged and worthy successor. Nevertheless, if symbolic dates are wanted, it seems fair to accept November 19, 1869, when the Hudson's Bay Company surrendered its trading monopoly and territorial claims, as the end of the old order of furs and October 21, 1876, when the first western wheat was shipped outward bound, as the date on which the wheat economy had its birth.

The Selkirk immigrants of 1811 carried a bushel and a half of seed wheat from Scotland and planted it in the Red River soil days after their arrival. They grew wheat for the next sixty-five years with varying degrees of success, but only for home consumption. But 1876 was different in several respects. First, the western farmers—most of whom were in Manitoba—changed seed that year, a change made necessary by the devastation caused by several years of grasshoppers. The new seed brought in from Wisconsin was the variety Fife, or Red Fife, discovered and developed by David Fife of Peterborough, Ontario. The wheat was red, hard, high yielding, and late in maturing, but it loved the Manitoba soil.

The other factor of importance was a poor grain crop in Ontario, so poor that seed merchants like Steele Brothers of Toronto couldn't find enough seed wheat to accommodate their customers. Members of the firm considered Manitoba as a possible source and instructed the junior member, R. C. Steele, to travel there and try to buy five thousand bushels. As the young man soon found, getting to Winnipeg wasn't easy. He was to travel to Chicago and St. Paul by train, then to Moorhead by stagecoach, and the rest of the way to Winnipeg by Red River steamboat. When he reached Moorhead, he discovered that the boat trip on the extremely loopy river was sure to be slow. Being in a hurry, he rented a team of horses and wagon and beat the boat to Winnipeg.

At Winnipeg, Steele met David Young of the firm of Higgins and Young, "Dealers in Boots and Shoes, Crockery and Glassware." Gladly the firm would accept the task of buying the wanted five thousand bushels of wheat or as near that amount as possible. From October 13 to 21, the *Manitoba Daily Free Press* carried the Higgins and Young announcement: "Cash for choice wheat for export to Ontario . . . 80 cents per bushel."

Higgins and Young received a commission of five cents per bushel, making the cost to Steele Brothers eighty-five cents per bushel, plus thirty-five cents for freight and cotton bags at twenty-six cents each. When they heard about this unprecedented cash offer, farmers lost no time in assessing their supplies. While Red River wives held bags, men shovelled to fill them. All trails seemed to lead to McMillan's mill close to the Red River, the point of delivery.

Nobody had much wheat to sell because nobody was growing much. It was soon evident that the country couldn't furnish five thousand bushels. The biggest single contributor to the order was G. R. Miller of Kildonan, who sold 204 bushels. All the wheat assembled totalled just 857 bushels and 10 pounds. That was all western Canada had to sell in 1876. It was carefully tied in 412 new bags and piled on the riverboat *Selkirk*, to be carried upstream and overland to Duluth, across Lake Superior to Sarnia, and by rail to Toronto. The western wheat created something of a sensation there.

"What's this?" men asked in astonishment. "Can Manitoba grow wheat like that?" Immediately there was a new eastern interest in homesteads and a transcontinental railway. The eastern buyers were back in the next year for more wheat. Then there was a shipment directly to Liverpool. Western farmers very quickly saw new reasons for growing more of the grain, and twenty-five years after 857 bushels and 10 pounds was all that the West had to offer, the country was selling 25 million bushels, most of it for export.

No Canadian commodity witnessed more extremes in fortune and misfortune than wheat, but it was this grain more than anything short of petroleum that stimulated western development and, perchance, Canadian prosperity. Revenue from wheat built villages, towns, and cities, paid for railways, and enriched the Canadian economy from coast to coast.

The Blessings of Climate

If an overseas candidate for emigration to Canada had heard what the critics were saying about the country, he or she would never have left home. For a long time, the pessimists outnumbered optimists by three to one. Canada was at the "ugly duckling" stage and receiving ugly comments which are now worth recalling for their entertainment value only.

Jacques Cartier started the defamations when, on his first of three voyages to the St. Lawrence River in 1534, he announced in his diary that along the whole north shore he didn't see one cartload of good soil, leaving him to believe that this was "the land God gave to [the Old Testament murderer] Cain."

Edmund Burke's opinion was scarcely less demeaning when he described the country as "a vast, barren, almost uninhabited country, lying in a cold region and with no commerce except furs and skins." Sir Archibald Alison, a British historian who apparently never cast an eye upon the Canadian countryside, found the most unkind words of all, that "seven-eighths of British North America is doomed to eternal sterility."

Less strident were the words of Madame de Pompadour, mistress of Louis XV of France, who at the fall of Quebec in 1759, said lightly: "It makes little difference; Canada is useful only to provide me with furs."

Lord Ashburton, who was England's appointee to sit with Daniel Webster to adjudicate the boundary dispute between New Brunswick and the state of Maine, allegedly said in a letter to John Quincy Adams, American ambassador to England: "I wish the British government would give you Canada at once. It's fit for nothing but to breed quarrels."

Pessimists were never popular; optimists fared better in public favour, but when compared with realists, neither would score high in reliability. Nevertheless, citizens of the early West were pleasantly surprised when John Macoun came to their attention after the publication of his 687-page book, *Manitoba and the Great North-West*, in 1882. The author, born in Ireland in 1831, was among those who fled the Irish Potato Famine and found himself chopping a farm out of the Upper Canada bush. A naturalist and botanist, he was in the West in 1872 as a member of a federal government survey party. He travelled extensively collecting plant specimens. In 1882 he was appointed to the position of botanist with the Dominion Geological Survey. Though in his book, he was guilty of some exaggeration, it proved to be a pleasant change and a partial contradiction of Palliser's report.

"The North-West," he said, "has the blessings of climate, not only exceptional in character but productive of results for the agriculturist which I believe to be unsurpassed in any other part of the world. . . . The rainfall of the North-West offers as favorable a contrast to that of other districts as the temperature. Rains usually come just when they are wanted and cease when vegetation no longer requires them and when their continuation would be detrimental to the harvest."[2]

Most westerners would not agree that rains fall precisely when needed and cease as though a great tap had been turned off when they are no longer needed, but Macoun was probably more correct than Palliser when the latter alluded to the Canadian plains as the "Great American Desert."

When he discussed the West's wheat-growing potential, Macoun was inspired to prophesy and oratory. "In a very few years," he said, "the crop will be limited by the means of export, and just as the carrying capacity of the roads increase, so will the crop. No man can doubt this for a glance at the map will tell him that there is actually no limit but the want of a market, to the wheat crop of the North-West. When the rulers of England awake, as they soon must, to the fact that within the Dominion of Canada there exists today as virgin soil, three-quarters of the wheat land of North America, and it is to her they must look for their future supplies of food whether it be beef or flour."[3]

Like other chronic optimists, Macoun wasn't always right, but he did much to strengthen confidence in western soil.

The Cochrane Ranche Company

Ideals in raising farm cattle came to western Canada from Scotland and England by way of Ontario. Not so the patterns for cattle ranching, which came from Texas by way of Kansas and Montana. Ranch traditions, western saddles, and many cowboy terms, like rodeo, chaps or chaparajos, bronco, lariat, and remuda, trace to Texas or Mexico. Even many of the founding ranch herds driven from Montana showed varying degrees of longhorn breeding that can be identified with Texas almost as easily as the Texas Rangers.

Small herds were driven north to the Alberta foothills in the 1870s, before the buffalo herds were completely destroyed. Senator Matthew Cochrane of Hillhurst, Quebec, was the first to select a big lease west of Calgary. He purchased six thousand cattle in Montana and had them driven to Big Hill, where today's thriving town of Cochrane perpetuates the rancher's name.

Cochrane, a mighty man in the area of livestock improvement in the East, gained his early wealth as a manufacturer of boots and shoes and his greatest fame as an importer of the best of the British breeds of cattle, notably the Bates strain of English Shorthorns. He was then caught up in a frenzied desire to engage in ranching in Texas, then a popular place with investors. When amendments to the Dominion Lands Act opened the way for large scale ranching, he was one of the first to respond.

Early in 1881, he travelled by way of Chicago to Fort Benton, Montana, where he obtained a buckboard vehicle and a team of half-broken horses and headed north toward the Canadian foothills, which he had not previously seen. Travelling near Waterton Lakes, he met John George "Kootenai" Brown, who was the first Caucasian to settle in the area. Brown affirmed that the foothills grass was as good as the best in Texas. "The buffalo were good judges of grass," the older man said, "and this was one of their favourite grazing grounds."

Cochrane continued north to Fort Calgary and west to Big Hill, where he was captivated by the combination of grass and water and mountain scenery. On his return to Fort Benton, he dispatched a telegram to Ottawa to record his bid for 100,000 acres of lease, for which he would pay one cent per acre per year. He then arranged to buy six thousand Montana cattle at an average price of eighteen dollars per head and have the I. G. Baker Company drive them from the border to the ranch for $2.50 per head.

The Cochrane Ranche Company, with the fifty-eight-year-old senator as president, was incorporated on May 14 of that same year. The next step was to hire N.W.M.P. superintendent James Walker to become manager of the new ranch.

In carrying out the delivery of the herd, the drivers made the mistake of moving the cattle too fast, and they arrived at Big Hill in poor condition to face the winter ahead. More than that, the cattle had not been rebranded as intended, and the first winter brought confusion and heavy losses. Cochrane, however, was undeterred and ordered more cattle to be driven from Montana in 1882. Again, winter losses were heavy because of unusual snow and cold, and the senator began to believe he should have located near Waterton Lakes.

Acting on impulse, he reorganized to give the Big Hill property a new name, British American Ranche Company, and leave it for sheep and horse production. He then obtained a second lease of 100,000 acres between Fort Macleod and Waterton Lakes and drove the big cattle herd to it. As luck would have it, weather conditions reversed in the winter of 1883–84, and while the animals on the range beside the Bow River were enjoying open grazing, the southern district was blanketed with heavy snow, and losses were high.

The British American Ranche was stocked with sheep and horses as planned and had its ups and downs. The Waterton Lakes range enjoyed better times, and notwithstanding the reverses of the first years, the southern ranch prospered and appeared to invite other big ranching enterprises, the North West Cattle Company—known in later years as the Bar U—started in 1882, the Oxley also in '82, the big Walrond in '83, and the Quorn in '84.

The Cochrane Ranche flourished until after the Senator's death in 1903. Two years later, the historic ranch was sold to the Mormon Church.

Sir John's Financial Empire

Sir John Lister Kaye wanted to be the top man in his own farm and ranch empire. Kaye was still a newcomer from England when he broke upon the western scene with the vivacity of a marching band. Throughout the late 1880s, he was undoubtedly the leading maker of agricultural news while making grand capital expenditures like a prime minister or premier on the eve of a general election.

While still a freshman in the West in 1885, he appeared as an associate of Lord Shaftsbury in a seven-thousand-acre farming enterprise at Balgonie, east of Regina. The operation, it seems, was too small for Sir John, and near the end of the next year, he announced the purchase of ten blocks of land along the main-line railroad between Balgonie on the east and Langdon on the west. Each parcel consisted of ten thousand acres, and the intent was to develop the land for farming and ranching and then divide it into small units to be sold to immigrants.

The dynamic little Englishman believed the cash returns from wheat would attract immigrant settlers, and the C.P.R. and Government of Canada—both in a hurry to settle the prairies—encouraged him. The government co-operated by exchanging homestead land for C.P.R. land to allow the railroad company to assemble land blocks for Sir John. The purchase price was generally one dollar an acre and the railroad company agreed to rebate the purchase money on all land brought under cultivation by a certain time.

Having bought the land, Sir John's spending spree was just beginning. He gave the impression that he could count only in terms of thousands. He admitted that he intended to spend $5.5 million, a staggering amount at the time, on land, buildings, and livestock.

The news of August, 1887, told of the purchase of 7,300 cattle from the Powder River Ranch Company, formerly of Wyoming. The cattle carried the brand "76," which explained why Sir John's chain of ranches went by the name Seventy-Six.

To meet his needs for work and breeding stock, Sir John bought five hundred work horses, including many purebred Clydesdale mares, in Ontario, eleven high-class stallions in Scotland, and twenty thousand sheep, which were trailed from Oregon and Washington and penned at Maple Creek until they could be allocated to the various ranches. To accommodate the flock's needs, he then bought five hundred purebred Cheviot, Leicester, Shropshire, and Cotswold rams in England. At the same time, he bought ninety-nine pedigreed Aberdeen Angus and Galloway bulls in Scotland. He also engaged 110 English workers to help prepare the prairie soil for cropping.

But the year following, 1889, was dry, and crops failed. Refusing to accept defeat by drought, Sir John resolved to irrigate the wheat land by hauling water in horse-drawn wooden tanks of twelve-barrel capacity. Forty-four such pine tanks were ordered in Winnipeg and placed in service. It made news, but it did practically nothing for the crop. What was obviously overlooked was the fact that it would require about 110 tons of water or forty trips with one of the water tanks to furnish even one inch of water for one acre. It made no visible impression on Sir John's vast prairie fields.

The dauntless fellow turned to dairying as a solution and ordered a creamery to be built at Swift Current. He ordered his ranch managers to start hand milking the unwilling Wyoming cows. It was said that the order was no more popular with the cowboys than with the unruly longhorns. Even the offer of a silver trophy for the ranch manager with the largest number of cows being milked by October, 1889, could not make the project a success.

Sir John was not lacking in imagination. He decided to operate his own slaughtering plants and retail meat shops; he would concentrate on the Calgary market. Sir John was then involved in beef from birth to boiling brisket, but there is no evidence that he reduced his operating losses thereby.

Sir John's mistakes were costly, and the English shareholders protested. The company was reorganized in 1893, and D. H. Andrews, who came to the ranch with the Powder River cattle, became manager. Sir John vanished from the prairie scene, except in memory. The West could claim him as one of many numerous colourful characters.

To Market

Jerome and Thaddeus Harper, prominent in British Columbia cattle history, crossed the continent from their home in Virginia to get a piece of the California gold rush in '49. They then turned their attention to trailing cattle from Oregon to feed hungry miners in the new gold rush on the Fraser River in British Columbia.

The first herd consisted of four hundred head. Making their own trail most of the way, the Harpers would cross the boundary at Osoyoos and drive toward Kamloops and over the Cariboo Trail to Barkerville, where beef commanded seventy-five cents a pound and quality didn't matter.

Before the last steer from the first drive was slaughtered, the Harpers were on their way to Oregon for another herd and then a third one. But the trade couldn't last forever, and the owners were left with a couple of hundred head of unsaleable cattle from the third drive. With foresight to delight a weather prophet, the Harpers had already obtained a spread of grazing land on the South Thompson east of Kamloops—still known as the Harper Ranch—and there they turned out some of the leftover cattle. They released the rest of the surplus animals to graze in the unlimited Cariboo country.

The cattle business was lifeless for a few years after the gold rush, but the Harpers were confident that their beef would be needed. They drove a few head to New Westminster, but the herd was growing faster than the demand.

Jerome, the older of the brothers, retired to live in California in 1870 and died there four years later. Thaddeus remained behind to keep an eye on the herd and brand the calves with the JH brand, adapted from Jerome's initials welded together. By 1876 Thaddeus knew he would have to quit the ranch or find a market. When a friend scoffed at the idea of finding a market, saying: "There is no market this side of Chicago," Thaddeus answered: "Chicago! That's an idea. Where is Chicago from here?" The friend didn't know for sure, but waved an arm to the southeast and said only: "A hell of a long way." Harper is said to have responded with the words: "I'll tell you more when I get back."

Harper didn't waste much time. On April 20, 1876, Victoria's *British Colonist* reported: "Mr. T. Harper proposes to take 800 head of beef cattle from British Columbia to Chicago. He intends to drive via Salt Lake and then take the railroad. At present there are a large number of cattle in the Interior; the market is limited and a band of beef cattle would hardly realize $15 per head. At present at Chicago, cattle will net over the cost of driving and railroad about $40 per head. . . ."[4]

The herd of eight hundred was gathered mainly in the Cariboo and started south on the Cariboo Trail. It was forced across the river at Savona, then driven to Kamloops, where more cattle were added from the Harper ranch. Harper, of course, was one of the eight or nine cowboys accompanying the herd. One of the riders was twenty-two-year-old Antoine Allen who had come from Oregon as a boy and lived with the Harpers. He told that all the riders were well armed and ever ready to use their guns. Progress was at the rate of ten or twelve miles a day. The drive was directed across the states of Washington, Oregon, Idaho, and into northern Utah, where winter weather overtook the travellers. Harper decided to wait for better trail conditions before continuing the journey to Chicago.

While they waited, a traveller with a team of mules and a wagon came in from the west and stopped to ask some questions about Harper's destination. "I think your cattle would fetch more money in San Francisco than in Chicago," he remarked.

"Do you think so?" Harper asked. "Then we'll drive 'em to San Francisco."

When the weather improved, the herd was turned westward to cross Nevada and California, to cross deserts, mountain passes, and Indian country all new to Harper. After eighteen months on the trail, the herd of about 1200 head was driven into San Francisco and sold on a good market. The Victoria press summed it up this way: "Some 18 months ago, Mr. Thaddeus Harper drove from British Columbia into Northern Idaho 1200 head of beef cattle. . . . Mr. Harper's band is now coming into market at San Francisco. The cattle are large and well grown beeves rolling in fat and have been sold at $70 per head."[5]

Thaddeus Harper rushed home to British Columbia to raise more cattle. With a minimum loss and a profitable sale added to the great distance travelled, the Harper drive should be remembered as one of the most notable in history. Poems and songs have been written about lesser deeds.

The Gold Rush of '98

Canada's most famous gold rush began on August 17, 1896 with a discovery on Bonanza Creek, deep in the Yukon and not far from the Alaska boundary. The find—made by a shabby-looking drifter, George Washington Carmack, and his native wife and two brothers-in-law, known as Skookum Jim and Tagish Charlie—was probably the most remote, most inaccessible, and most inconvenient gold discovery on record.

Local prospectors, like vultures coming together to feast upon a fresh kill, converged at once to stake claims on hitherto obscure Bonanza Creek. News to the outside world travelled no faster than a funeral procession, however, and almost a year passed before Canadian and foreign newspapers carried the headlines that excited prospectors and gamblers everywhere, inspiring them to pack their bags and enquire: "How do we get to Bonanza?"

There was no simple answer to that question. Although there were three or four possible routes, all were difficult or costly or both. The easiest route was the longest, an almost all-water course of at least 2500 miles down the Mackenzie River to the Delta and then west via the Rat and Porcupine rivers to the Yukon River, flowing from far-away Dawson City.

The shortest routes were the extremely hazardous land and water journey north or northwest from Edmonton and the overland expedition north from the British Columbia Interior to Teslin Lake and an all-water journey from there. Writer James MacGregor believed that 1500 people elected to go via the Edmonton route, and 725 reached their goal.[6] Another author, W. G. Hardy, says that of an estimated 2000 who started from Edmonton, only 30 succeeded in going all the way.[7]

The most popular route, of course, permitted train travel to Vancouver and boat service from there to Skagway or Dyea at the upper end of the Lynn Canal, which penetrated the Alaska Panhandle almost a hundred miles inland. At either of these wild coastal locations, travellers were confronted with the necessity of packing supplies and equipment over the awful climb to the summit of Chilkoot or White Pass. The dangers were about equal; both paths meandered upward at an angle of 35 degrees. Transporting the required ton of food supplies as well as equipment, which ranged from lumber and sawmill machinery to at least one partly dismantled piano, was bound to take weeks of heavy toil. For those who had horses, the packing was easier on the men but a cruel killer of the animals, as the name, Trail of Rotten Horse Meat, which was applied to the approach to Chilkoot Pass, indicated.

Beyond the chosen and often stormy pass, the trail dropped down to Lake Lindeman and the headwaters of the Lewes and Yukon rivers, leading to Dawson City—and gold—some five hundred dangerous water-miles to the northwest. Once at the river, there was a general rush to construct boats and rafts on which to carry the inescapable freight.

An estimated twenty-five thousand men and a few women started over the pass and down the rivers in 1897 and '98. Needless to say, not all succeeded. Many were obliged to spend a winter beside the frozen river, and some perished. But when spring returned and ice left the rivers, the waterways to the mouth of the Klondike River at Dawson City resembled a gay regatta as boats and rafts of all sizes and shapes bobbed along. Still, nobody felt at ease until the deathtrap waters of Miles Canyon and Whitehorse Rapids were behind him. Most travellers chose, wisely, to portage around those troubled places and accept delay rather than face the dangers; some didn't choose as wisely and lost in the gamble.

The mounted police did well in maintaining control and order on the travel routes and in Dawson City, where the rocket-like rise in population made it the biggest centre in western Canada except for Winnipeg. The wisdom of the police in requiring every incoming miner to bring a ton of food supplies was soon recognized. Even so, food prices soared, especially for fresh foods, which were in short supply.

It is unlikely that Canada will ever again witness such a gold-inspired stampede. The rush of '98, '99, and 1900 was without parallel in many ways, although it did not follow that a big proportion of the miners became rich. If the total value of gold recovered in these years could be compared with the total costs of travel, living in the North for a year or more, and failure to collect wages for lost time by 100,000 aspiring miners, it is doubtful if the gold would have matched the costs.

Klondike Cattle

The 100,000 gold-seekers flocking to the Klondike brought big appetites with them. They might have been packing flour, oatmeal, sugar, and tea and still have faced possible famine in perishable foods like milk and eggs and fresh meats. Wild game in the region offered slight relief, but if all the meat-hungry miners became hunters of deer, moose, and caribou, the wild things would have vanished quickly.

What could be done to alleviate the need? There was one hope: western farms and ranches more than a thousand miles away had the cattle and the men who were ready for the challenging task of delivering them to Dawson City. The practical incentive was the prospect of converting cattle worth three cents a pound at home to dressed beef selling for as much as a dollar a pound in the distant North.

Ed Fearon of Maple Creek was the first prairie man to act. He left late in the spring of '97 with one hundred four-year-old steers and an old milk cow, Bessie. He took them over the Chilkoot Pass and placed them on rafts at Lake Bennett. It took five months to make the delivery, but he gained a piece of the dollar-a-pound reward. Other prairie cattlemen followed in the next year: Billy Henry from High River, Burchill and Howie from Brandon, the Tuxford Brothers and Thompson from Moose Jaw, and F. O. Sissons of Medicine Hat.

Billy Henry, who died in 1971 at the age of 104 years, had the distinction of taking Pat Burns's cattle into the North on two occasions. The first herd—250 big four-year-olds—was loaded on freight cars at High River, but before the cars reached Calgary, there was a train wreck, and 65 of the cattle were killed. The remaining cattle, however, were reloaded and sent on their way. At Vancouver, the cattle, 22 saddle horses, and feed were loaded on a 1200-ton scow—a glorified raft—and the big load was drawn away by a C.P.R. tugboat.

Unloaded at Skagway some days later, the cattle were started inland on what became known as the Dalton Trail. "It took from the 1st of July to the 20th of September to reach the mouth of the Pelly River, where we made rafts seventy-two feet long and thirty-six feet wide and slaughtered the cattle and horses and piled the carcasses on them," said Henry. By good fortune, the carcasses were at Dawson just hours before the river froze over. They sold 75,000 pounds of beef to the mounted police for seventy-five cents a pound, and most of the balance went to miners at a dollar a pound. Horsemeat and hides sold for dog feed at fifty cents a pound. The trip was a success, and Henry and his men were back home nine months after leaving.

Norman Lee, driving two hundred cattle from his Hanceville Ranch in British Columbia's Chilcotin region, was not as lucky. Lee was a young Englishman who settled in the Chilcotin in 1887 to trade in furs and raise cattle. He heard of the race to find gold at Klondike, and he concluded that by driving a herd straight north from Hanceville, he could bring his animals to Teslin Lake, which by his map, had a water connection with Dawson.

On May 17, 1898, Lee left home with two hundred heavy cattle, thirty pack and saddle horses, and five cowboys. The drive continued without much change of direction for four and a half months when, sure enough, he reached Teslin Lake. There he slaughtered the cattle and piled the carcasses on rafts, which he and his cowboys made on the spot. Each of the two rafts measured forty feet by sixteen feet.

Lee figured that his plan was working well, but the rest of the story is tragic. After two days of slow travel, a storm came up. It drove the rafts on coastal rocks, wrecking them and causing almost complete loss. Thankful to be alive, Lee and his men walked back to Teslin and, with a few local people, returned to the scene of the wreck. They salvaged thirty quarters of beef—the slim equivalent of seven and a half carcasses from the handsome herd that started about five months earlier. The enterprise ended in failure, but it was no worse than the fortunes of another British Columbia cattleman, John Harris, who followed the same course. He reached a point within two hundred miles of Dawson City only to have his raft-loads of beef trapped in winter ice with no hope of recovery.

Lee turned toward home, tramping through the winter snow on foot, to begin ranching again. It was the way of the frontier.

Seager Wheeler, Wheat King

Most boys want to be six-footers; Seager Wheeler was short, and it changed his life. It led him to go to the Canadian West, where he became the country's unquestioned Wheat King.

Growing up on the Isle of Wight, off the south coast of England, a boy's dreams were unlikely to range far beyond fishing, smuggling, and going to sea. Young Wheeler's heart was set on joining the British navy, but when he was old enough to apply, the "Nivy" wouldn't have him because he was "an inch too short up and down and another inch too short round about."

With a touch of bitterness, he resolved to go to Canada and see what the authorities there meant by "free land." It was 1885—Rebellion year in the West—when this sixteen-year-old boy from the village of Black Gang, accompanied by his mother and sister, arrived at Moose Jaw. They spent their first nights on the floor of the immigration hall trying to sleep.

Wheeler needed a job. He had left school at eleven and gone to work, and he had to take what work he could get. He dug cellars, painted houses, and worked on nearby farms, generally earning a dollar a day and saving some of it.

After saving a little and borrowing two hundred dollars from the Temperance Colonization Society in Saskatoon, he filed on a homestead near Clark's Crossing, where he lived for a time in a dugout on the river bank. But he wasn't happy with the soil on his first homestead, and when he heard that the C.P.R. was offering land at Rosthern, he inspected it and bought a quarter section for three dollars an acre. He was able to finance the purchase of the three homestead essentials, a pair of oxen, a wagon, and a walking plough. He displayed his natural interest in planting when the first chore to get his attention was the moving of seedling poplars, maples, and caraganas to his chosen homesite.

He broke sodland for wheat and in due course planted Red Fife, the high-yielding and good milling variety that broke many homestead hearts because it was late in maturing and a frequent victim of frost. He found joy in working with soil and plants. He hadn't learned the technique of hybridizing, but he could select superior plants to effect improvement. Soon he attracted the attention of the professional plant breeders, including Dr. Charles Saunders, whose new wheat variety, Marquis, was being circulated in 1910. It was a cross between the familiar Red Fife and the early maturing Hard Red Calcutta, and the hope was that the hybrid would inherit the best of both parents.

Saunders was anxious to have his new wheat tested on western soil and sent Wheeler a package of seed in time for the 1911 planting. Wheeler was delighted and bought a few additional pounds of the same variety. The crop did well, so well that after the harvest, he decided to send an entry to the Provincial Seed Fair in Regina. Wheeler's Marquis won the championship.

One of Wheeler's neighbours, happy about the success, said: "Seager, there's a World Fair at New York. Why don't you enter your Marquis?"

Wheeler laughed and said: "An entry from Rosthern would have no chance," but the neighbour persisted. Wheeler sent the entry and, being busy, forgot about it until a month or two later, when he received a message that his wheat had won the world championship and the thousand dollars in gold offered by Sir Thomas Shaughnessy, president of the C.P.R.

The prize was presented at a banquet in the Palliser Hotel in Calgary at which Wheeler was the guest of honour. Following the presentation, as the story has been told, Wheeler promptly passed the prize back to the president, saying: "Thank you, Mr. President. Now you take it as my final payment on the Rosthern land I bought from you."

The critics said Wheeler's success with the wheat was a fluke, that it would never happen again. But the critics were wrong. The little Englishman sent a second sample for international competition and again won the world championship, then did it a third time, a fourth, and a fifth, after which he offered to retire. But he had done far more than win five world wheat crowns: he so inspired other western growers to pursue the same goal with Marquis wheat or its derivatives that they completely dominated international wheat competition for the next seventy-five years.

Honours were showered upon the westerner who was too short for the Royal Navy, including an honorary degree from Queen's University in Kingston. It was the first time a man of the soil had been so recognized.

The Aberdeen Angus of Glencarnock

Seager Wheeler dignified 1911 by bringing a world championship for wheat to Saskatchewan. The very next year, James Duncan McGregor, already an agricultural leader and nation builder, won similar international honours with cattle of his favourite Scottish breed, the black, polled Aberdeen Angus. Taken together, these two events probably did more than anybody realized to change the image of the West.

For McGregor, winning the championship at the Chicago International Fat Stock Show represented just one more in a series of bold and successful ventures. He was born to Scottish parents at Amherstburg, Ontario, in 1860 and came west with his father in 1877, before the railroad grade reached Winnipeg. He and his father became dealers in cattle and horses at Portage la Prairie and, from 1881, at Brandon.

In 1889, Hon. Walter Gordon-Cumming imported forty Aberdeen Angus cows and three bulls from Scotland and placed them on the Quorn Ranch in the foothills of Alberta. Shortly thereafter, McGregor became a partner in the cattle and then bought the herd and moved it to the Glencarnock Farm at Brandon.

His next venture was in the Klondike, where he represented the Government of Canada as Gold Commissioner at the time of the gold rush. When he returned from the Klondike in 1904, he settled more seriously into agriculture, especially cattle breeding, alfalfa promotion, and farm fairs. He was largely responsible for organizing the Brandon Winter Fair and the first "baby beef" shows for boys and girls.

But his successes in 1912 and their impact upon the West were like a mountain peak towering above the lesser peaks in a range. His herd of purebred Aberdeen Angus cattle had become the biggest in Canada, and his show herd was going over the Canadian show circuit with regularity. J. D. McGregor and James Bowman of Guelph, Ontario, were the leading contestants, and the former was winning most of the championships. Then, without much publicity, McGregor began selecting and fitting a herd for the highest livestock court on the continent, the Chicago International.

The results of the judging came as a surprise to western farmers, who didn't even know that the McGregor cattle were in Chicago. And what a surprise! The McGregor herd bull, Leroy 3rd of Meadowbrook, won the grand championship for males of all ages; Violet 3rd of Congash, a cow that Mr. McGregor had selected in Scotland after she placed first in her class at the Highland Show, was chosen reserve grand champion female; Queen Rosie of Cullen was the first-prize two-year-old heifer; and the Glencarnock herd entry, composed of herd bull and four females, was also the winner.

That was not all: the most coveted award of the show had always been the inter-breed championship for fat steers; this time the distinction came to Mr. McGregor's two-year-old entry, Glencarnock Victor.

So surprising and convincing was this sweep of championships that the American cattlemen gave the McGregor Aberdeen Angus farm a new name, the "Ballindalloch of America," taking the name from that of the leading herd in the homeland of the breed, long the source of the world's best breeding stock.

The people at home in Manitoba were elated, although there were skeptics, as usual, who were inclined to interpret the big win as an accident, saying: "Don't expect to see it happen again. Lightning never strikes twice in the same place, you know." But McGregor, like Wheeler, returned to Chicago with another fat steer, Glencarnock Victor II, the next year and won the grand championship. It was the first time in the history of the great Chicago show that a private breeder and feeder had won the supreme championship twice. The Scottish judge said the Manitoba steer was the best he could recall seeing.

McGregor returned Victor II to Brandon for display at the Brandon Winter Fair, where the great steer could be seen and enjoyed by thousands of visitors. The champion, like a guest of honour, was given the best accommodation and had thousands of visitors who paused to admire "Victor II, the Toast of 1913." A few of the visitors with Scottish roots were said to have repeated the words used to praise another hero of Clan MacGregor, the famous Rob Roy: "MacGregor, despite them, will flourish forever."

James Duncan McGregor bred more champions, many more, and served the country in many more ways. He was Canada's food controller during World War I and filled the office of Lieutenant-Governor of Manitoba between 1929 and 1934. He died a year after retiring from that office.

1915: "The Harvest Was Great"

The forces of adversity seemed to delight in testing the patience of newcomers to farming and ranching, and great was the pain thereof. Stockmen would never forget the cruel winters of 1886–87 and 1906–07, which left dead animals outnumbering the living in many parts and the smell of putrefying flesh blanketing the countryside. There were years of glanders, swamp fever, mange, anthrax, blackleg, and even the odious foot-and-mouth disease, as there were those when crops suffered and failed because of drought, floods, hail, grasshoppers, or rust, or when markets were paralysed.

But most years were moderately rewarding, and periodically there would be a year in which Nature excelled herself, a year in which soil and weather co-operated to send crop growers on a record-making spree. Such was 1915, a year when the unprecedented harvest of cereal grains in all parts of the Canadian West would have astonished even Ceres, the Roman goddess of grain and harvests. Farmers were able to meet debts due on the first of November, pay for new machinery, build farm houses that would retire the homestead shanties, submit big orders for winter clothing and other goods selected from Eaton's catalogue, and even allow a few western farmers and their wives to pay their first winter visit to California. They never stopped talking about 1915.

Nothing could make the agricultural people forget the awful realities of World War I, then in its second year, and the awful price being paid in lives and dollars and property. Immediately following Britain's declaration of war against Germany on August 4, 1914, Prime Minister Robert Borden spoke for the Canadian people, offering Britain every possible support. The first of the more than half a million Canadians who saw active service were in the front-line trenches by February of 1915. By that time, the enemy's plan to employ submarine warfare to blockade Britain and force the government to choose between surrender and starvation was in operation. Canadian farmers heard the pitiable call for more wheat and other foods. "Food will win the war," they were told again and again.

All things considered, the record crop of 1915 looked like heaven's approval of Canada's purpose. Its size was nigh unbelievable. The total western Canadian wheat crop had exceeded 100 million bushels for the first time in 1906; five years later, in 1911, the same area produced 200 million bushels for the first time; and four years after that, in the notable year of 1915, the West's wheat crop was above 300 million bushels for the first time. The crop was, for the first time, predominantly Marquis wheat, and the general average was 26 bushels per acre.

Nor was wheat the only grain making records that year. Oats, barley, rye, and flax were no less productive. The oats crop on the big Noble Farm at Nobleford, north of Lethbridge, was believed to have made a world record for yield. Charles Noble, who had started homesteading west of Claresholm in 1904 and broke his land with a walking plough and team of oxen, responded to the wartime pleas for greater production in 1915 by planting about 9,000 acres of recently acquired land and was preparing for yet a bigger acreage the following year. In 1915, he got 300,000 bushels of oats from 3,091 acres—an average of approximately 100 bushels per acre. That same year, a measured field of 1,000 acres produced an international record for that big a field of 126 bushels per acre. At the same time, a field of 100 acres, which Noble called his "test plot," gave him the amazing yield of 130 bushels per acre. Western editors were quick to declare Noble the "Oats King of Western Canada."[8]

That's the way it was in 1915, and for obvious reasons, Thanksgiving Day that year held special significance. Rev. A. Mahaffy's Thanksgiving message, printed in the *Daily Albertan*, admonished city dwellers for their folly in pursuing two recent booms, one in real estate and the other in Turner Valley oil, both ending in area depressions. The wild promotions and speculations, he said, were "morally and economically vicious," and those who were responsible were "reaping what they sowed." He noted that speculation does nothing to create food and meet other basic needs. It was the season for special thanks for the Canadian soil and its munificence: "Granaries, roothouses and corrals," said the writer, "are full. The season was not perfect but the harvest was great."[9]

Chapter 5

Rich Land; Harsh Environment

Winter of Suffering

For ten years after Constable Whitney released his small herd of cattle to face the southwestern winter, friendly chinook winds visited with reassuring frequency, and ranch stock survived without recourse to haystacks. It was easy for inveterate optimists and idlers to presume that chinooks would be unfailing, making it unnecessary to spend time and toil on making hay.

The memorable winter of 1886–87 silenced the optimists and cost much more in livestock losses than expenditures for making hay would have totalled in ten years. The snow and cold came early in October and remained almost unbroken until spring. To make matters worse, many ranges were overstocked and overgrazed, leaving them with little to offer for winter grazing. The first animals to suffer were the thousands of young stocker cattle brought to the southwest from Ontario and Manitoba farms. These unfortunate critters had but poor resistance to cold and took to wandering as if trying to find their way back to the eastern barns in which they were raised and where they banqueted on clover hay and sliced turnips. They were the first to give up the struggle and perish.

The small amounts of hay in stacks or storage were hopelessly inadequate, and such hay as was offered for sale soared in price. At a time when the best beef cattle were bringing about 2½ cents a pound, an inflated price of forty dollars per ton for hay was practically prohibitive. Hence, as a cause of deaths on the range, hunger ranked close to cold and storms.

As L. V. Kelly, author of the often-quoted book *The Range Men*, reported the calamity in tones of sadness: "The rabbits died; the lynx left; the herds of antelope starved in hundreds, the poor brutes wandering into the very settlements where they were often killed on the streets. . . . The I. G. Baker Co. cattle were scattered widely through the South and suffered frightful loss. . . . Sixty per cent of this herd was wiped out in the winter of 1886–87."[1]

Kelly, who is one of the best sources of information about the losses, noted that while the cattle losses represented a terrible blow to Alberta ranchers, the losses were even higher in Montana, Wyoming, and the Dakotas. He mentioned also that the Stoney and Sarcee Indians were about the only beneficiaries of the cruel winter and feasted "sumptuously on the fat beef that lay scattered all over the hills of the West."

From Kelly's accounts, it appears that the average loss in the area that was to become Alberta was 25 percent, but in the Calgary district, it was between 50 and 60 percent, and around Medicine Hat, 50 percent.

Horses, being instinctively able to paw the snow to give themselves access to the dry grass below, fared considerably better than the cattle and some ranchers, after taking heavy losses in cattle, elected to change from cattle raising to specialize in horses.

A few cattlemen were forced into bankruptcy, but most survived and pledged to cut and stack enough hay to prevent a recurrence of the winter tragedy in the years ahead. But human memory is short, and the lessons of 1886–87 were soon forgotten. By 1905, cattlemen were again falling into the dangerous habit of gambling on getting through the winter without stockpiled hay. Then they were caught.

Exactly twenty years after the distressing year of 1886–87, it happened again, in 1906–07. Actually, this time the losses were higher. Prairie fires combined with overgrazing left the ranges with limited reserves, and as in 1886, the winter came early and harsh. Adding to the dangers, many range cattle were still suffering from mange, and the widespread adoption of barbed-wire fences caused cattle drifting with winter storms to "bunch" in the fence corners and perish there.

The Calgary district reported a 60 per cent loss of cattle. Not many ranchers escaped. George Lane of the Bar U Ranch west of High River told of counting twenty-four thousand cattle at the onset of winter, of which only twelve thousand could be counted in the spring. In the great sweep of country between the Red Deer and Missouri rivers, the estimated loss was 40 percent. It was the cruelest winter of all for range livestock and was followed by the "spring of rotting meat."

The Big Business in Buffalo Bones

For many prairie homesteaders, the unexpected sale of buffalo bones—like butter and eggs in later years—furnished their first grocery money.

When the North-West Mounted Police made their historic march westward in 1874 and reported seeing the plains "black with buffalo" in places, the North American bison population was believed to be well over fifty million. Like mosquitoes, they were difficult to count and the estimates might have been little better than wild guesses. In any case, they were numerous. Ten years later, in 1884, the noble prairie race had vanished completely, a victim of the predator white man and his new guns. The United States and Canadian governments did nothing to halt the wanton slaughter that brought the prairie race perilously close to extinction, both accepting the belief that total destruction of the wild herds would make it easier to persuade the Indian people to accept reservation life.

Of those who participated in the big kill, most profited by the sale of hides at two dollars each, and others who enjoyed the bloody exercise for recreational reasons reported a "good time." The hides were sold for tanning; the carcasses were allowed to rot. All that remained visible was a scattering of bones becoming white with age, making burnt-over areas of prairie look like stony fields of black summerfallow.

The gathering and shipping of buffalo bones to fertilizer plants and certain refineries wanting bone charcoal began in Kansas. Sales amounted to $2.5 million before Canada's old buffalo range was served by railroads. Canadian collections began immediately after the Canadian Pacific rails reached Moose Jaw. Thereafter, many prairie homesteaders relied upon bones, for which they received six dollars per ton, to pay for their groceries.

Moose Jaw, at the centre of what was once good buffalo country, may have been the first prairie point to gather and ship bones from the West. The local newspaper of November 7, 1884, reported: "Mr. Dolittle who has been in town for some time collecting bones for a Philadelphia firm shipped three carloads to that place last night."[2]

In the next year, 1885, more than a hundred carloads were shipped from points on the main line of the C.P.R., and in 1886, the volume more than doubled again. Regina, Moose Jaw, Swift Current, Medicine Hat, and Maple Creek became leading shipping points. Many smaller places adopted bones as their primary business. Branch line communities followed. Saskatoon became a clear leader, supporting many Métis from Batoche and Duck Lake who made bone gathering their full time occupation. Using Red River carts hauled by either oxen or horses, they began gathering near the town and then worked areas ever farther out, leaving deep ruts in what became known as the Bone Trail, which entered the town from the southwest.

When recession in the early 1890s forced the American buyers to temporarily suspend bone purchases, the Métis continued to bring their loads to Saskatoon, until a pile of bones awaiting shipment stretched for a hundred yards along the railroad and contained the bones of an estimated 168,000 buffalo, according to the *Saskatchewan Herald*.

James Leslie, R. W. Dulmage, and Mrs. Grace Fletcher were the Saskatoon merchants who handled most of the bones. Leslie told that he accepted more bones than cash in return for groceries and supplies. He alone sent 750 carloads to the American buyers from his town, and he admitted that Mrs. Fletcher shipped more because she had more friends among the Métis. Her best known customer was Edouard Dumont, brother of Gabriel Dumont of North-West Rebellion fame. Not very provident, he invariably overdrew on his bone account and ended each season with a net debt to Mrs. Fletcher. When she would remind her customer that he owed her money on the year's transactions, his reply was always the same: "Don' worry, Mrs. Fletcher, you wait till next summer; I bring you more bones."

It was James Leslie's opinion that he and his two competitors together shipped between 3,000 and 3,500 carloads of bones from Saskatoon over the years. Each freight car, he explained, was expected to contain the skulls and other bones from 250 buffalo, weighing about 20,000 pounds. From these figures it would seem that the total Saskatoon shipments would represent 60 million pounds of bones from about 750,000 buffalo.

A few conservation voices were raised to halt the export of bones, among them that of the editor of the *Nor'West Farmer*. "The bones will ere long be required at home," he said. "Even the reputed fertility of the prairies cannot afford the loss of the best of all fertilizers being exported. Keep the bones and use them."[3]

The Frank Slide

Surviving residents of the little mining town of Frank in the Crowsnest Pass said that they remained in a state of semishock for six years after the awful morning of April 29, 1903, when Turtle Mountain seemed to fall apart. An estimated ninety million tons of rock crashed down the mountain side, destroying homes, streets, and a section of railroad. It forced a diversion of the Crowsnest River and was presumed to be one of the two or three most devastating rock slides in history. On the human side, about seventy lives were lost; estimates varied between sixty-six and eighty.

The Turtle Mountain coal was discovered only three years before the tragedy. Mining operations started in the spring of 1901. There had been an elaborate official opening with the Hon. Clifford Sifton, Minister of the Interior, in attendance. The mine and village seemed to have a bright future. By the beginning of April, most of the mine workers and their families were living on the townsite located in the attractive river valley. Then came the blow: part of the mountaintop fell off and thundered into the valley, literally burying part of the village under broken limestone up to a hundred feet deep. Houses vanished; the people in them had no chance to escape. There was no warning but the faint rumbling noises heard from within the mountain, but according to one man, "old Turtle was always rumbling a little."

It happened at 4:10 A.M. About the only residents who were securely insulated from the crushing blow were those on the night shift and working far under the mountain.

No one knew what force could have caused the mountain to cleave after it had stood steadfastly for aeons. There was speculation that the removal of coal had changed the thrust of the mountain's weight, but nobody was convinced. The possibility that gasses had formed deep within the mountain and then exploded was considered. A slight earthquake in that part had been recorded three years earlier; perhaps it was the culprit in opening a crack in Turtle Mountain.

Technical people believed that a repetition wasn't likely but did not totally dismiss the possibility, and after a few years, mining was discontinued for precautionary reasons.

The toll in lives had been devastating, but there had been what seemed like miraculous turns in events. There was the discovery of a baby girl, still in night attire, alone and shivering on top of fifty feet of freshly broken rock and apparently uninjured. There was the heroic performance of the brakeman on a C.P.R. freight train that passed at the foot of Turtle Mountain just seconds before the rails and roadbed were swept away and buried deep in limestone rubble.

Crewmen on the train said that the sudden roar of the falling rock was enough to drown out the noise of the locomotive. The track behind them had been completely obliterated. There was immediate concern about the Spokane Flier travelling between Spokane and Lethbridge and already due to pass Frank. Running late, the engineer could be expected to attempt to clear the village at top speed. Brakeman Sid Choquette recognized the danger of a terrible wreck and dashed away over the mile-long rock pile. It was a dangerous course, and he fell a few times into crevices of unknown depth, but Choquette succeeded. He reached the clear track in time to flag down the high-speed passenger train and almost certainly averted another disaster with the potential for even greater loss of life. One writer told that when the passengers on the fast train heard of the brakeman's action, they subscribed at once to the purchase of a gold watch inscribed with words of appreciation for Sid Choquette.

Then there were the men who were on the night shift in the mine when the deadly slide occurred. The rumble was very clear to them, and they sought to leave by the usual exit, but it was blocked by broken rock. They hastened to an auxiliary outlet, but it was also blocked. The men began to dig frantically where they sensed a chance to escape, and they succeeded. The next test of human endurance for some of them was finding that their homes and families had been buried in the deadly rock pile.

The Buffalo: Destruction of a Noble Race

Like the story of the passenger pigeon, the slaughter of the North American buffalo or plains bison herds was terrible. It was strange and sad that hunters would take the destruction of a noble race so lightly and then work so hard to effect a faint recovery. If it brings tears to human eyes and new resolves in support of preservation of nature's treasures, the debacle might still serve a useful purpose.

Most of the killing took place within a period of ten years. When the North-West Mounted Police were making their famous trek westward in 1874, Constable E. H. Maunsell wrote that they camped on Milk River Ridge during an autumn snowstorm. They awakened in the morning to find the countryside "covered with buffalo" as far as they could see. He and Colonel Macleod believed they saw a million buffalo at one time.

It is pointless to attempt more than wild guesses about the buffalo population at that time. Whether 20 million or 100 million is the better figure is of little consequence; the amazing fact is that ten years after the mounted police were viewing a sea of buffalo from Milk River Ridge, the great wild herd had vanished, destroyed by the new rifles in the hands of men thinking only of the two dollars they hoped to collect for every hide.

"Buffalo Bill" Cody reported killing 4,200 in his "best year." J. A. "Dad" Gaff, who took to ranching in the Cypress Hills, claimed to have bettered Cody's record with a kill of 5,200 in one year in Kansas. Neither the Canadian nor the U.S. governments took steps to halt the slaughter, convinced, apparently, that total destruction of the herds was the only way to convert the prairie Indians to reservation life.

Two Manitobans, Charles Alloway and James McKay, the 350-pound halfbreed strongman, possessed the imagination and will to capture buffalo calves for breeding in captivity. They captured three calves in 1873 and three more in '74, placing them on McKay's farm west of Winnipeg. When McKay died four years later, there were thirteen in the herd. They along with three hybrids were sold to Samuel Bedson, warden of Stony Mountain Penitentiary, for one thousand dollars. The herd continued to grow, and Bedson was obliged to sell after ten years. He shipped eighty-three head to "Buffalo" Jones of Kansas for a reported fifty thousand dollars.

Jones sold the herd in about 1893 to Charles Allard and Michael Pablo, who were ranching on the Flathead Indian Reserve in Montana. The partners already had a herd of buffalo of Canadian origin there. Whether history or legend, the story of those buffalo began with a Montana Indian, Sam Walking Coyote, who was having mother-in-law troubles. Leaving his wife behind, he fled to Canada, but after several years, Sam became homesick and resolved to go back and seek forgiveness. He needed a present for his mother-in-law. But what could he offer the irate lady? He caught four buffalo calves, taught them to follow him and set out for the Flathead Reserve. The peace offering worked wonders, and the little herd grew until it too was sold to Allard and Pablo.

Allard died in 1896, and Pablo was left with the biggest herd in the world. By 1906, Pablo's buffalo numbered almost 800, and the herd came to the attention of the well-known pioneer Norman Luxton of Banff, who was quick to conclude that Canada had the strongest sentimental claim to it. He took his conviction to his friend, Hon. Frank Oliver, then Minister of the Interior in the Laurier government. Oliver agreed that the herd should be brought back to Canada. He convinced his cabinet colleagues, and negotiations were started, ending in the purchase of 716 buffalo of all ages for $245 per head.

Rounding up the animals and loading them on freight cars promised to be a stupendous task, especially in the rough country. Seventy-five of the best cowboys and best horses were obtained, but the first of three roundup attempts was judged a failure. The buffalo proved unmanageable on the long drive, and many good horses were killed. Pablo called a temporary halt and ordered the construction of a heavy plank fence from the buffalo range to the railroad corrals. The idea was good, and the drive along the fence was easier. It was still an uncertain operation, but the loading of the buffalo on reinforced rail cars was accomplished. Several trainloads of all-buffalo cargo left on the 1200-mile journey to a 197 square mile range near Wainwright, Alberta and to Elk Island Park, east of Edmonton. Wainwright was at once the centre of world buffalo interest and continued to be until 1939, when buffalo trouble loomed again. With war worries and a need for an artillery range, the government acted in haste—perhaps too much haste—and ordered liquidation of the great herd at that location.

The Regina Cyclone

Regina's thirty thousand citizens were in a holiday mood, suffering only from the extreme heat of that Sunday afternoon, June 30, 1912. Tomorrow would be Dominion Day and the forty-fifth anniversary of Confederation, and people were making ready to celebrate appropriately. That a cyclone might be aimed at the capital city was about the last thing being considered, for it was a common boast that cyclones and earthquakes were practically unknown in this new land.

But cyclones never serve much advance notice. Late in the afternoon, storm clouds rolled in with uncommon suddenness, looking black and angry. Lightning flashed, and frightening peels of thunder caused a few buggy horses on the street to bolt out of control. Parents in the park collected their children hurriedly. Those who had gone out in canoes on Wascana Lake to get away from the heat turned toward shore and paddled fast, but so quickly did the storm strike, some of the canoeists didn't quite make it to the shore—at least not by canoe. One young man, Marshall by name, still on the water when the blast came, was lifted through the air and dropped on dry ground. Exactly what happened was largely conjecture, but when Marshall regained consciousness on the grass of Victoria Park, it was clear that the wind at the peak of its intensity had picked him up, with or without the canoe, and dropped him from about treetop height some distance away.

Another canoeist was less fortunate. Philip Steele was one of two young fellows in a canoe; both were lifted from the lake and dropped roughly on the nearby land. One of the boys survived; Philip Steele died.

The cyclone's behaviour was like nothing of earlier record. The path of its onslaught was neither long nor broad. The swath of devastation was only about three blocks wide, mainly between Lorne and Smith streets, and about a couple of miles long. But within the limits of the swath, which happened to coincide roughly with the centre of the city, buildings, big and small, became victims. Among those that fell were two churches, the city library, the Y.M.C.A. and Y.W.C.A., and hundreds of homes that were either carried away or demolished. Freight cars were blown off their tracks, and grain elevators were toppled. Total damage to buildings was estimated at $10 million in the values of 1912, representing more than a million dollars per minute after the cyclone struck at 4:48 P.M.

Communication was still at a primitive stage, and most Regina residents living outside the narrow corridor of destruction were unaware of the magnitude of the damage until the storm had passed and they left their homes to determine if the city escaped harm. Only then did they discover how close their own homes were to the area of near total destruction. When these unsuspecting citizens discovered the wreckage, hundreds of them removed their coats and went to work in search of possible victims buried under the debris. A few people were found alive, but more were found dead; twenty-eight people were known to have lost their lives, and many more were injured. Hundreds of Regina families were homeless.

Naturally, the city was in a state of shock on Dominion Day, and there was no celebration. There was enough emergency work to keep every volunteer busy. Sympathetic friends in neighbouring villages, towns, and farming communities responded as prairie neighbours would be expected to respond. Relief came in the form of money contributions from distant parts of Canada. The Government of Saskatchewan contributed $25,000 forthwith and offered a loan of up to $10 million for city reconstruction. The Government of Canada gave $30,000, and the neighbouring province of Manitoba gave $10,000. The Grand Trunk Railroad contributed $5,000, and so did the Calgary *Herald*.

The people of Canada, through their governments, were saying very clearly to Reginans: "Your misfortunes are our misfortunes too."

Passenger Pigeons by the Barrel

September 1, 1914, was the day on which "the lights went out forever" for the graceful and beautiful passenger pigeon, which once filled our skies. It should have been the first annual day of mourning for bird lovers everywhere and all people who abhor the wanton slaughter of animals. Such an observance might have helped to prevent North Americans from forgetting one of the most shocking biological tragedies in their history.

The most spectacular scenes in the decline and disappearance of the "passengers" took place south of the international boundary. Slaughter was the heaviest there, but it would be a mistake to believe that the pigeons were American property more than Canadian. The huge flocks migrated as far north as the Mackenzie River Valley, and Pigeon Lake, by its name, gives a hint of the huge flocks that settled there, in what is now central Alberta, in nesting season. The author's father, Alexander MacEwan, who came to Manitoba in 1889, told of seeing the Assiniboine River Valley at Brandon when there were pigeons "in almost every tree."

So large were the flocks seen in the wooded regions during migration that according to writers who saw them, they cut off the light from the sun, making midday appear like dusk for hours at a time. Alexander Wilson, a leading American ornithologist, told of seeing a flock of close to two billion birds in Kentucky and of men with guns who were said to have killed as many as forty birds with one shot.

The flocking instinct is strong, and even at nesting time, the passengers remained close together, so close that every tree in a chosen area would have a nest. Norman Luxton of Banff, recalling his boyhood years beside the Red and Assiniboine rivers at Winnipeg—from whence came one of the two mounted passenger pigeons seen in the Luxton Museum at Banff—told of seeing tree branches broken by the weight of pigeons roosting on them and of trees so discoloured by pigeon droppings that the boy who tried to climb them "never got his clothes quite clean again."

Many early observers believed that until the spectacular decline in about 1890, the passenger pigeon ranked first in bird population on the continent. Their double misfortune was that their meat was delicate and tasty and they were easy to kill. Rev. George Grant, who accompanied Sandford Fleming across the prairies in 1872, remarked about the large numbers of game animals. He was particularly impressed by "pigeon with rice and curry for breakfast." The heavily muscled breasts gave the birds a special epicurean appeal and hastened the slaughter. They were easy to shoot and easy to catch by netting, and a professional hunter might kill three or four barrels of the birds in a day. Fifty cents per dozen carcasses seems to have been the prevailing price in eastern city markets, to which the birds were shipped in carloads.

Taking pigeons for shipment to eastern cities like Boston, Philadelphia, and New York became a leading industry in Wisconsin. A single community in that state was reported to have shipped one hundred barrels of pigeons per day for forty days in 1871. Such killing, of course, was more than any species could stand. There were warnings, but the words of advice were apparently lost, muted by the merry jingle of cash returns, and the slaughter continued for a while. The serious decline in the bird's population was recognized in the 1890s, and only rarely was a wild pigeon seen after the beginning of the twentieth century. There was discussion about the need for statutory protection, but it was too late. Nature's balance had been seriously disturbed, and when the bird's numbers had been shockingly depleted, the few remaining passenger pigeons seemed to lose their desire to survive. Biologists became alarmed and made a frantic attempt to save the species, but by 1909, only two passenger pigeons remained, both in captivity in the Cincinnati Zoological Gardens, both twenty-four years old, and one or both believed to be sterile from age.

Ornithologists, in desperation, offered rewards for living specimens that would bring a ray of hope for the dying species. There was no response. The zoo's male pigeon died as old birds must do, and finally, on September 1, 1914, the twenty-nine-year-old female, Martha, died too, the last of a race that had known incredible numbers.

It was the end of another sad chapter in North American history. The race that had withstood glaciers, earthquakes, disease, and other enemies was unable to withstand the entrepreneurs who would sell birds—or any natural resource for which there was a market—by the barrel.

The Whooping Crane: Back from the Brink

Canada's record in wildlife conservation is a mixed bag of successes and failures. In too many cases, the strange pleasure of hunting, the monetary returns from trapping, and the ease and presumed convenience of practices causing pollution have hurt the cause of conservation. It was the cash return from the sale of buffalo hides that decimated the huge bison herds that occupied the western plains just a little more than a century ago. Likewise, it was the human influence that led to the extinction of the passenger pigeon, the great auk, the Labrador duck, and the Eskimo curlew, and the near-extinction of many others, including the California condor and the whooping crane.

Only in rare cases have birds and animals come close to extinction without going all the way. As Canadians should know and appreciate, the beautiful whooping crane is one of the few seriously endangered birds that, with the help of wildlife conservationists, made a significant comeback.

Being big and migratory and perhaps tasty to humans, the "whoopers" lived dangerously, especially when making their long flights between wintering areas near the Gulf of Mexico and nesting grounds far north. In pioneer years, they were known to nest in parts of the southern prairie provinces, but with the influx of settlers, the big birds retreated further north. The last known nesting in settled parts of the West was at Baliol in western Saskatchewan in 1922. For some years following, the cranes flew more deeply into the North to nest at sites where they were able to hide from human eyes.

An important development occurred in 1937, when a Texas peninsula jutting into the Gulf of Mexico with a fifty-five-mile coastline was named the Aransas National Wildlife Refuge. It had grassland, marshland, tidal flats, and lakes, everything to make it a perfect winter home for the cranes, which already nested there.

But whooping crane numbers were falling. The first annual count, made in 1938, revealed only eighteen birds in existence. Clearly, they needed more help. Hunters along the flyway were urged to be extremely careful about their targets, but accidents will happen, and the warnings were not enough. The count for 1941 brought more gloom: it had fallen to a total of fifteen birds. The odds seemed to be against survival. A single tragedy at the nesting site or in the course of migration could mark the end of the race.

It was decided to start breeding the big birds in captivity. The experiment was conducted at New Orleans, and two chicks were hatched there in 1956, but one nestling disappeared, and the second one died. Nobody gave up hope, however, and the following year, as conservationists around the world watched for news, two adult birds in the Audubon Park Zoo at New Orleans, the same parents that lost their offspring in 1956, produced two more. These did well, but there was no assurance that cranes raised in a zoo would ever adapt to the wild. Workers wanted a better plan—and they found it.

First in a series of events was the discovery in 1954 of the whoopers' summer nesting place beside the Sass River in Wood Buffalo National Park. Creatures of habit, the cranes, which mate for life, had been returning there year after year. With fresh resolve, the wildlife specialists were determined to protect the isolation of the region.

By 1962, the wild flock showed slight improvement in numbers: thirty-three adults and five juveniles. There were, as well, a few more whooping cranes in zoo cages. Still it wasn't enough, but a bright prospect appeared in 1975 when an attempt was made to establish a second wild flock. Fourteen eggs were removed from the Wood Buffalo Park site and flown to a sandhill crane nesting area at Grays Lake in Idaho. The eggs were placed in sandhill crane nests in the hope that the eggs would hatch and the young whoopers would accept the migration habits of their foster parents. It was a first-class hunch: four young birds flew south with the sandhill cranes to winter in New Mexico and back to Grays Lake in the spring. The new migration pattern was the only one the young cranes knew, and they were quite satisfied with it. A second flock of wild whoopers was achieved, providing a measure of the survival insurance the wildlife workers wanted.

Whooping crane prospects were at once improved. By 1985, the overall count confirmed 84 wild birds ready to make the spring flight from the Texas refuge to the Canadian North, 35 in the Grays Lake flock, and 35 in captivity. The reassuring total was 154 whooping cranes, ten times as many as in 1941. Human effort and imagination had triumphed in saving a race of birds.

"We Two Nations"

Fifty thousand Canadians and Americans assembled on July 14, 1932, to share a solemn promise to pursue peace between their two nations and witness the official opening of the International Peace Garden. It was situated plumb in the middle of the 4,000-mile or 6,500-kilometre boundary, and visitors could stand boldly with one foot in Canada and the other in the United States without fear of breaking crossing rules. There on the naturally scenic hills misleadingly called mountains, the new park had been created from two contiguous contributions of land, one from the state of North Dakota and the other from the province of Manitoba, and together comprising 2,200 acres.

The idea of a peace garden was conceived by Dr. Henry Moore of Islington, Ontario. Moore, after coming to Canada from England, taught horticulture at Cornell University and Ontario Agricultural College. His idea was presented for the first time at a convention of the Professional Grounds Management Association on August 7, 1929. A guest speaker at the convention, Moore's proposal for an International Peace Garden was instantly popular. He and two others were appointed to a committee to consider possible sites. Encouraged by enthusiasm on the part of the professional gardeners and their desire to make their own contribution to the cause of understanding between the two countries, Moore visited all the promising boundary sites. In September, 1931, his committee submitted its recommendation strongly favouring the Turtle Mountain location, about fifteen miles south of Boissevain, Manitoba, and about fifteen miles north of Dunseith, North Dakota.

The governments of the United States, Canada, Manitoba, and North Dakota responded favourably to requests for funding in spite of the drought and Depression, and construction plans were advanced quickly. Work began on the big stone cairn and essential buildings. Not many undertakings were completed by the day of the opening, but people came in great numbers, obviously more impressed by the ideal than the physical structure. Henry Moore was present on that dry and dusty July day and was beaming with justifiable pride.

Visitors crowded close to the fieldstone cairn to witness the unveiling and bow their heads as the dedication was read by Bishop Thomas of Brandon:

> To God in His Glory, we two nations dedicate this Garden, and pledge ourselves that as long as man shall live, we will not take up arms against one another.

Many organizations and groups participated both physically and financially in expanding the garden's facilities: the Masons of Manitoba and North Dakota built the Masonic auditorium; the veterans' organizations paid for the handsome Carillon Bell Tower; the Manitoba Horticultural Association provided the arboretum; one of the genuine showpieces, a beautiful floral clock, was a gift of the Bulova Company; the I.O.D.E. backed the Birch Grove picnic grounds; and the Order of the Eastern Star was responsible for the building of the Peace Chapel right on the boundary. There were dozens more such gestures of support and approval from organizations wishing to declare their loyalty to the principles expressed by the garden, which so clearly belonged to all residents of the two countries.

Further west on the same border and in the same year, another scenic region was being dedicated to North American peace. The Waterton-Glacier International Peace Park resulted from the "marriage" that united the exquisite Waterton Lakes National Park on the Alberta side and the equally lovely Glacier National Park on the Montana side for a total of 1,754 square miles of rugged grandeur.

Canadians and Americans have thanked God for a long boundary adorned with precious jewels like peace gardens and peace parks instead of barbed wire and gun emplacements, and for years, Rotarians and others have met at these parks for symbolic Hands across the Border exercises.

Looking for Grass

There is reason to believe that the sheep drive from Kentucky to the Selkirk colony in 1833—about 1600 miles in four and a half months—was the longest and most notable in world history and marked the starting point for the sheep industry in the West. Nothing like it would happen again, some people said, but exactly one hundred years later, there was the no less remarkable Eppard drive, which deserved more acclaim than it received. The Rae-Campbell drive of 1833 covered more miles, but the Eppard adventure took longer and faced more horrendous obstacles along the way.

With the hardiness and resourcefulness of his Dutch forebears, Iowa-born Marrion Eppard and his Saskatchewan-born wife and five-year-old son, Kenneth, were small-farm residents near Estevan in the southeast corner of Saskatchewan. They were wearied by drought, Russian thistles, and mortgage collectors, and in the spring of 1933, Eppard was ready for a change. He repeated the family options to his wife and asked: "What will it be? We can sell our sheep and apply the money we get to the farm mortgage, or we can let the mortgage company take the land and we'll keep the sheep and look for grass." Mrs. Eppard knew that by voting to hang onto the mortgaged farm, she would have been sure of a roof over her head, but intuition told her they should keep the sheep.

The day of departure from the farm was set to follow immediately after shearing and the sale of the wool. With the cash returns from the wool, they paid some local debts, bought a supply of food essentials, and had $3.40 left over. Eppard placed a mattress, a stock of food supplies, and some personal belongings in the wagon and hitched his two Percheron horses to it. Mrs. Eppard and Kenneth took their seats on a twelve-inch plank placed across the wagon, and the lady took the reins.

Eppard then whistled for his dog, a Border collie that was really his assistant manager of sheep operations, and turned the flock westward on the road allowance. Mixed feelings rose within them all: regrets, of course, and a sense of release from debts and thistles. He had no idea where he would go, but his wife as driver of the wagon would follow close behind. Travel wouldn't be fast. The sheep would have to graze as they travelled and would largely set their own speed.[4]

Day after day the Eppards followed their flock of over three hundred sheep and lambs. Night after night they slept in or under the wagon. By summer's end they were in southeastern Alberta, south of the town of Foremost. There, compassionate local people offered an empty granary in which the Eppards might winter and a stack of straw from which they could draw winter feed for the sheep. A borrowed stove and a roll of tarpaper winterized the granary, and when groceries were needed, Eppard dressed a lamb and bartered the carcass.

Spring came. It was then one year after the Eppards had driven away from their former home to find grazing land for their sheep. Clinging to their westward course, they entered the Crowsnest Pass. Mountains were closing in on them, and they worried about coming to a dead end. When they came to Kimberley, where many young people had never seen a sheep, the Eppards learned that there was neither road nor trail across the mountains. There was a path up the east side of a mountain to a lake with good fishing. It was an approach to Rose's Pass, but it would be impossible to take sheep over it, he was told, and it was grizzly bear country. His only hope, they told him, was to drive south to Creston and then come back north on the opposite side of the Cascade range, a journey almost as difficult and of much greater distance.

Eppard sharpened his axe and began working on the fisherman's path toward the top of the pass, and after weeks of cutting, clearing, and bridging coulees, he had a rough opening through which the three Eppards drove and pushed the sheep to the top and down the west side of the mountain. Eppard returned to the base of the pass on the east side to recover his wagon and team and drove to Creston and back on the west side of the range to meet his family.

The next obstacles were the Kootenay and the Lower Arrow lakes. Paying with mutton, Eppard was able to rent what looked like glorified rafts with motors. From Needles on Arrow Lake, the Eppard wagon and flock were back on the trail, bearing westward. After two long summers of travel and one cold winter in a granary, the Eppards arrived at Vernon in the Okanagan Valley and found the reward of security and good grazing.

Prairie Farm Rehabilitation

Soil and water were the gold coins of western agriculture and the western economy. Any malfunction in one or both could spell disaster, as it did in the dry and wind-blown thirties. If Capt. John Palliser could have returned to see the grim plight of the Palliser Triangle, he might well have said: "I told you so."

By the middle of that unfortunate decade, many prairie farmers were abandoning their land. Hope was fading, and informed people were telling the Bennett government that the country was letting its water get away before it had used it and that soil resources were dwindling fast, partly by depletion and partly by wind and water erosion. Minister of Agriculture Robert Weir, a Saskatchewan farmer, understood and agreed it was time to bring the public's best effort to the conservation of soil and water.

The Prairie Farm Rehabilitation Act, passed on April 17, 1935, was intended to furnish muscle and money with which to pay for conservation and recovery of security. It was to have a life of five years, and although money was as scarce as drinking water in Saskatchewan, a budget of $4.75 million was set. The act would be in effect in Manitoba, Saskatchewan, and Alberta. The immediate emphasis, logically, would be on catching enough water to meet living needs. Farm dugouts and reservoirs to catch and hold runoff were already in use in places, but many more were needed, and the new P.F.R.A. administration undertook at once to create them.

George Spence, who had come from the Orkney Islands, homesteaded, and sat as an elected member in both Ottawa and Regina, was already the acknowledged doyen of soil and water conservation. He was appointed to be the first director of the P.F.R.A. administration. He sounded the battle cry when he declared, with a good Orkney accent: "I believe it is nothing short of a crime to allow water to run across this dry land, down to the ocean, without making an effort to conserve and use it."[5]

The new administration had 50 new dams or reservoirs built in late 1935 and 800 more in the following year. Ultimately, the list of new water basins for farm homes and small herds numbered 110,000. To this could be added 12,000 stock-watering dams and a growing number of larger irrigation dams to serve entire communities. Of the latter, the St. Mary River Dam southwest of Lethbridge was able to bring water to almost 100,000 acres in its first phase.

The Gardiner Dam, the most spectacular effort of all and the most controversial, was planned to furnish water for irrigation, hydro power, domestic needs, and recreation. Work on the dam began in 1959 and was completed eight years later. The dam stood like a monument in the dry prairie area. The big Diefenbaker Lake, which rose behind the dam, changed the Saskatchewan landscape and served recreational needs well. Irrigation was slow in becoming popular with the people for whom it was intended, but it was accepted.

P.F.R.A. development brought the mistakes in early land use into view. Farm families had to be moved from submarginal lands to areas offering reasonable security. Questions were raised about utilization of the abandoned farmland, but the answer came quickly: even the poorest of the lands on which homesteaders had mistakenly settled were capable of growing grass, and useful community pastures emerged.

The principle of such pastures had been advocated by Saskatchewan's Robert Sinton at the National Live Stock Association meetings in Ottawa in 1908 but remained more or less dormant until revived by the reassessment of areas of abandoned land in 1937. Sixteen community pastures ranging from 6,000 to 25,000 acres were established in the drier parts of Saskatchewan in 1937, and ten years later, there were seventy-five such big areas of well-fenced and supervised pasture land. Comprising 1,412,860 acres, the pastures supported 67,900 cattle and horses and 2,966 sheep. By the best rehabilitation techniques and re-grassing where needed, the carrying capacity of the range was increased dramatically.

P.F.R.A. workers heard increasing calls for their healing techniques. The arrest of drifting soil, control of salinity of soils, and restoration of fertility became major objectives. Tree distribution for shelterbelt planting, a federal service since 1902, was in 1963 taken over by the P.F.R.A. and co-ordinated with other rehabilitation undertakings. By 1985, federal tree nurseries in Saskatchewan had furnished more than 450 million trees for western planting. Such programs are costly, but most westerners believe P.F.R.A. is worth it.

The Red River Flood

Manitoba's Red River—often called the Red River of the North to distinguish it from the Texas Red River—figured prominently in the fur trade, in the fortunes of the Selkirk settlers after 1812, and in the introduction of freighting by steamboats on western waterways after 1859. In addition to all that, the river made its own flood history, a chapter that was too soon forgotten or too readily ignored.

To most, the Red River gave the impression of an even-tempered thing wanting to get to Lake Winnipeg on a straight course without wandering needlessly around the country. But, like a man who appears mild and gentle but reserves the right to go on an occasional "bender," the Red River possessed a potential for ugliness.

The biggest Red River flood of record was in 1826; it drove all the Selkirk settlers to higher ground at Bird's Hill or Stony Mountain. When the settlers returned a month and a half later, their homes and other buildings were gone; to the last log, they had floated away. The floods of 1852 and 1861 were almost as big as that of 1826, but still bigger than the big one of memory, 1950.

With no Red River flood of extreme proportions for sixty-two years, residents of the area came unsuspecting and unworried to 1950, even though weather conditions offered a perfect set of circumstances for flooding: a previous autumn with unusually much rain, a winter with heavy snowfall, a late spring, and more rain with it. When weather reports from Minnesota and North Dakota, from whence the waters of the Red originate, sounded a warning, Winnipeg engineers took stock of their sandbags and the condition of their dikes.

On April 11, Winnipeg citizens received a solemn warning that their river could be expected to overflow its banks in parts of the city. The message carried a rider that the flood waters might rise to the same level as that of two years earlier—which was too high for comfort. Some dikes were raised, and steps were taken to deal with possible ice jams. The flood crest, it was reported, would likely reach Winnipeg about the end of April. No serious trouble was expected from the Assiniboine. Daily flood bulletins were promised. It didn't seem particularly frightening, and the Winnipeg pace didn't change.

Upstream, snow and ice were melting slowly, but there came a change to warmer weather about mid-April, bringing fresh surges of water. Winnipeg reported its first flooding on or about April 21. By this time, the upstream towns of Emerson and Morris were really flooded. Aerial surveys at the beginning of May showed 150,000 acres south of Winnipeg flooded. On May 5, flood water cut the railroad connections with towns south of Winnipeg.

At that time, the Canadian army was called in to direct relief operations; they would remain until May 31. Hospital patients were evacuated from areas threatened by flooding. By May 7, the water was nine feet above the "minimum flood stage" and still rising. Federal government departments were called to assist. Winnipeg was in a state of emergency, and rural people, especially those with livestock needing care, had to rely entirely upon their own resources. Aerial photos now showed the Red River looking more like a lake than a stream, up to twenty miles wide.

A mass exodus from Winnipeg and towns in the valley was in progress. Close to 100,000 residents—mainly women and children—departed to stay with relatives and friends elsewhere. Some wondered if their homes would remain standing.

The flood peak of 30.3 feet came on May 19, much later than expected. Even more surprising was that the water remained at or close to the peak for about ten days. The decline was slow. The water remained above the recognized flood stage for fifty-one days. But as the flood fell, residents returned to their homes, often to find them seriously damaged and uninhabitable. A Red River Valley Board, backed by both federal and provincial funds, was set up to assist in repairing or rebuilding. It was a multimillion-dollar undertaking and it took time.

Residents wondered what they could do to see that such a disaster did not happen again. Public workers embarked upon a survey that led to the construction of the gigantic floodway to take floodwater from the river at a point above the city, convey it by means of the huge ditch around the east side of Winnipeg, and return it to the river north of the city. Thoughtful Winnipegers were grateful that they had passed the catastrophic flood of 1950 with only one loss of life and that they now had the floodway to prevent evermore a flood disaster of the magnitude of 1950.[6]

Henry Hind's Vision

In 1858, Henry Youle Hind, professor of chemistry and geology at Trinity College in Toronto, stood at the elbow of the South Saskatchewan River and caught a vision of a massive dam at that point. His thoughts, however, were not on irrigation or hydroelectric power or even recreation; rather, his motivation was the thought of a river diversion to send the South Saskatchewan water into the Qu'Appelle Valley and on to the Assiniboine and Red rivers, thereby furnishing a thousand-mile water highway to connect Fort Garry with the Foothills. He was excited about the idea of achieving so much with an eighty-five-foot dam and may have temporarily forgotten his main purpose for being there.

Hind and Captain John Palliser were both in the West at that time, on similar business but serving different masters. Palliser's assignment was from the imperial government; he was expected to determine if Rupert's Land had some better use than for support of the fur trade. Hind was to report to the government of the Province of Canada; he would advise if the country was worth annexing. It is doubtful if Palliser and Hind ever met.

Hind's dam, if it had been built, would have been well within the bounds of the Palliser Triangle, where its author saw drought as the great obstacle to cropping. Hind's concept of river diversion was forgotten, but time brought increasing interest in using the river's water for irrigation, and a dam built primarily for irrigation and power became a popular political issue. A government-authorized study failed to make a strong case for the dam on strictly economic grounds, but that did not discourage the politicians. In the years following the extremely dry thirties, western leaders of all parties wanted to appear as champions of a big multipurpose dam scheme.

After much discussion, in 1958—exactly one hundred years after Hind saw the elbow and got the inspiration—the governments of Canada and Saskatchewan agreed to build the one hundred million dollar dam installation. P.F.R.A. workers, who had mounting experience in water developments, would be responsible for the planning of the main dam and the auxiliary dam needed to control the flow into the Qu'Appelle.

That main dam would become one of the largest earth-fill dams in the world and one of the biggest construction projects in Canadian history. It would be 64 metres, or 208 feet, high, about a mile and a half long, and half a mile wide.

The dual dams and the big artificial lake behind them, located close to the centre of the Palliser Triangle, captured public imagination in all parts of the continent, and small wonder. The statistics were staggering. The earth and clay moved to become the body of the big dam amounted to 35 million cubic yards, which would explain the great concern shown about footings or foundations. The new lake created by the dam was about 135 miles long, with a shoreline of 475 miles. Covering close to 100,000 acres, or 40,000 hectares, the lake could store 6 million cubic feet of water.

Construction began in 1959, after ten thousand guests gathered to witness the official sod turning, a charge of dynamite set off by Prime Minister Diefenbaker. After he had pushed the button, he observed wryly: "That's easier than doing it with our old potato shovel." It was the first step toward a reservoir that might irrigate three-quarters of a million acres of cropland in thirty-six municipalities and generate 416 million kilowatt hours of hydroelectric power per year with water that normally flowed unused to Hudson Bay.

Another hundred thousand urban residents hoped that the same reservoir would assure reliable water supplies at kitchen taps on farms and in towns. Citizens of Regina, Moose Jaw, Saskatoon, and Brandon believed the new lake would be their best hope for water security.

There remained the matter of conferring names upon the dam and the lake; with two governments and three parties involved, it wasn't easy to get agreement. There might have been logic in a name like Henry Hind Dam, but the Hind name was no longer meaningful. In the end, the names chosen were Gardiner Dam, honouring former Saskatchewan premier and federal minister of agriculture Jimmy Gardiner, and Lake Diefenbaker, honouring former prime minister John Diefenbaker.

Completion of construction on the South Saskatchewan River megaproject made a fitting addition to Canada's centennial of Confederation celebration in 1967, and regardless of what the critics said about the hundred million dollar investment, most westerners approved.

Foot-and-Mouth Disease in Saskatchewan

Bad news is most shocking when it comes without warning, like the headlines blazoned across the nation on February 25, 1952: FOOT-AND-MOUTH DISEASE CONFIRMED IN SASKATCHEWAN.

Before sundown on the day the news broke, federal servants of the

Health of Animals Branch and additional mounted police converged upon Regina to assume command in the emergency. Strict quarantines in the area of the sick cows were ordered at once. Agricultural conventions and activities like bull sales were cancelled. The livestock markets were suddenly paralysed, and western people knew they were in trouble.

"Looks like a deathblow to the livestock business in Canada," people were saying gravely. The chance of eradicating the insidious disease appeared slim because the infection was found to have had a long head start on diagnosis. "If we had caught it two or three months ago, we might have eradicated it," a Regina man said in March, "but the infection has had time to get into our wild animals and if our deer and northern buffalo get it, we'll never see the last of it."

The story of Canada's first and only outbreak of the disease that plagued European countries for centuries seemed to have started on a dairy farm near the village of McLean, east of Regina. The farmer called the local veterinarian, who inspected the sick cows and said they had vesicular stomatitis. He prescribed something and went on his way, but he did report the illness to the provincial veterinarian at Regina. The latter discussed the case with the federal officer, and they agreed that the disorder was probably stomatitis and justified a quarantine.

Some days later, when the sick cows in the first herd appeared to be recovering, a neighbour's cows were showing symptoms of the same malady. Then the "stomatitis" appeared in cattle at the Burns feedlot in Regina. A quarantine was imposed, only to be lifted before the real trouble was even suspected.

Somebody in the veterinary service sent medical specimens to the federal laboratories in the East. On February 25, everyone's worst fears were confirmed, and the big headlines brought nation-wide shock. The deepest gloom was in Saskatchewan, where farmers and ranchers understood the seriousness of the disease. There was but slight assurance in the reminder that the United States had, years before, experienced an outbreak of foot-and-mouth disease and had succeeded in eradicating it. A four-pronged Canadian policy was adopted forthwith: first a rigid quarantining; next the slaughter of all cattle suspected of carrying the infection; then deep burial of carcasses; and finally, vigorous disinfecting.

The very day after the disease was diagnosed, heavy bulldozers from P.F.R.A. sheds were moved into position to begin excavating through six feet of frozen ground to make deep trenches for the mass burial. The first grave was two hundred feet long, sixty feet wide, and ten feet deep. As soon as the digging was completed, the hateful task of slaughter commenced. The unfortunate animals were herded into the pits where they were dropped immediately by mounted police rifle fire, covered with lime, and buried under ten feet of clay and heavy soil. The animals slaughtered included 1069 cattle, 129 pigs, 97 sheep, one goat, which happened to be the mascot of the Saskatchewan Roughriders football club, two horses, 1,610 poultry, and 13,192 hens' eggs.

While the slaughter and burial were in progress, a search was underway for the original Canadian source of infection. An immigrant boy hired to do chores on the farm east of Regina was a suspect, but nothing concrete resulted. At this point, however, nothing was more important than the big job of eradication, which was proceeding in a masterly way. The result was the best possible reply to the pessimists who said it would never be done: Hon. James Gardiner, federal minister of agriculture at the time, declared publicly on May 20—less than three months after the disease was correctly identified—that in his personal opinion, the disease was already buried deeply in the Regina gumbo. The skeptics were sure he had spoken too soon, but the minister was right. On August 19, 1952, slightly less than six months after the outbreak was announced, eradication was made official.

It was a great national triumph. Canada was again free of foot-and-mouth disease and, thirty-eight years later, is still free of it.

Chapter 6

People and Places

Gateway to the West

In the race to become a great city, Winnipeg had some geographic advantages: It was situated on the site of the Selkirk Settlement, where the first real experiment in western farming occurred. The site had been chosen with considerable care from 116,000 square miles of virgin country. Also, its geographical location practically forced immigrants to pass through this acknowledged Gateway to the Promised Land. The city's inheritance of history, geography, water, and soil, which in the words of W. L. Morton, was "as slippery as grease and as tenacious as glue" when wet, was altogether unbeatable.

Such circumstances gave Winnipeg a long head start in the race to become the West's first incorporated city. The goal of incorporation wasn't won easily, however, making the day of incorporation, November 8, 1873, even more of a triumph.

The citizens of Winnipeg were more enthusiastic and in a bigger hurry than the legislators. A committee of citizens, taking their instructions from a general meeting, prepared the first bill of incorporation, but when it was presented to the provincial legislature, it was not found acceptable. When it was amended to suit the provincial law-makers, it was no longer acceptable to the citizens' committee. Donald Smith—later Lord Strathcona—was sitting in the legislature at the time and was blamed for spreading fear of a rapid rise in city taxes after incorporation. His long association with the Hudson's Bay Company and his status as a big property owner and hence a big taxpayer in Winnipeg couldn't be overlooked. Citizen patience dropped, and anger at the provincial government and legislature grew to the unpardonable length of the use of tar and feathers on the Speaker of the legislature. The perpetrators of that despicable crime were never apprehended.

Winnipeg's first civic election following incorporation was on January 5, 1874, and it too raised some eyebrows. The contest for mayor was won by Frank E. Cornish, who received 383 votes; his opponent, W. F. Luxton, a school teacher and journalist, collected 179. Together, the votes totalled 562. What was not explained was how 562 mayoralty votes could be counted in an election in which the voters list showed only 388 names.

One of Cornish's first duties as mayor and chief magistrate was to hear cases against transgressors. He had, it seems, celebrated his victory well, perhaps too well, and legend has it that a hangover left him feeling guilty. He paused long enough from his duties to lay a charge of disorderly conduct against himself; then, leaving the bench, he moved down to the prisoner's dock and pleaded guilty, returned to the magistrate's chair, and ordered that the guilty person pay a fine of two dollars. He promptly paid the fine and went on with other court cases with a good conscience.

There were notable names on that first aldermanic list, among them J. H. Ashdown, a widely known merchant who was secretary of the citizens association that drafted the first bill offered to the legislature in support of incorporation; John Higgins, another well-known merchant; Alex Logan, who was Winnipeg's mayor at a later date; and Archibald Wright, who had arrived from Fort Carlton in 1869 and opened for business as the first harnessmaker. He added to his list of distinctions by being arrested by Louis Riel in that same year and later made agricultural history by bringing the first Holstein cattle to the West and to Canada, a purebred cow and bull that were placed on his extensive farm about four miles west of Fort Garry on the Assiniboine River.

It was an exciting year in Winnipeg. The number of buildings in the city doubled in Cornish's first year as mayor. The weekly *Free Press*, established on November 9, 1872, became a daily on July 6, 1874. Winnipeg people saw the last annual Indian dog feast in '74, when two hundred Indians assembled for the alleged delicacy of roast dog.[1] The first railroad hadn't been laid, but there were seven sternwheel steamboats carrying freight, and a railroad was in the planning stages.

The stage was set for a real-estate boom. As it turned out, the year marked the beginning of a moderate boom, which led into the even bigger boom of 1881, when short and plump Jim Coolican was conducting real estate auctions several nights per week. Winnipeg's real-estate King, Coolican, wearing a fur coat, plug hat, and diamond cuff links, was a symbol of boom-time madness.

The Mennonites

The Mennonite group that reached Winnipeg by steamboat on July 31, 1874, was the first big party of immigrants to the West since the coming of the Selkirk Settlers half a century earlier.

The group came from Russia, where they had lived and farmed for a few generations, but they and others of their sect, made distinctive by their devotion to their faith and frugal way of life, possessed no homeland they could call their own. Their religion had its roots in the Anabaptist movement of the Reformation in 16th-century Europe. A much-persecuted people, the peace-loving Mennonites spread from Switzerland, Germany, and the Netherlands to Russia and other parts of Europe and then to the United States and eastern Canada. The first Mennonites in Canada came by way of Pennsylvania to settle in the

Niagara Peninsula and elsewhere in Upper Canada after the American Revolution.

The mass departures from Russia were caused by fear of losing the few freedoms they possessed and the immunity from military service that had attracted them to Russia in the first place. In their search for a homeland, a deputation of Russian Mennonites travelled to Canada in 1873 and made an inspection of central and southern Manitoba by means of a horse-drawn wagon, provided courtesy of the government of the young province. Officials of the Dominion government promised full exemption from military service, freedom of religion, and a good measure of freedom for church schools.

There was still the question of finding a big block of land that would be to the Mennonites' liking. The Canadians' advice was guided by the recommendations of Captain John Palliser, who had unhesitatingly pronounced the "Fertile Belt," which spread like a crescent north of the shortgrass plains, as the best country for farming. Mennonite emissaries ignored the advice and asked for a reservation in the open country south of Winnipeg. The government representatives saw no reason to argue and agreed to set aside a reserve consisting of eight townships southeast of Winnipeg, east of the Red River and extending as far south as Rat River, the area in which the town of Steinbach would become a showpiece. The government also promised that if this block of land proved to be less than enough, another reserve would be marked on the west side of the Red extending as far back as the Pembina Hills. That "West Reserve" was needed, and on it, in time, farming and urban communities like Winkler, Altona, and Gretna prospered. Here developed Canada's first permanent farm settlement on the open plains, a monument to the Mennonite pioneers.

To the astonishment of spectators in and around Winnipeg, the Mennonite determination to "settle for" this flat prairie land, which happened to resemble what these people were farming in Russia, proved the soundness of their judgement.

The sixty-five families that arrived on that last day of July were just the forerunners of the more than 6,000 people comprising 1,200 Mennonite families that settled on Manitoba farm lands in a five-year period. They employed many of the methods they had used in Russia like summerfallowing, co-operating by using communal pastures, and the characteristic clusters of farm buildings usually at the centre of a block of farms. There were social and practical advantages in such arrangements but in time, the collective pattern disappeared.

More immigrants came from time to time. The biggest wave consisted of twenty thousand who came to Canada after World War I, most of them to the West. Manitoba continued to have the greatest concentration of Mennonite population, in urban communities as well as on farms. The province was thought to have fully one-third of the Mennonites in Canada. Winnipeg might well qualify to be the Mennonite capital of Canada, if there was such a thing. It is there that the Canadian Mennonite Central Committee came to have its headquarters. Distinguished for its distribution of charity and the efficiency with which the service is conducted, the committee has become one of the most effective relief institutions in the world.

A New-World Paradise

Hard on the heels of the Mennonites came the Icelanders. Traditionally, their way of life was very different, but the two groups had one thing in common: both knew exactly what they wanted to find in Canada. The Mennonites wanted level and open land, while the Icelanders, whose lifestyle on their former small, forty thousand square mile home island had demanded a combination of small-scale farming and large-scale fishing, wanted opportunities for the same here.

The small subarctic land has been called "an island of glaciers and volcanoes." On the map, it looks something like a dishrag hung over the Arctic Circle to dry. Its greatest length would equal the distance between Prince Albert and Weyburn in Saskatchewan. A growing population coupled with serious limitations of soil, forests, grass, and living space forced many of the Island's sons and daughters to seek their fortunes elsewhere.

Various countries with northern frontiers wanted the hardy Icelanders as immigrants. The Icelanders probably retained some sentiment for the North American continent their Viking ancestors had discovered a thousand years ago and were interested in settling in Canada and the United States. President U. S. Grant was enthusiastic about a proposal to settle Alaska with Icelanders and placed a naval training ship at the disposal of an Icelandic scouting party; it was used extensively, but no settlers responded.

There was more interest in Canada. After Iceland's Mount Hecla erupted and destroyed much grassland, many families were ready to move. A party of 150 came to Ontario and took land at Muskoka in 1873. A second and larger group, about 365, left Iceland in September, 1874, to go to the United States. They were intercepted by a Canadian promoter in Quebec who convinced the travellers to go to Kinmount, Ontario—not far from the first party—instead. Kinmount proved disappointing, and on the advice of Rev. John Taylor, the immigrants became interested in Manitoba, especially a location on the west side of Lake Winnipeg, where settlers heard they would find soil and good fishing and a water course all the way to Winnipeg.

They sent a scout to verify the account, and his report proved convincing. Some of the immigrants had left Kinmount to settle in Nova Scotia, and they returned to travel west with their friends. Two hundred and eighty-five persons—eighty-five families—arrived in Winnipeg on October 11, 1875, and then travelled north to build cabin homes and make ready for winter.

The place was given the name Gimli, said to mean "paradise." Almost as often, it was called New Iceland. In the early years, Gimli was not within the limits of the original "postage stamp" province of Manitoba. If they were to have something resembling local government and order, the newcomers would have to do everything for themselves. Democratically, they named essential committees and then a central committee with wide powers. What was often called the Republic of New Iceland lasted for about ten years, until the Manitoba boundaries were extended west and north to include the "republic." The "homemade" administration was one of the wonders of the frontier, and when the area was finally absorbed by the expanding province, the organization was so efficient that it could be turned over to the province as a ready-made municipality.

The record of success was a tribute to Sigtryggur Jonasson, who had masterminded the organization and was the first chairman or president of the republic. He was also the first Icelandic member of the Manitoba legislature.

The Gimli settlement made a big impact upon the province of Manitoba and the West, largely through its sons and daughters. Author Margaret McWilliams, writing in 1928, caught the essence of the Gimli contribution in a few words: "Their most famous representative is the explorer [Vilhjalmur] Stefansson, who was born on the shores of Lake Winnipeg in 1879. At the time of the celebration of the fiftieth anniversary of their coming, they claimed in the West 18 members of the Legislatures, two Rhodes Scholars, 19 professors, 40 lawyers and 40 doctors—a remarkable percentage out of the 16,000 who now live in Canada, of whom 12,000 are in Manitoba."[2]

Another settlement, Markerville, Alberta, was founded by fifty men, women, and children who came by way of the United States in 1888. The name honoured C. P. Marker, a leader in the dairy industry at Markerville and in the province. The most famous Markerville resident was Stephen Stephansson, who homesteaded in the district and became the greatest Icelandic poet of modern times.

John Ware: "One of God's Gentlemen"

Even before the gaiety of Alberta's inauguration day had subsided, a cloud of sadness fell over the southwest. John Ware was dead. The greatly loved Negro rancher and former Carolina slave was regarded as the ablest cowboy rider of his time and perhaps the greatest of all time. His first journey northward, from Texas to the Canadian foothills, was by saddlehorse in 1882. In the years that followed, his estimated travels in a stocksaddle totalled about 250,000 miles, six times the circumference of the earth.

The irony of it all was that his death on September 12 occurred when his saddlehorse put a foot in a badger burrow and fell on him, breaking his neck. The body was shipped from the ranch, near Duchess, to Calgary for burial.

On Ware's first visit to Calgary, he noticed a "Man Wanted" sign in the window of a trading store on Atlantic Avenue. But when the manager saw Ware and noted his colour, he quietly removed the sign and explained: "We've decided not to fill that position." In the intervening years, the true measure of the black man had been recognized, and Ware became one of the most popular people in the ranch country. At the time of his death, the place that once snubbed him witnessed the public tribute of the biggest funeral ever seen there.

John's memories of Carolina slavery were ugly. He had worked hard and had suffered. Having never gone to school, he couldn't read or write. It was told that he never had shoes on his big feet until he was twenty years old. Shoes and schools were not for slave boys. When the slaves gained their freedom at the end of the Civil War, he went to Texas to escape memories of slavery. Although he had never ridden a horse in his life, he joined a cattle drive of Texas Longhorns to the North. His work ended in Idaho in 1882.

Tom Lynch of High River was in Idaho at the time to take charge of a herd to be delivered to the North West Cattle Company on the upper Highwood River. Lynch wanted an experienced cattleman to help him, and he approached Tom Morrow, a knowledgeable Texan, and asked him to hire on for the trip to the Canadian foothills. Morrow said that he intended to ride back to Texas but that he wouldn't mind seeing the Canadian grass. "I'll go if you'll hire my pal too," he said.

"Do you mean John Ware?" Lynch replied. "He's a Negro, and I don't want him. I never saw one who knew anything about cattle and horses. I just want you."

"You heard my terms," said Morrow. "You hire both of us or I won't go."

"All right," Lynch replied with disgust. "If that's the way you feel, I'll hire you both."

The drive started. Morrow rode near the front of the herd, overseeing. John Ware, on a broken saddle and a decrepit horse, was at the rear, getting the dust. He was not very happy. Mustering his courage, he went to Lynch and said: "Boss, would yo mind giving me a litta betta saddle an a litta woss hoss? I'd like to try them."

The other cowboys sensed a chance for some entertainment. They advised Lynch to give the big fellow a "betta saddle and that bad horse that hasn't been ridden yet."

The outlaw horse was snubbed to a wagon wheel, and a good saddle was buckled on him. "There," said Lynch. "If that's what you want, let's see what you can do." The cowboys got ready to laugh. John mounted, and the horse was cut loose. It jackknifed, bucked, and corkscrewed. The horse tried everything, but the onlookers didn't get their laugh. What they saw was the most perfect ride they could remember. John was at once promoted to the front of the herd.

After reaching Highwood River, Lynch paid off his men. When he came to Ware, he said: "John, will you stay and work for us?"

John considered briefly and replied: "Boss, I intended to ride back to Texas, but if you'll hire my pal too, I'll stay."

"I don't need your pal, but I need you, so all right, I'll take both of you," Lynch answered with a smile.

John saved his money, bought a few cows, and got a small ranch on Sheep Creek above Millarville. He built a log house and married Mildred Spence, whose family was living at Shepard, east of Calgary. When the herd became too big for the Sheep Creek range, the Wares obtained another on the Red Deer River east of Calgary. There, John met his death.

John's herd had grown to almost a thousand cattle and a few hundred horses, and his fame went far. He was powerful enough to upset a horse and hold it upside-down if a blacksmith was having trouble in shoeing and nimble enough to walk from one side of a crowded corral to the other on the backs of the cattle inside. Best of all, nobody could have a better neighbour.

The Baptist minister conducting the funeral service said: "He convinced me that black is a beautiful colour, one that was reserved for God's most cheerful people. The one whose remains we bury today was indeed one of God's gentlemen. His example and message on brotherhood should be entrenched in our hearts."

Whitewood's French Aristocracy

For a few years in the late 1880s and early 1890s, the best place in Canada to observe the latest Paris fashions in women's clothes was tiny

Whitewood, about one hundred miles east of Regina, North-West Territories.

Most immigrants to the Canadian West in those years were peasant people dressed in homespun with sheepskin coats, but there were two notable exceptions: first a colony of well-to-do Englishmen who followed Edward Pierce to a location about forty miles south of Moosomin in 1883. Because these Cannington Manor settlers did not have to rely entirely upon homestead returns, they were able to escape the worst of pioneer hardship and pursue a happy blend of cricket, horse racing, tea at four o'clock each day, and essential farm work. Cannington Manor was about as distinctive as Panama hats would be in the Arctic—at least until the coming of the French counts.

The first indication of a farming interest on the part of a group of French aristocrats was in 1885 when, strangely enough, a French-speaking German, Rudolph Meyer, appeared to inspect the district and make some land selections along the valley of the Pipestone River south of Whitewood. He was followed a short time later by the Count and Countess of Roffignac whose attractive valley farm became widely known as Rolandrie Ranch.

Then came Count Joumillhac, whose Richelieu farm on the north side of the river became an object of interest to French and other settlers pursuing high ideals in mixed farming. Among his special lines of production were Thoroughbred horses for racing, cavalry horses for the French army, sheep including Shropshire rams brought from the home of the breed in England, dairy cows to support a cheese factory, and various new field crops. Count de Soras appeared to have the most consistent interest in sheep and must be reckoned with when the history of the sheep industry is under review.

However much these French adventurers were attracted by frontier freedoms, they displayed a genuine interest in making a contribution to new-world agriculture. They were imaginative and various new avenues of production were considered and tried, but for one reason or another, their new enterprises failed to be very rewarding. Wheat and coarse grains were already the most popular crops in the country when the French tried chicory and sugarbeets. Both grew well in the Pipestone Valley soil, but because of difficulties with either marketing or processing, they failed to become popular. The beets were a success in the fields, but the facilities for making sugar were never installed. The chicory was likewise a field success, but markets were limited, and almost at once the supply exceeded the demand.

Several members of the distinguished community took to dairying and might have become leaders in the production of conventional lines like butter and common cheese, but again, in their determination to introduce new lines of production, they achieved nothing more useful than to find that the Canadian market was not ready for the exotic Gruyère cheese. With generous help from Count Joumillhac, a cheese factory was built. The subscribers had the satisfaction of turning out Gruyère cheese of highest quality, but with no market interest in the big balloon-like balls of cheese, the cheerful owners could think of no better solution than to use them for a mammoth cheese-rolling sweepstakes on the Pipestone hillside: the Frenchman who, with a push, could roll his ball of cheese the farthest into the valley was the winner.

If the French community had a business and social centre, it was the Rolandrie Ranch, which witnessed lively and glamorous times as well as serious times. About once a year, the ladies and gentlemen of the settlement staged a very formal ball in Whitewood. It may have been presented for the pleasure of the non-French spectators as much as for those who attended. Citizens of the town and beyond watched with intensity as elegant coaches driven four-in-hand by coachman in full livery brought the richly dressed and perfumed guests from their farms. The occasion presented scenes that the country had not witnessed before or, perhaps, since. It was always a night marked by stylish clothes, classical music, French wines, and Parisian manners, about which the more permanent residents talked in superlatives long after the last of the counts and countesses moved back to Paris.

Saskatoon: Born to the Temperance Tradition

Saskatoon was established with a clear and high purpose: to furnish a community thoroughly isolated from booze in all its evil forms. A separation of 150 miles from the nearest railroad town, Moose Jaw, seemed to offer a reasonable guarantee of insulation from the wicked John Barleycorn.

The idea of an alcohol-free colony in the West was hatched in Methodist Church circles in Toronto and facilitated by the federal government policy of selling big tracts of Crown land beyond the twenty-four-mile zones bordering the C.P.R. right-of-way to colonization companies at prices as low as one dollar per acre. The Temperance Colonization Society was organized in Toronto in 1881, following which an application for an isolated block of land in the North-West Territories was submitted to the Department of the Interior.

A publicity campaign to recruit settlers was launched at the Toronto exhibition that same year, and the response was overwhelming. The following June, a committee consisting of John H. Lake, who was regarded as the father of the scheme, S. W. Hill, and George Grant was to proceed to the territories to inspect the areas suggested by the government and make some decisions. The committee took a private surveyor along to help find good land.

The party travelled by way of Chicago to Winnipeg and Moosomin, which was as far as passengers could go by rail. Taking to the trail, they then travelled through Fort Qu'Appelle and the Touchwood Hills to Clark's Crossing on the South Saskatchewan River. At Fort Qu'Appelle the little party was joined by James Hamilton and his son, Robert, who brought with them valuable practical knowledge of western farming. The Hamiltons came to stay and were the first to stake out a farm for themselves and build a house.

Clark's Crossing, already served by a ferry, was within the bounds of the colony's land allotment but considered too far from its centre for a permanent colony townsite. The committeemen turned south but stayed close to the river.

John Lake told that after studying various possible townsites, he and his colleagues fixed upon section 27 and gave it the attractive Indian name Minnetonka. But days later when an Indian presented Lake with a handful of berries and informed him they were saskatoons, the leader fell gleefully upon the name and immediately renamed the town.

The members of the advance party returned to Toronto to report favourably on the allotment of land and prepare for the great migration in the spring of 1883. By this date it was possible for the settlers to travel as far as Moose Jaw by train. There they took to the 150-mile trail to complete their journey with horses and wagons. Indeed, it was possible by that time to ship the freight by rail as far as Medicine Hat and then route it to Saskatoon by riverboat. This was obviously the easier way of getting equipment and supplies to the destination.

Recalling the events of that year, Lake wrote: "I left Toronto May 1, 1883, reached Winnipeg by the evening of the 4th, arranged for scows, cables, lumber, shingles, doors, sash, tin, nails, etc., to be sent to Medicine Hat and floated down the Saskatchewan to Saskatoon. . . . I came on to Moose Jaw, took the trail and reached the colony on 29th of May. I found the Government surveyors were surveying our land along the river and farther north in long, narrow [riverlot] strips, like Halfbreed lands at Red River."[3]

This method of survey was totally unacceptable to Lake, and he was so upset that he proceeded at once to Ottawa, where he saw the prime minister and registered his complaint. As a result, a telegram was sent at once instructing the surveyors to quit the riverlot survey plan forthwith and get on with the square township layout.

The lumber arrived by river on August 27, and in Lake's words, "We all rejoiced." Houses were built and plans made for winter fuel. As it turned out, it was a brutal winter, and there was much hardship in the colony. As Lake noted: "God and the people alone know how they pulled through."

But pull through they did and the colony and its town prospered.

Three years after the coming of the first settlers, they held their first fair. Twenty-three years after coming, with many of the original settlers still there to see it happen, their booze-proof colony was incorporated as a city, with James Clinkskill as the first mayor.

Chief Crowfoot, Native Statesman

The Lethbridge *News* of May 7, 1890, reported the death of Chief Crowfoot. He was revered by his own people, and to him members of the white race owed a debt of gratitude, probably much greater than they realized.

"The Chief had been ill for some time," the article stated, "and on Tuesday last, Dr. George was summoned and found him suffering from pneumonia. The scene in the teepee of the dying Chief was exceedingly impressive, there being about 40 Indians assembled, including the three wives of Crowfoot and Medicine Men from both camps. . . . The day before yesterday, Sapoo Muxima [Crowfoot] went into a swoon and his relatives, believing him dead, killed his best horse before the teepee for his use in the Happy Hunting Ground. He, however, revived. When the great Chief breathed his last, his death was taken quietly; he had told the Indians not to mourn and to make no noise. A few days before his death a will was drawn up for him and in this document he left his house and one of his medals to his favourite wife, the rest of his medals and horses to his brother, Three Bulls, who is now Chief. The Medicine Men received 15 horses. . . ."[4]

No smoke arose from the camps the day of the leader's passing because no fires were kindled. Nobody took food. The constant beat of the tom-tom was for a dead hero.

Nobody was sure of Crowfoot's age at the time of his death, but it was thought to be about sixty-nine years. The Indians didn't show much interest in bookkeeping and vital statistics—the fact of a person being alive was proof enough that he had been born, and after that person's death, the time and place didn't matter—but if he was sixty-nine years old, it meant that his birth coincided with the union of the two big trading companies, the Hudson's Bay Company and the North West Company.

Crowfoot was the second son of a Blackfoot chief and the second son to carry the Crowfoot name. The first son was murdered when he visited the neighbouring Snake Indians to offer a pipe of peace. Infuriated by this breach of Indian honour, the dead man's younger brother—known thereafter as Crowfoot—led a Blackfoot party on a war of revenge and won a notable victory.

The young Crowfoot became a skilful horseman and encouraged his followers to cultivate horsemanship. The Blackfoot tribesmen were the first Canadian Indians to have horses and soon gained supremacy with them. Horse stealing was a favourite Indian pastime, and the Blackfoot people demonstrated that they could excel in that also. Like other tribes, the Blackfoot saw nothing evil in stealing horses as long as it was the original owners' privilege to steal them back, and hence it was more of a game than a crime. The mounted police, however, refused to see it this way. Like the Nez Percé Indians of Idaho, the Blackfoot may have learned something about horse improvement by selective breeding, but there is no evidence that they did. Perhaps they chose to believe that by discriminate stealing they could still ride the fastest horses.

Crowfoot was not without a few eccentricities. One of his vagaries was the white man's umbrella, and after acquiring one, he carried it constantly when riding his horse. It became a common spectacle on the reserve to see the great chief riding across the range, rain or shine, under the shelter of his beloved umbrella. For him, it was one of the white man's better achievements, one that made it a little easier to forgive the new race for its evil contributions like liquor, which the chief hated, and the awful diseases that had caused death and suffering among the native people.

Most important in the white man's relationship with Crowfoot were the four occasions from which the chief's honour and uncompromising honesty were the means of saving lives and avoiding frontier bloodbaths: First, in the months following the chief's first meeting with Colonel James F. Macleod of the N.W.M.P., he promised to work for understanding and peace between the police and his Indians, and did. Second, when he responded to the proposal for Blackfoot Treaty No. 7, he declared that he would be the first to sign the treaty and the last to break the promise. Third, by rejecting overtures from Sioux Chief Sitting Bull, he frustrated plans for a united Indian force to drive the whites from the buffalo country. Finally, he refused the invitation from Louis Riel and Gabriel Dumont to join the Métis in a campaign to win back the Indian country and freedoms of bygone years.

The First Big Fair

The territorial exhibition of 1895, the biggest event of its kind in the West, was a born-in-Regina idea, although there was never agreement about the individual in whose mind it was conceived.

There was already a positive agricultural-fair tradition in eastern Canada. There, the internationally recognized Toronto exhibition had grown from a "seedling" planted by the Agricultural Association of Upper Canada in 1846. As well, a venerable fair had been held annually at Windsor, Nova Scotia, since 1765. It was not only the oldest in Canada, but it had the best claim to being the first in North America.

But while Regina's fair dwarfed other western fairs and exhibitions, it wasn't the first in the West by any means. That honour would belong to Victoria, British Columbia, for its agricultural fair of 1861. Winnipeg might have had the first fair on the Prairies in 1871 had it not been for misfortune: the cattle and horse entries were tied to the fence and ready to enter the judging ring when a rumour of an impending Fenian raid from the south nullified all plans, and the fair ended before it was really started.

Pioneers in many parts, however, thought well enough of fairs that they organized them even before their districts were served by railroads; so it was with Portage la Prairie, Fort Edmonton, Prince Albert, and Saskatoon. Regina conducted fairs from 1884 and gained experience that was to be of value in 1895.

Lieutenant-Governor Charles Herbert Mackintosh was one of the enthusiastic supporters of the big Regina show and was influential in obtaining a federal grant of twenty-five thousand dollars. The Regina town council responded by pledging ten thousand dollars, and the territorial government, although struggling to pay for essentials, promised five thousand dollars. The C.P.R., instead of pledging cash, offered free transportation to and from the exhibition for all exhibits.[5]

Regina residents reacted by presenting a striking demonstration of co-operation and volunteerism. The lieutenant-governor drove a team of horses and carriage for the benefit of guests, and Frederick Haultain, premier of the territories, drove another team and wagon and hauled water in barrels from Robert Sinton's good well on Albert Street to the fair.

Property on the west side of the town was obtained to provide a permanent home for Regina's fairs. The site was practically without buildings at the time, but tents big and small appeared suddenly, like mushrooms, and visitors were promised the biggest fair west of Toronto. The prize list was inflated to $19,000, the most generous ever offered in the West; visitors were promised "an education for 25 cents."

Canada's governor general, Lord Aberdeen, officially opened the show on July 29. All the exhibition essentials were present: Scottish bagpipes, seven bands, the Musical Ride by the mounted police, football, broncobusting, horse races, and auction sales. In the livestock section, a primary attraction at that time, there were more breeds than anybody had seen at one time and place before. There were eight breeds of sheep in competition, six or seven of pigs, and four breeds of draft horses, including the Belgian, which many people had never seen before. The prizes, ranging up to $32 as first prize for mature stallions, were effective inducements and so were the promises from the mounted police to buy all prize winners in the light-horse classes for $125 per head.

For the first time in the West, Shorthorn cattle—or Durhams as they were then called—were effectively challenged by Herefords, from the herd of William Sharman of Souris, and Aberdeen Angus, entered by J. D. McGregor of Brandon.

One of the feature classes of the exhibition was intended to reach to the heart of the mixed-farming ideal; it demanded that each entry include no less than twelve items: five draft horses; five general-purpose horses; four pedigreed cattle, one to be a bull; four grade cattle; four ewes and one ram; five pigs; two bushels of Red Fife wheat; two bushels of feed barley; two bushels of black oats; two bushels of white oats; two bushels of two-rowed barley; and two bushels of six-rowed barley.

Then there were classes to meet timely needs; typical was the special prize of $500 for the best fire extinguisher of local invention and costing not more than $2 per day to operate. It was the territorial exhibition—novel, challenging, and in tune with the times. When it ended, thousands of visitors were impressed, and hundreds of Regina citizens were proud and exhausted.

Sifton's Favourite Immigrants

Canada wanted homesteaders—thousands of them—who would accept quarter-section farms in return for hard work, loyalty, and ten-dollar filing fees. People in distant lands thought the proposed deal sounded too good to be true and had to be convinced that it was real.

Icelanders followed Mennonites, and then came the French, Germans, and Hungarians to establish settlements and make good. But the response was too slow for Canadian leaders. The silver-tongued and polished French Canadian Wilfrid Laurier became prime minister in 1896 and, much impressed by the carefully considered views about immigration being expounded by the new Member of Parliament for the constituency of Brandon, Clifford Sifton, appointed him Minister of the Interior.

Sifton had begun his political career in the Manitoba Legislature in 1888 and was the attorney general in Premier Thomas Greenway's government for several years. Now, he entered his federal portfolio with the enthusiasm of a boy tackling raisin pie. At once, the call for settlers was trumpeted in far parts of the world. He recognized the huge potential for immigrants among the Slavic people of Eastern Europe, especially the peasant masses, unschooled and handicapped by poverty, in the provinces of Galicia and Bukovina in the old Austro-Hungarian Empire. There, rumours of free land in Canada and the possibility of escape from oppression and compulsory military service had already resulted in two courageous souls, Ivan Pylypiw and Wasyl Elyniak, venturing forth. They were attracted by homestead land at Deep Creek, south of today's Josephburg, Alberta. A few more came in '94. Then, as the Sifton campaign became more effective, Ukrainian settlements sprang up at Dauphin and Stuartburn and Ukraina in Manitoba and Wakaw in Saskatchewan. Altogether Canada received almost 300,000 Ukrainian immigrants.

A Ukrainian Orthodox Church was built at Gardenton, Manitoba, in 1897; schools were built without delay; and scores of Ukrainian newspapers and magazines were published across the West after the beginning of the present century.

Sifton remained proud of his choices for immigration and settlement on western land. As he surveyed the Ukrainian occupation of a broad ribbon of parkland—John Palliser's Fertile Belt—extending from south of Dauphin to Edmonton, he was glad to defend his concept of "quality" in settlers. "I think," he wrote, "a stalwart peasant in a sheepskin coat, born on the soil, whose forefathers have been farmers for ten generations, with a stout wife and a half-dozen children is good quality. . . . I am indifferent as to whether or not he is British born. . . ."[6]

The census of 1901 showed 5,600 Ukrainian-Canadians, most of them on farms and in the West. Eighty years later, the total was above half a million, many of them in towns and cities. The biggest urban concentration was in the City of Winnipeg. Still, farming was the Ukrainian's first love, and as a hard-working and resourceful farmer he will be remembered. His humble but warm and well-ordered home with plastered exterior and thatched roof bespoke thrift and practical skills.

The Ukrainian immigrants of Sifton's time were indeed eager to make homes on the land and stay there. But their children of the second and third generations moved into all walks of Canadian life, and with marked success. They entered the professions and public life. Large numbers volunteered for active service in World Wars I and II. Sons and daughters took their places among the scientists and great scholars of the nation. Some wore the uniforms of leading athletic clubs and teams, like Walter "Turk" Broda, who became a hockey hero with the Toronto Maple Leafs; some became leading farmers, like members of the John Skrypitsky family of Mundare who won the Alberta Farm Family Award; others, many others, reached into the highest levels of public life to become reeves, mayors, members of Parliament, and even, with Ramon Hnatyshyn's appointment in 1990, governor general of Canada.

The Doukhobors

It was 1899, three years after the Hon. Clifford Sifton had set in motion the new and aggressive programme to attract immigrants, and the arrival of seven thousand Doukhobors from Russia looked like the first big dividend from the investment. Canada would prove to be a new and strange experience for the Doukhobors, and the Doukhobors were an equally new experience for Canadians.

As far as anybody knew, the intensely serious Russian sect of peasant and pacifist people began with a breakaway segment from the Russian Orthodox Church about 250 years ago. They renounced church denominations and found their spiritual strength within their collective conscience. They were vegetarians and believers in communal living as a manifestation of charity. They were hard workers, but their unbending convictions led to conflicts with the Czarist regime. If the Russians believed they could persecute these dissident people into conformity, however, they were wrong.

Russian Count Leo Tolstoy showed sympathetic interest in the Doukhobors, and so did some English Quakers. They suggested that the oppressed people go to western Canada, and a few Doukhobors visited in 1898. The Government of Canada agreed to reserve 750,000 acres in the West, promising religious freedom and exemption from military service.

The Doukhobors accepted and sailed in four ships, landing at St. John, New Brunswick. The big party, mostly women and children, entrained to the West. A few stopped at Brandon or Winnipeg for the winter, while others continued to Yorkton. The land reserved for them was in three districts, two of them in the Yorkton-Kamsack area and one at Blaine Lake. The people were anxious to start building and cultivating. Lack of money was a handicap, but the newcomers possessed muscle and enterprise, and after locating their land and agreeing upon locations for the communal villages, the men hired out for wages, which were deposited in a community fund. The women remained behind to build log houses and cultivate the first gardens and crops. Refusing to enslave God's other creatures like horses and oxen for ploughing—and owning no such animals anyway—the women harnessed themselves to walking ploughs in teams of twelve and managed very well to bring their first small fields to production. They whitewashed their log houses and made acceptable furniture. Uncompromising vegetarians, they refused not only meat in their diets but even eggs and cows' milk, which properly belonged to the calves. Neighbours looked on with surprise and some ridicule, but the Doukhobors lived by their conscience. Those critics who warned superciliously of nutritional problems had to admit, finally, that no people of the frontier possessed more stamina and better health.

Their acknowledged leader, Peter Verigin, who had been banished to Siberia by Russian authorities, was able to join his people in Canada in 1902 and received a genuine welcome. He built a big and handsome house and lived richly. He was "Lordly Peter Verigin," but a prudent leader and one who might be described as a benevolent dictator.

The settlements progressed; they built good roads, installed some of the first telephones, and adopted good farming methods. Still, there were conflicts, some between the people and the government and some internally. The government could not bring itself to change the Dominion Lands Act to accommodate the whims of a single group and insisted that homesteads be registered in the names of individual homesteaders. The policy was contrary to Doukhobor views about private ownership. Further conflict arose over compulsory education and government demands that births, deaths, and marriages be registered officially.

As a result of these differences, some of the Doukhobor homesteads were cancelled and there were protest marches and some nude parades. At the same time, there was trouble between Doukhobor and Doukhobor. At first, one organization, the Christian Community of Universal Brotherhood seemed to satisfy everybody, but new groups appeared to represent changing concepts, the most radical of which—the Sons of Freedom, centred at Krestova, British Columbia—was blamed for burning schools in a dispute with the government over education.

After 1908, there was a big movement of Doukhobors from the prairies to British Columbia, notably Castlegar, Grand Forks, and Brilliant, until most of the Doukhobors of Canada were in that province. The people were changing, though, and before long, Doukhobors were found in every walk of Canadian life. But as one who knew them well in Saskatchewan and British Columbia said: "They are still dedicated people and good neighbours."

The Barr Colonists

Rev. Isaac Montgomery Barr, from whom the Barr Colony scheme of 1903 took its name, was an Ontario-born clergyman, a brilliant visionary, but one who was less than successful at bringing his grand ideas to reality. His parents, Rev. William and Catherine Barr, were Irish, staunch Presbyterians who came as immigrants to Halton County, Ontario, in 1846. Their first son, Isaac, was born the following year. As a young man, he was noticeably nonconformist. He left his parents' church and embraced the Anglican faith and then went on to become an Anglican priest. Ever restless, he moved from one church diocese to another in Canada and the United States.

Barr left the ministry late in 1901 to join Cecil Rhodes in a settlement undertaking in South Africa.[7] One way or another, he became enthusiastic about serving both England and Canada by helping to transplant middle-class English families to farm land in western Canada. Officials in government were willing and eager, and in 1902, he secured a land reservation of fifty-six townships of crown land immediately east of today's city of Lloydminster on the present-day Alberta-Saskatchewan border.

Having secured the land, he embarked upon a campaign to attract English candidates for emigration, especially those interested in farming on the Canadian frontier. He hoped to attract about six hundred Englishmen who would accept pioneer conditions and have sufficient start-up capital. He arranged for a ship, the SS *Lake Manitoba*, a ship formerly used to take troops to South Africa during the recent war. At this point, an unsuspected problem arose: instead of hearing from six hundred interested people, he had a list of over two thousand men, women, and children attracted by the prospect of free land for homesteaders. Barr was not inclined to refuse anybody.

The sailing date from Liverpool was March 31, 1903, and Rev. George Exton Lloyd was appointed chaplain for the party. Lloyd, who was later bishop of Saskatchewan, said afterward that 1964 passengers were taken on board, and it was evident that conditions would be terrible. The boat was overcrowded, sanitation was unsatisfactory, and food was inadequate and unpalatable. To make matters worse, a hundred or more family dogs were taken and had the freedom of the ship. The temper of the passengers deteriorated. There being no one else to blame, all complaints were directed at Barr. It reached the point where the poor fellow locked himself in his cabin in order to escape the angry mobs.

The ship docked at St. John, New Brunswick, on April 12. The C.P.R. had trains ready to take the colonists to Saskatoon, the nearest rail point to the land reservation, but there was delay because of lost baggage, for which, of course, Mr. Barr was blamed.

When the four trains were finally loaded and moving there was another outburst of complaints. The new immigrants were overcrowded, dissatisfied about sanitation, and unhappy about having to sleep on the wooden seats of the cars.

In Saskatoon, there was more confusion about baggage, like in

St. John, only worse, and the government tents that were to be used by the newcomers were late in arriving. Patience was needed; eventually, the tents arrived, and Saskatoon took on the appearance of a tent city.

The two-week stop at Saskatoon proved to be a bonanza for local merchants; the colonists bought food supplies, clothing, axes, walking ploughs, horses, and oxen. Prices rose sharply, and the English visitors renamed the town: Saskatoon became "Soak-it-to'em." The town residents watched as the English shopkeepers and clerks prepared for the trail and their homesteads. They saw men who had just bought horses in harness making chalk marks on the animals to show where the harness should be placed the next day, and they saw rodeos daily as men struggled with horses and oxen they did not understand.

The worst was yet to come: the long trail journey on wet ground to the Promised Land, to be called Britannia. Horses and oxen were undisciplined, and the wagons were repeatedly stuck in mud and sloughs. Some of the colonists gave up and turned back. Mr. Barr was blamed. It seemed that everybody was against him, and he finally withdrew and left the role of leadership to Mr. Lloyd.

For Rev. Isaac Barr, it was a sad finale. He probably had the best of intentions, but the task was too much for him, and his tormentors showed no mercy. He did not return to the settlement but went, in time, to Australia and died there. But the colony he founded was on good land and, after a full share of mistakes and pioneer misfortunes, became one of the most prosperous agricultural districts in the West.

The Calgary Stampede

Calgary's Stampede story began with Guy Weadick, a long, lean, voluble New Yorker who ran away from his boyhood home to be a cowboy. According to Weadick himself, he ultimately came to be "half cowboy and three-quarters showman," which wasn't bad for a person who never got beyond grade five arithmetic. He saw Calgary for the first time in 1905 when touring with a vaudeville troupe in which Negro Will Pickett was billed as a steer wrestler and Weadick as his manager. When he came again three years later, it was as a rider with the Miller Brothers' Wild West Show performing at the Dominion Exhibition.

This time, Weadick became friendly with H. C. McMullen, who was with the C.P.R. In the course of their discussions, they agreed that Calgary would be a most suitable place at which to stage a big rodeo, one that would present range history in a popular light. The swashbuckling Weadick went on his way but did not forget Calgary, and in March, 1912, he returned for serious talks with local businessmen about financial backing for a prestigious rodeo. The merchants listened politely but were cautious and said a city of sixty thousand wasn't big enough. "Try Pendleton or Cheyenne," they advised.

"Let's talk to George Lane of the Bar U Ranch," McMullen advised Weadick. "He'll be at the Alberta Hotel tomorrow."

Lane listened to Weadick's sales talk and then drawled: "I'll talk to a couple of friends. See me in two days."

The friends Lane wanted to see were Pat Burns and A. E. Cross, both cattlemen of prominence, and they added another cattleman, A. E. McLean. Lane agreed to be chairman of the little group. Their decision was to back Weadick's proposal to the extent of $100,000, with the understanding that the contests would be on a high plane and contestants would get a "square deal." Weadick would be manager, and he promised to have some of the best contestants, two hundred Mexican Longhorn cattle, and three hundred of the meanest horses. The date was fixed for September 2 to 5, and a premium list offering $20,000 in prizes was prepared.

It promised to be a world-class show. The Indians were the first to arrive; they pitched their tepees in Victoria Park. The Duke and Duchess of Connaught and their daughter, Princess Patricia, came for the opening day; they remained for three days, in spite of heavy rains. And as Weadick promised, the top rodeo performers on the continent were present.

It was expected that the American cowboys, who had more rodeo experience, would capture the major prize awards, but there were some surprises. In the saddle bronc contest, Tom Three Persons, a Blood Indian from the reserve near Cardston, was doing very well. Courtesy of the Inspector of Indian Agencies, he had been released from the mounted police cells at Fort Macleod a few days early in order to attend. Coming into the finals, he had what most spectators saw as a misfortune in drawing the notorious bucking horse Cyclone, the reputed man-killer in a band brought in from the United States. The big black gelding had rarely been ridden, and the words on most tongues were: "Poor Tom; this'll be the end of the show for him."

The finals in the bronc riding were called, and Cyclone, as always, leaped explosively from the chute and bucked his best, which had always been enough to unload his rider. But this time, his best was not enough. As the crowd roared with delight, the contest ended. Tom Three Persons dropped from his saddle, champion of the most important contest in the show. Adding to local satisfaction, Calgary's Clem Gardner stood beside Three Persons as the All-Around Canadian Cowboy Champion.

The four-day Stampede, Canada's first big rodeo, came to an end with special praise for Weadick, Three Persons, and Gardner. The show had lived up to the organizers' highest hopes and paid its way without drawing upon the guarantee pledge that had been furnished by the highly respected "Big Four" cattlemen. The feeling was widespread that the Stampede—with Weadick as manager—should become Calgary's annual summer frivolity.

It didn't happen right away. Weadick went on his way, travelling to far parts of the rodeo world, but when he came again in 1923, it was to stay. He became a permanent part of the "common-law" union between the Calgary Exhibition and the Stampede, which was soon to become a world-class show. Weadick remained as manager for a few years, and he chose to make his permanent home in the Alberta foothills; his final resting place is at High River.

The *Eye Opener*

Bob Edwards, who started and published the Calgary *Eye Opener*, was a strange fellow, but when they buried him on a November day in 1922, they buried an important part of the Old West.

That he was often caught in controversy was not surprising. He might have called himself a Conservative in politics, but at heart he was a bold reformer. Although he needled the churchmen, he practised the charity of St. Paul. After making life miserable for the politicians, he condescended to be a candidate for election to the legislature and won. And although he made light of his drinking habits, when the future of the booze business was about to be determined by plebiscite in 1915, Bob was working seriously for prohibition.

One of his fellow editors called him a "journalistic hermaphrodite." He gave the impression of having been "born in a brothel and bred on a dungpile,"[8] but a churchman who knew him well said admiringly: "Such qualities of heart and mind we shall never see again." On the other hand, Robert Gard, who came to Alberta in 1943 with instructions from the Rockefeller Foundation to collect and record Alberta folklore, sat across a lunch table from the writer of these lines and said: "Speaking as an American, it is my view that if Bob Edwards had lived longer and had the ambition to do it, he might have completely overshadowed Mark Twain."[9]

Edwards was born in Scotland in 1859 or 1864; the exact date was in doubt, but this didn't matter in the least to him. A "rolling stone," he tried journalism in England and France, cowboying in Wyoming, and farming in Iowa. He came into Canada from the south in 1895. He travelled by train to 16th Siding, north of Calgary, soon to be renamed Wetaskiwin. There, after working at odd jobs, he decided to start a weekly paper. He wanted to call it the Wetaskiwin *Bottling Works*, partly because the town at that time had a population of "287 souls plus three total abstainers," but on better advice, the paper's name was changed to the *Free Lance*. It was very popular at first, until the blunt and honest editor made many bad friends. He moved to publish at Leduc, then Strathcona (south Edmonton), then to Winnipeg to work for the *Free Press*. But Edwards couldn't work for another person, and he bounced back west to High River, where one of his Wetaskiwin friends had relocated. There, Bob started the *Eye Opener*. He promised it would be published "semioccasionally," meaning as often as Edwards had enough reading matter to fill the columns and was sober enough to get it out.

He lasted two years at High River. On a suggestion from lawyer extraordinaire Paddy Nolan, with whom Edwards formed a staunch and lasting friendship, he moved to Calgary. The *Eye Opener* was renamed the Calgary *Eye Opener*. The circulation of the renegade paper, again published "semioccasionally" by an editor who had no printing press, no typewriter, no secretarial service, and no subscription list, began to rise. The more rules of journalism the editor broke, the higher, it seemed, went the circulation, until he had the highest circulation of all papers published west of Port Arthur.

He hated snobbery and the society columns fashionable at that time, so he decided to include an "Eye Opener" society column in the paper. Edwards's column, riotously funny, became the most widely read column of its kind and served effectively in bringing the conventional society columns to ridicule.

He advocated many still-unpopular social changes like voting rights for women, old age pensions, and subsidized hospitalization. In 1915, he surprised everybody—especially his friends—by endorsing prohibition. He published a special edition of the paper to help win a favourable vote. Bob was on another drunk on voting day, but the *Eye Opener* had done its work, and Edwards was given much of the credit for the success of the vote.

In 1921 when Alberta was preparing for a general provincial election, Bob's friends asked him to be a candidate. His answer was given with a laugh: "No," he said, but he was told that since he had been a constant critic of people in public life, it was now his duty to stand.

Bob didn't lack conscience, and when he thought about this challenge, he said he would run, but he added that he wouldn't make a lot of speeches about himself: he'd make one speech. He did. It lasted one minute. Edwards, running as an Independent, one of twenty candidates running for six Calgary seats, finished with the second highest number of votes and was elected, as was his friend, Rev. Robert Pearson, also as an Independent. Pearson asked Edwards to promise that he would not take a drink of liquor of any kind during the session. Edwards promised, and it is believed that he never took another drink. It led Rev. Pearson to say in congratulating Edwards: "Bob, there must be more joy in Heaven over one old boozer who quits the habit than over ninety-nine Methodists who never took a drink."

Anahareo, Grey Owl's Mentor

Grey Owl faked his identity beautifully. He convinced Canadians and the world that he was indeed an Indian, a conservationist worthy of the hero worship he enjoyed for many years. His wife, Anahareo, a true Mohawk Indian, appeared in a minor role with him. She never tried to be spectacular, but it was she who converted Grey Owl from a rough-and-ready trapper to a man of sympathy for animals. Thirty-seven years after Grey Owl's death, Anahareo was the recipient of the Order of Nature, presented by the International League for Animal Rights. The first such award had been given posthumously to Dr. Albert Schweitzer, a world figure who died in Africa in 1965; the second was awarded to Canada's Anahareo.

Taken together, the lives of Grey Owl and Anahareo possessed all the ingredients for a best seller. Their first meeting was beside Lake Temagami in Northern Ontario in 1925. Grey Owl had just pulled his canoe ashore when his roving glance fell upon the attractive nineteen-year-old Indian girl. He was momentarily mesmerized. She too was impressed by what she saw, but she was in no hurry to let him know it. He came again and again and then invited her to visit his trap-line cabin. She accepted, and what was to have been a one-week visit lasted ten years.

Critics said she was only Grey Owl's common-law wife, but she answered sternly, saying that they were married in an Ojibway Indian ceremony and considered themselves as much husband and wife as if the union had been solemnized in the best cathedral in London or Rome. But Anahareo did have a worrisome problem: she was in love with a trapper but hated traps and trapping. She told Grey Owl of her anxiety; he just laughed, but she had no intention of changing her convictions. She reminded him again of a lynx she couldn't forget. It had been caught by one foot in one of his traps and was slowly dying from hunger, thirst, and pain. The poor creature had eaten all the poplar bark it could reach and all the snow near the trap. Worse, it had chewed the flesh from its upper leg in an effort to cut it off and gain release. "Then and there," said she, "I vowed that I would never trap again."[10]

As if to help her win Grey Owl to her beliefs, two small beavers—McGinty and McGinnis—orphaned when their mother was caught in one of Grey Owl's traps, came into her life. She raised them, and soon they won the heart of the trapper. He vowed that he would never trap another beaver. Later, he vowed he would never trap anything again.

McGinty and McGinnis were followed in the Grey Owl household by another pair of beavers, Rawhide and Jelly Roll. They accompanied Grey Owl when he entered the Federal Parks Service at Riding Mountain National Park in Manitoba and then at Prince Albert National Park in Saskatchewan. Rawhide and Jelly Roll became national favourites, as well known as their owners.

Grey Owl died on April 13, 1938, and was buried beside his beloved Saskatchewan lake. Only then did Canadians learn the truth about Grey Owl's pedigree: he was an Englishman whose real name was Archie Belaney and had no Indian blood in his veins whatever. But regardless of his real identity he left some important messages for Canadians and the rest of the world. And for those messages, the thanks should have gone to Anahareo.

Daughter Dawn, who was born at Ajawaan Lake in 1932, confirmed that it was her mother who brought the great change to her father, Grey Owl, and sent him on his way to distinction. "She was never given the credit she deserved. Her encouragement and compassion marked the course," Dawn said. "I mentioned this to her one day and told her if it hadn't been for her, my father would never have accomplished what he did." To this, Anahareo answered: "No, not me; it was McGinty, McGinnis and me."[11]

Anahareo wrote one book, *Devil in Deerskins: My Life With Grey Owl*. Throughout that book, in letters and in press items there ran the golden thread of compassion for all living things. "Can't we live at peace with Nature," she asked, "or will we destroy the earth for a few more dollars?"

Anahareo's finest hours came in her later years, when she renewed her opposition to the cruelty of trapping. "All this ghastly suffering, ladies, is the real cost of your fur coat."[12]

"Can't we control our greed?" she asked a reporter interviewing her in her seventieth year: "What kind of greed is it that would risk destroying the earth for a few more dollars?"[13]

Chapter 7

A New West

A New Century, a New Vision

By the end of the nineteenth century, the highly prejudiced views expressed by the old traders about western soil and its productivity had become laughable. It was a good sign when Sir George Simpson's recorded remarks about the "poverty" of western soil were repeated only to produce laughter.

The new and popular pastime was in making extravagant predictions about future exports of wheat, dairy products, meat animals, coal, minerals, forest products, and a hundred other things the world's people needed. It was a mixed list but agriculture was still the "Toast of the Time."

With the timidity of a bashful farm boy venturing onto a dance floor for the first time, Canada sent a big entry of products from all parts of the dominion to the Paris exposition that ran from April to November, 1900. Canada won 88 gold medals, 105 silver medals, 92 bronzes, and enough diplomas to paper the inner walls of a horse barn.[1]

That year of 1900 and the following year were like a springboard from which Canadians would plunge into the uncertain waters of the twentieth century. Almost at once, Canadians had to pause to mourn the passing of Queen Victoria, whose death on January 22, 1901, came after a record sixty-four years on the British throne. The eighty-one-year-old queen was succeeded immediately by her son, who became King Edward VII.

Another reason for distress was that Britain was at war with the South African Transvaal and the Orange Free State, and Canadian troops and horses were sent to support the British cause. The first Canadian contingent, made up of 57 officers and 1224 men, sailed late in 1899; more followed, including Strathcona's Horse, which left on March 16, 1900. It was financed entirely by Lord Strathcona, whom the West knew as Donald Smith before he was elevated to the peerage. The Strathcona company consisted of 537 officers and men and 573 horses. Many of the men and most of the horses were from the West.

Petroleum in 1900 meant practically nothing to the West, although the *Canada Year Book* gave a hint of its potential, stating in the 1901 issue: "Petroleum has been found in Quebec, Nova Scotia and New Brunswick and particularly in the North West Territories where it seems certain there is an immense unexplored oil region, but it is in the County of Lambton, Ontario, where most of the oil has been and is obtained. Oil Springs and Petrolia have been the largest producing districts. The oil is obtained at a depth of from 370 to 500 feet."[2]

Forestry and mining were expanding rapidly, but it was in agriculture that the most significant changes were being seen. The 1901 count showed 511,073 farms in Canada, 63,332 of them in the West. The majority of western farms were of homestead size, and new homesteaders were flocking into the West at an accelerating rate. Homestead entries totalled 10,023 in 1901, the first time such numbers rose above 10,000. It was a reflection, of course, of the rising flood of immigration—a total immigration list of 55,747 in 1901.

There were 1,869,000 acres of wheat planted on the prairies in 1900, a record acreage, but it was not a good year for wheat. It was one of those very dry years, and the average yield was recorded as 9.1 bushels per acre. As if to atone for nature's failure, however, the next year was particularly generous and the average yield was 25 bushels per acre; in that favourable year, prairie wheat production passed 50 million bushels for the first time. It was a most acceptable way to celebrate the twenty-fifth anniversary of the first shipment of wheat to leave the West, the historic shipment of 857 bushels and 10 pounds that left Fort Garry by steamboat in October, 1876.

Cattle ranching may have passed its peak, but the number of cattle on farms was increasing at a rapid pace. The West was proving its suitability for all classes of livestock, although sheep numbers were declining, as was the number of draft oxen, which had performed much of the pioneer toil to bring the country to a state of cultivation. The decline of oxen followed as soon as farmers could obtain and pay for horses. Horses were much more successful than oxen in making friends, but it wasn't very long after that landmark year that mechanical giants driven by steam and later gasoline began to displace the faithful horses—but that's another story.

The Horseless Buggy

Horseless buggies, the lowliest form of automobile, had their day in the West, albeit a short one. Winnipeg claimed the earliest one, a misshapen thing that, when first seen on the streets of that city in June, 1901, looked more like an orphan farm democrat searching for a horse than an automobile. It had a one-cylinder motor and ran on three wheels. Its owner and driver, Prof. E. B. Hendrick of St. John's College was praised for his courage.[3]

Southern Alberta was next. In 1902, Billy Cochrane of High River took spring delivery of a four-wheel, four-seater, steam-powered Locomobile with a total weight slightly less than that of one of Cochrane's range horses. Bob Edwards, editor of the widely known High River *Eye Opener*, recorded the event, adding a touch of "Edwardian" sarcasm directed at the neighbouring village: "Billy Cochrane of High River has introduced the first automobile into Alberta. High River is the pioneer of progress. Okotoks still clings to the Red River cart. . . ."[4]

So incomprehensible was this new car to fellow cowboys that one of them, seeing it in fast motion on a range trail with Cochrane inside, was struck with fear that his boss was being carried away by the strange monster. He instantly turned his horse and pursued at full gallop. Overtaking the vehicle, he threw his lariat and caught the machine by a front wheel. The well-meaning fellow then got an explanation he could understand.

Soon after the steamer auto became a familiar spectacle on foothills trails, Calgary's John Prince bought a Rambler and J. S. Young, editor of the Calgary *Herald*, obtained a McLaughlin, leading Bob Edwards to note that "the first thing a man with a new car runs into is debt."

Joseph H. Morris bought Edmonton's first automobile in May, 1902, and two years later the same car became the first in what is now Alberta to have a licence. Two years later there were forty automobiles in the new province. In 1906, a provincial automobile act was one of the first pieces of legislation passed. Thereafter, owners were required to register their motorized vehicles and display their registration numbers. Licence plates were not furnished by the government, but owners were free to make their own. The principal public interest was in the legal speed limits. Ten miles an hour was the upper limit in towns and cities and twenty miles an hour on country roads, except when a motorist was passing a horse-drawn vehicle from the rear, when the maximum speed was ten miles per hour. Although the implication was not noted in the act, the obvious practical result was that it would be impossible for a car to get past a horse and buggy travelling at eleven or more miles an hour.

Edmonton, by this time, had an enterprising auto dealership, Carriveau and Manuel, that was making both sales and history. In March, having made a sale to W. H. White of Calgary, Carriveau agreed to deliver the car overland by its own power. Some people said it couldn't be done, but Carriveau had courage. He left Edmonton at 10 A.M. on Saturday, and reached Red Deer at 7 P.M. that same day and Calgary at 7 P.M. on the second day. The driver's best speed was on a stretch of "good" road between Lacombe and Red Deer, covered at the daredevil speed of thirty-five miles an hour. He figured that gasoline consumption averaged about ten miles per gallon, judged to be favourable in light of the roads, or absence of roads.

The journey was considered a triumph, and three weeks later, Carriveau and Manuel's new shipment of "benzine buggies" was selling like popcorn at a circus. Almost at once, Edmonton began boasting that it had more automobiles per capita than any other city in America.[5]

Exactly seven days after this report appeared, Edmonton citizens read about a runaway involving a horse and buggy belonging to Mr. Manuel of the car dealership. The frightened horse had bolted and collided with a telephone pole, breaking its leg and injuring Mr. Manuel. It was an unfortunate accident, but since it happened at a time of heated controversy about safety in travel, automobiles gained an unplanned endorsement, and while Mr. Manuel was recovering from the accident caused by his horse, his auto business soared.

Meantime, the pioneer steamer car imported by Billy Cochrane was sold to Charles Jackson, a Calgary resident of prominence. He drove the historic Locomobile with pride. By good fortune, it is one of the horseless carriages preserved in the sanctum of the Glenbow-Alberta Institute museum in Calgary, there to be studied and loved forever.

Frederick Haultain and Responsible Government

Manitoba became the fifth Canadian province in 1870, and British Columbia the sixth in 1871. Saskatchewan and Alberta waited with mounting impatience for almost thirty-five more years before being admitted to Confederation. For much of that long period, the North-West Territories had nothing resembling self-government.

It was a blessing for the cause of democracy when English-born Frederick Haultain came west in 1884 to practise law at Fort Macleod. Three years later he ran in a by-election to fill a seat on the council of the North-West Territories and won. He found the council an impotent body composed of both appointed and elected members, all of whom bowed to the domination of the lieutenant-governor, who controlled expenditures and accounted only to the federal cabinet.

Haultain led the demand for change, which came gradually. The council was replaced by a legislative assembly, which was granted the right to authorize expenditures up to the amount collected by the local administration, a paltry sum. More important, however, was the provision for an executive committee of four Members to "advise" the lieutenant-governor in matters of finance. Haultain was chairman, and inasmuch as the new committee bore some resemblance to a provincial cabinet, the chairman became "Mr. Premier." A further amendment in 1891 brought the assembly a step nearer full responsible government with more money to spend.

Still the federal government resisted the assembly's petitions for provincial recognition, at least on Haultain's terms, which had been approved by the assembly. He insisted that the area be set up as one province rather than two, that public lands be placed in the ownership of the province, and that responsibility for schools and school policies be placed with the province as stated in the British North America Act.

But these conditions were not acceptable to the prime minister and were disregarded. With a general election approaching in 1904, though, the prime minister promised the necessary legislation. Early in 1905, Parliament was presented with the Saskatchewan Act and Alberta Act. The area between Manitoba and British Columbia and from the international boundary northward to the 60th parallel of latitude would be divided into two provinces.

The two acts would take effect on September 1, 1905, and Haultain's requests concerning Crown lands, school policies, the number of provinces, and a name, Buffalo, suggested for the more westerly province, were ignored. More than that, Haultain was ignored. Most people expected that this man, the popular "premier" of the area and the principal exponent of the autonomy plan, would be recognized by the prime minister and named the provisional premier of one of the two provinces to serve until an election was held. But it was not to be. The prime minister may have thought Haultain too aggressive or seen him as a political threat in the federal field. Anyway, G. H. V. Bulyea, who sat with Haultain in the territorial assembly, was appointed to the office of lieutenant-governor of the new Alberta. He, in turn, no doubt carrying out the wishes of the prime minister, named A. C. Rutherford, the foremost Liberal in Alberta, the provisional premier. In Saskatchewan, A. E. Forget, who had been lieutenant-governor of the territories, was now appointed to the same high office in Saskatchewan. Again reflecting the wish of the prime minister, he invited Walter Scott, the Liberal member of Parliament for Assiniboia, to accept the office of provisional premier. The appointees were all Liberals.

Haultain may have been a Conservative at heart in federal politics, but he was an Independent in the territories and had successfully discouraged party politics in the assembly. Although he may have been head and shoulders over all other public figures in the West at that time, he was rudely bypassed by the Ottawa luminaries of 1905.

Alberta's inauguration as a province was at Edmonton, the provisional capital, on September 1. It was an impressive event. To allow the prime minister and certain other dignitaries to attend both inaugurations, the Saskatchewan event was on September 4. The birth dates of the two provinces were made official, and in the elections that followed, Alberta's Rutherford and Saskatchewan's Scott—with generous help from Ottawa—saw their party triumph and were confirmed as premiers.

Haultain ran and was elected in a Saskatchewan riding and became the leader of the opposition. In 1912 he was appointed chief justice of Saskatchewan and left politics. Four years later he was honoured with one of the few knighthoods conferred upon Canadians. He may be remembered as Sir Frederick Haultain, but even more he deserves to be remembered as a man of sterling integrity, a westerner with the rare gifts that make statesmen of only a few.

The Big Tractors

When horses first won favour over oxen for field work, it was the start of a fast-moving farm drama. Later, the big, slow-moving, cumbersome steam tractors would make inroads upon the use of horses, and finally, the noisy gasoline tractors would win out over both horses and steamers.

By 1908, breeders of draft horses were becoming worried about the growing threat to the horse business, and the makers and salesmen of tractors were becoming impatient for more trade. The farmers were confused. Like the organizers of other exhibitions, the managers of the Winnipeg Industrial Exhibition recognized their duty to bring these groups together. They fixed upon a light agricultural motor competition, to be conducted in conjunction with the 1908 Winnipeg Industrial Exhibition. It would be conducted under strict competition rules and be open to the world.

It was their first effort, and there were misfortunes. Manufacturers were timid, and tractor entries were few; mechanical troubles, on the other hand, were many. One operator broke his steering chain and rammed a hole in the exhibition fence, which suited the Winnipeg boys, who were normally obliged to climb over. One entrant had a breakdown, but he returned to the contest; two others had troubles and didn't return. The third day was marred by rain, and the Winnipeg gumbo mud completely immobilized the heavy tractors. When competition resumed on the fourth day, the roads were still wet, and the tractors, with no more traction than pigs on ice, spent parts of the day in the ditch. One way or another, the first motor show was disappointing, but Winnipeg directors promised a bigger and better motor show the next year.

It was bigger and better. It had more entries and better weather. The gasoline tractors were more numerous, but the steamers still had loyal friends. Most tractors were from United States factories, but three were entered from Britain. Many of the tractors carried the names of makers that would become increasingly familiar, names like Case, International Harvester, Avery, Rumley, and Marshall.

Of the twenty-two tractors entered, five were steamers. Weights varied from 3,000 to 40,860 pounds, the heaviest an Avery 90-horsepower steamer. Prices for gasoline tractors in the 1909 competition ranged from $1,700 for a 20-horsepower International Harvester unit to $3,400 for a 60-horsepower Marshall and Sons tractor. For steam tractors, the prices rose from $3,250 for a 60-horsepower Marshall and Sons model to $4,050 for a 110-horsepower Case.

The giant of the show was a 120-horsepower Rumley steamer weighing 20 tons and pulling a 14-furrow John Deere plough. Each ploughshare cut a standard 14 inches, so the tractor was turning a total swath of 196 inches, or a little more than 16 feet, which meant that a farmer could plough almost two acres on every round of a half-mile field. During the competition, the big Rumley ploughed 4.23 acres in 75 minutes and used 580 pounds of coal, a figure that will seem strange to Canadians of a later generation, who think of car economy in terms of miles per gallon or kilometres per litre. The operator of the big Rumley could boast of ploughing at 137 pounds of coal per acre, or 15 acres per ton of coal, in Winnipeg's heavy clay. It wasn't the most economical record, but it was impressive, and spectators did not see many more performances like it.

The high-scoring tractor was one of only slightly less size and power, a 110-horsepower Case that started the test with a 12-furrow gang plough and finished with an 11-furrow plough because of the extremely heavy soil. It ploughed 3.6 acres in 62 minutes on 442 pounds of coal. Among the gasoline burners, the International Harvester Company took the gold medal on the performance of its 1-cylinder, 20-horsepower model pulling a 3-furrow plough. It turned 1.09 acres in 75.5 minutes on 1.5 gallons of gasoline per acre.

The motor competition of 1909 was the most important demonstration of tractors staged anywhere in Canada up to that time. Farmers with notebooks seen following their favourite tractors up and down the furrows, hour after hour, testified to a new interest and enthusiasm. It was a style setter, and the mechanical revolution that followed was as significant as the Industrial Revolution had been in Britain a century earlier.

Stumbling Upon Oil

Peter Fidler—the first trader in the Alberta North, the second white man to grow a garden there, and the first to be accused of murder—walked over the world's most fabulous deposit of oil-in-sand along the Athabasca River a little more than two hundred years ago and didn't know it was there. About a hundred years later, John George "Kootenai" Brown, known for his irreverent language spoken with a cultured British accent, was sure there was oil in his region of Waterton Lakes. He asked his Stoney Indian friends to let him know if they ever saw anything that looked like a mixture of coal oil and molasses on pond water or oozing from the ground. He did locate enough oil to meet his needs in lubricating the axles of his wagon.

About the same time, Lafayette French, another Foothills character, watched a native lady dress his injured foot with what he recognized as crude oil, and he bribed her to show him where she found it. It was indeed petroleum that was seeping from the ground. A derrick was set up for an oil operation, and a small amount of oil was recovered.

These were small traces, and nothing much was achieved until William Stewart Herron appeared in the lovely Turner Valley. Herron had the benefit of experience in silver mining at Cobalt, Ontario, and the searching instinct of a prospector. When hauling coal from Black Diamond to his farm at Okotoks in 1911, his gaze fell upon a scum of oil on the water where he crossed Sheep Creek. He was so intrigued that he bought the land, got the mineral rights, and moved to make his home beside the creek.

Herron had faith. He invited William Elder and A. W. Dingman, both interested in oil, to drive out from Calgary for a visit. As the story has been told a few times, Herron led his visitors to the creek, where he planned to unveil the evidence. There, he coyly produced a frying pan and two eggs, lit a match to the tiny natural gas leakage, and proceeded to fry the eggs. It was a demonstration that needed no words. The visitors were convinced, and the Calgary Petroleum Products Company—later taken over by Royalite Oil—was formed, with Mr. Dingman as managing director.

Drilling began on January 25, 1914, and on May 14—109 days later—the drillers, despite the primitive methods of the time, made the historic Turner Valley strike at a depth of 2,718 feet. They called it Dingman No. 1, and it caused a furor in Calgary the like of which had not been seen there since the peak of the real estate madness.

Early the next day, every available Calgary automobile was in service on the road to the valley, about thirty-five miles away. People who could not get motor transportation hired livery horses and drove in buggies. The city visitors dipped their fingers into the oil, sniffed it, and tasted it to find proof that it was real. In the ensuing days, literally hundreds of companies were formed to prospect for oil or deal in oil stock, and hopeful customers stood eagerly in long lines. Only a few of the companies drilled wells, and still fewer struck oil. But the city that had fretted so recently as the amazing real estate boom was followed by the inevitable post-boom slump was suddenly back in a high state of buoyancy.

Dingman No. 1 lived up to expectations. There are pictures of six-horse teams hauling oil in tank wagons from the valley to the railroad at Okotoks. But many other wells did not prove to be great successes, and the valley field slumped until 1924, when Royalite No. 4 blew in from a deeper zone. It was like tapping a new and better field, and until the great Leduc field was discovered in 1947, Turner Valley continued to be seen as Canada's best petroleum treasure, well deserving the praise it received.

Women Win the Vote

It is fortunate that women are forgiving souls, otherwise many more men would have gone to their graves with the stigma of having harshly delayed the female right to vote, even into the enlightened years of the present century.

The campaign to win the vote for Canadian women was decidedly less militant than the suffragette movement in England, where the enraged women demonstrated that they could break windows and battle with the police as effectively as men. But in technique and determination, the Canadian women were in no way backward, and every province had its dedicated leaders. The task was never easy, and the principal opposition came from men in government. The witty prime minister, Sir John A. Macdonald, did nothing to help the cause of women's suffrage by treating it lightly. When an angry suffragette demanded to know the difference between the prime minister and herself, he allegedly answered, very seriously: "Madam, I cannot conceive."

One of the first Members of Parliament to show an approving interest was Nicholas Flood Davin, who in 1895, as an aging but very recent newly-wed, moved formally for the preparation of a bill to extend voting privileges to Canadian women. His motion was greeted with ridicule by most of his fellow parliamentarians. In the debate that followed, they repeated time-honoured platitudes of love and affection for the ladies, admirable creatures who were "too good and too pure" for the rough-and-tumble of political life and should not be encouraged to leave their homes and kitchens. "We think too highly of our women," said another parliamentary orator, "to let them become degraded in public life."

Davin's motion was defeated, of course, but the House of Commons and the country were to hear much more about the mounting demand for votes for women. Manitoba was the first province to legalize the extension of the vote to women. According to Miriam Green Ellis, a first-hand observer, Nellie McClung, who "spearheaded" the drive, deserved most of the credit for the result. The bill was introduced by the Norris government and passed on January 28, 1916.[6]

Nellie McClung was born Nellie Mooney on October 20, 1873, the first of six children born to her Scottish-Canadian mother and Irish-Canadian father on their Grey County farm in Ontario. While Nellie was still a baby, the Mooneys moved to Manitoba to farm in the Souris River Valley. There being no school in the area, Nellie didn't attend one until she was ten years old, but no time was wasted: six years later, she was admitted to the Manitoba Normal School in preparation for a teaching career.

Her first school was in the country near Manitou. There she met Mrs. McClung, wife of the local Methodist minister and a committed worker for temperance and women's rights, who was to shape the course of the young woman's life. There was an immediate bond of admiration between the new teacher and the minister's wife. Nellie admitted later to saying that if she could have chosen her own mother-in-law, Mrs. McClung would have been her first choice. Later, Mrs. McClung's son Wesley returned home from college, where he was enrolled in Pharmacy. There was a romance, then a wedding, and Miss Nellie got both the husband and mother-in-law of her choice.

After a few years spent, a few books written, and a few babies born at Manitou, Nellie and Wesley and their family moved to Winnipeg, a city that seemed to be waiting for somebody like Nellie McClung. She plunged into the still-uncertain waters of temperance and women's rights and was encouraged, but before the Manitoba legislation was passed, the McClungs moved to Edmonton.

Where Nellie McClung was living didn't matter much, though, because she could see challenges everywhere. Her support and leadership on all fronts helped to bring victory and voting rights to the women of Manitoba in January, 1916, then to Saskatchewan on March 14, 1916, and Alberta on April 19 of the same year. The equivalent legislation was passed in British Columbia on April 5, 1917, making the Canadian West a solid bloc of official approval for the new and broadened democracy.

Nor did the removal of old voting prejudices end there: on May 24, 1918, by Act of Parliament, all female citizens of Canada, twenty-one years of age or older, qualified to vote in federal elections, and from July 1919, the women of Canada could become candidates for election to the coveted seats in the House of Commons. Nellie McClung saw it all and had reason to be very proud.

The Great Flu Epidemic

After more than four years of fighting, killing, and destroying, after an awful cost in lives and public spending, the savage struggle of World War I ended. At 11 A.M. on November 11, 1918, joy and sorrow mingled as never before. Soldiers who had been courting death in the war zones would be coming home, but the reunions would be marred by haunting thoughts of the sixty thousand young Canadians who would never return and thousands more who would return with permanent disabilities.

One enemy was decisively beaten, but nobody could have anticipated that another killer would advance, this time invisibly and with almost equal lethal power: Spanish influenza. It had been reported recently in Spain, but it did not originate there. It was probably the same disease, or a close relative of it, that had taken a heavy toll in both the Old World and the New from time to time through history. In any case, in 1918, it was as much a stranger and a mystery as if it had never occurred before. Nobody was familiar with its secrets. There was no known cure and no sure prevention for the cruel killer.

And cruel it was. After the huge Canadian losses in the war, it seemed unthinkable that an enemy as imperceptible as a virus could take another fifty thousand Canadian lives in a few weeks, almost as many as the Canadian war dead.

After inflicting its harshness upon the armies engaged in war, the flu was believed to have been carried westward across the Atlantic by returning troops. Then, moving like a prairie fire, the infection swept from east to west. Practically no parts escaped. Regina, in the middle of October, had 150 cases; the mayor of Saskatoon presumed that his city had no reason to be alarmed, but both cities were largely demoralized by the flu a few days later. Isolation of communities by quarantine was tried in some parts, but without success. No district was safe from attack.

Hospitals, doctors, nurses, and volunteers made hasty preparations for the emergency, which was more serious than anybody had expected. People of all ages proved vulnerable, although deaths were more numerous among the very young and very old. Barring complications, the sickness did not last more than a few days, but the complications—mainly in the form of pneumonia—were the principal killers, and the deaths were many. Doctors and other medical workers regrouped and prepared to be overworked, but they were among the first victims. Sick people were given the best possible care, but it wasn't enough. The suppliers of funeral services could not keep abreast with the soaring number of deaths.

Although there was no sure cure, there was no shortage of home remedies, none of which emerged with glory. Antibiotics were totally unknown, and medical people had little more to recommend than aspirin and lots of water and bed rest. The most popular medicine was brandy, which in dry provinces was obtainable from druggists at two dollars per six-ounce bottle, but only with a doctor's prescription. In at least one province, however, the gravity of the epidemic led the government to waive the required prescription. It made less work for the overworked doctors and very much more trade for the pharmacists—but with druggists increasingly used as brandy merchants, the government decided to withdraw the relaxation order. Both flu victims and perpetually thirsty citizens were obliged to return to their doctors for their alcoholic "medicine."

Home remedies were numerous and sometimes entertaining. There were those who regarded Epsom salts as a cure-all, and its consumption soared. Raw onions found their supporters, as did eucalyptus oil, hydrogen peroxide, and small doses of kerosene, none of which gained much credibility. The use of silk or gauze masks to cover mouths and nostrils and thereby restrict the movement of germs was general and even mandatory in many districts.

In the West, the peak of the memorable flu epidemic came in the late part of October and the first half of November. There was a light return of the trouble in 1919, and everybody hoped it had ended there. It didn't end, but it seemed likely that there would never be another flu epidemic like that of 1918.

The Winnipeg General Strike

Canada's labour force came to the end of World War I with some legitimate gripes. Wartime inflation without commensurate wage increases had left workers with reduced purchasing power, and unrest was growing. The prospect of rising postwar unemployment led them to demand pay adjustments and collective bargaining rights. Their demands were not extreme, although the labour movement of the time was believed to have leaders with strong Marxist leanings who were pointing suggestively to what Russian revolutionary workers did for themselves in 1917.

An important labour conference at Calgary in March, 1919, gave delegates a chance to become familiar with the "One Big Union" concept. A proposed constitution was unveiled, and back of it was the principle that capitalism was the labouring man's enemy and that the time was at hand for more and bigger general strikes.

The metal workers and the building-trades unions—both big

groups—walked out on strike on May 1 after employers refused to negotiate with the large group and the workers baulked at the idea of each individual union coming to the bargaining table separately. Both sides were adamant, and union bosses decided to call a general strike. It wouldn't last long, the leaders said, and labour, making a fine display of its strength, would emerge as the winner.

The general strike was called on May 15, and most Winnipeg services came to a halt. Factory and industry workers were at once off the job. Postmen and firemen didn't report for duty. Stores were without clerks. There was no milk or bread delivery. The city police, however sympathetic they may have been to the strike, were not called out; it was the strike committee's concession to the cause of law and order.

A big and enthusiastic citizen's committee was organized to perform many public services. The volunteers did well, but generally, the city was close to being paralysed.

Governments at all three levels watched with understandable concern and did not hide their disapproval of the strike. When things became disorderly, the federal government was asked to intervene with military force. Military support was denied, but a strong detachment of mounted police was rushed to the troubled city. The government then ordered all strikers who were on the federal payroll to go back to their work at once or face the possibility of dismissal.

At this point the strike took an ugly turn. On government instruction, eight of the strike leaders were arrested, and then two more, including J. S. Woodsworth, who later sat in the House of Commons. As might have been expected, the strikers and their sympathizers, who included many war veterans, became more defiant. On June 21, a large crowd of strikers and their friends gathered on Main Street, in front of city hall. The mayor called upon the mounted police to disperse it. As the police moved in, stones and bottles were hurled at them and being overwhelmingly outnumbered, police lives were in danger.

It looked like revolution in the guise of strike, and Mayor Gray seized the opportunity to read the Riot Act from the steps of city hall. Again an angry mob formed, and the mounted police charged the crowd and fired some shots. One man was killed, and more were wounded.

It was a sombre moment and held lessons for everybody connected with the strike. Even the strike leaders were ready to acknowledge the futility of continuing the struggle. If there was a termination date, it was June 25, when the end of the strike was announced by the labour organizations. There was still the matter of court trials for the fourteen strike leaders who had been arrested and released on bail. Some received jail terms, but they were not common criminals, and most of them became prominent and highly respected citizens in society.

It is difficult to find much good in the strike. For the workers, it was an unprofitable experience, and for Winnipeg, it was one of the most unfortunate events in civic history in Canada.

The Soil Surveys

If Canadians could live their pioneer years over again, they would demand a soil survey first and accept a delay in the Dominion Lands Act and the hasty give-away of land, at least until they had a moderately reliable inventory of their soil resources. By advancing their soil surveys some fifty years, they might have prevented fifty thousand mistakes in land settlement.

To state the obvious, the better time for a soil survey is before settlement rather than after. For half a century following the passing of the land act, most newcomers to the West chose their locations and land on the basis of accessibility and scenery and then discovered too often that they were saddled with second-rate soil, even unsuitable for cultivation in some instances. Too often the land-seeker, carried away by the landscape, didn't examine what was below the surface. Soil surveys weren't undertaken until many innocent immigrants had settled, fenced, built, cultivated, and planted, until they finally became convinced of the necessity of abandoning the work of several years.

The fact was that western soils were extremely variable in composition and productiveness, and when blanketed with native vegetation, appearances could be dangerously misleading. Western soil ranged from deep to shallow, from acid to alkaline, from heavy clay to light sand, and from highly fertile to degraded and eroded. Even in colour it was variable, so much so that colours were accepted to identify the principal soil zones in the grain-growing regions: brown soils dominated in the drier parts of the prairie southwest or short-grass plains; then there was the dark brown soil zone to the north, and the highly regarded black soil, spread like a crescent to contain the park belt that appeared so attractive to Captain John Palliser when conducting his survey from 1857 to '59; and deeper in the tree region there was the big area of grey bush soil that required special attention in cropping.

The earliest soil studies in Canada were conducted in Ontario by the Department of Chemistry at the Ontario Agricultural College in about 1914. In the West, it all started in Manitoba in 1917.

Professor Joe H. Ellis of the soils department at the University of Manitoba—himself a pioneer in western soil studies—gives the main credit for the introduction of the surveys in the West to Professor A. J. Galbraith. Galbraith came to the Department of Chemistry at the

Manitoba Agricultural College in 1915 from the corresponding department at Guelph. He convinced the proper representative of the Manitoba government to pay his modest expenses and began in 1918 a one-man survey at Arborg. To him, said Joe Ellis, "must go the credit for introducing the concept of a provincial soil survey . . . and arousing in at least one of his students an interest that bore fruit later."[7]

According to Ellis, the soil survey and soil investigations initiated as provincial projects were continued as a co-operative endeavour between the Manitoba Department of Agriculture and the University of Manitoba. "By 1970 approximately 45 million acres had been covered by the Manitoba Soil Survey."[8]

The soil survey work in the West didn't become general until after 1920. The best of it was carried out by the federal and provincial governments and the provincial universities working together. Alberta was in the field in 1920, Saskatchewan in 1921, Manitoba returned to it in 1927, and British Columbia started in 1931. Even though it was being funded with public money, a few pioneer names deserve special mention, mainly from the University side: Professor F. A. Wyatt of Alberta, Professor A. H. Joel of Saskatchewan, and Professor Joe Ellis of Manitoba were most conspicuous at the outset.

In all the participating provinces, the surveys progressed with no more than minor interruptions. As work was completed, the results were made available in reports and in the form of maps to people who needed the information.

Considered in total, the western soil surveys and the resulting reports and maps were unfortunately late in relation to the rush of settlement, but circumstances made it so. For present-day Canadians living on the land and those entrusted with the making of public policy, the soil surveys are still monumental assets. Indeed, students of public affairs may be hard pressed to name a better Canadian investment.

The Wheat Pools

World War I elevated wheat to a position of unprecedented importance and kept it there until the last shot was fired. It was no wonder. Overseas countries were struggling to get enough wheat for bread, and enemy submarines were struggling to send wheat cargoes to the bottom of the ocean. Western growers were anxious to increase production in spite of dwindling work crews. Winnipeg prices rose to $3.00 per bushel, basis No. 1 Northern, in May, 1917, and the Canadian government, more concerned about holding prices back than encouraging a further rise, appointed a Board of Grain Supervisors with wide powers of control. The board fixed the price at $2.40 per bushel, which was an acceptable price, but farmers were already worried about what would happen at war's end.

To meet the farmers' clamour, the first Canadian Wheat Board was formed in July, 1919, to operate one year. Farmers begged for the board to be continued, but the government, it seems, was as anxious to get out of the wheat business as the Winnipeg Stock Exchange was to get back in. Futures trading resumed at once. Wheat prices rose briefly and then began a long decline. The stability furnished by the board was gone, and the favourable prices were going too.

Producers pleaded for another national wheat board and were alternately angry and frustrated at the thought of Winnipeg grain traders, who had never planted a pound of wheat or stooked a stook in their lives, making far more money on wheat than the growers. They began to wonder if they could market their own grain co-operatively. Western farmers were not strangers to co-operation by any means: they already owned many co-operative elevators. They had strong leaders such as Henry Wise Wood, president of the United Farmers of Alberta. He had come from Missouri in 1905 and had served as a member of the Board of Grain Supervisors in 1917. He contended that the time had come for growers to act for themselves, and he approved a proposal from the Calgary *Herald* and Edmonton *Journal* to invite the California mogul of co-operative marketing, Aaron Sapiro, to visit Alberta and advise farmers on what they should do.

It was already late in the 1923 growing season, but Sapiro agreed to come. He quickly brought prairie enthusiasm to a boiling point. "Stop dumping and start merchandising," he challenged. With Sapiro's encouragement, Alberta farmers and others began the quest for signatures that would commit 50 percent of the province's wheat acreage to the pooling programme for five years. Starting on August 20, they had to end the drive on September 5. The farmer canvassers were so busy that some of them didn't find the time to harvest their own crops. At the cut-off date, the commitments totalled 2,558,095 acres, a little short of the objective, but it was close, and members of the committee decided to proceed with plans for the 1923 pool.

Saskatchewan growers fixed their objective at six million acres and allowed 12 days for the sign-up. They didn't reach the minimum acreage and decided to defer the plan until 1924. The Manitoba experience was like Saskatchewan's, but the infant Alberta Wheat Pool succeeded in marketing 30 million bushels, selling it at an average price of $1.01 per bushel for No. 1 Northern wheat at Fort William. The farmers were pleased.

Saskatchewan was fortunate in having the leadership of James Alexander McPhail, a forty-year-old bachelor farmer from Elfros who knew all about farm problems, and he guided the sign-up. On June 16, 1924, he wrote in his diary: "Wheat Pool over the top today." The Saskatchewan Pool had 46,509 signed contracts and a comfortable margin over 50 percent of the province's total wheat acreage. Likewise, Manitoba completed its drive in 1924. In July of that year, representatives of the three provincial pools met to form a central selling agency, Co-operative Wheat Producers, Limited, with Saskatchewan's McPhail as chairman, Alberta's Wood as vice-chairman, and Manitoba's C. H. Burnell as secretary.

At that point, the three wheat pools together made up the biggest producer co-operative in the world. Memberships rose to 140,000, backed by 15 million acres. The drive to renew pooling pledges and sign up new pledges at the end of the first five years proved comparatively easy.[9] Still, there were troubled times ahead, like the thirties, when everything went wrong. The pools didn't escape the Depression, but recovered from bankruptcy to occupy a bigger place than ever in the agricultural life of the West and Canada.

A Railroad to the Bay

Pioneer generations were well aware of the cost of living far from Liverpool, Antwerp, and other world markets. They became convinced that to improve their position, a railway connection with a seaport on Hudson Bay was needed to shorten shipping distances. The shipping distance from Saskatoon to Liverpool by way of Hudson Bay was a thousand miles shorter than by the Great Lakes and Montreal. Providence seemed to have created that great arm of the sea reaching inland toward wheat country to benefit the Canadian West.

Rarely was there a pioneer convention in the West without a resolution asking the Canadian government for the early construction of the much-needed railway to the bay. Various private companies obtained charters to build such lines if the government declined. The most promising was the Winnipeg and Hudson Bay Railway and Steamship Company initiated and promoted by the tireless Hugh McKay Sutherland. In 1886, he announced an official sod-turning and reported that he had ordered the needed steel rails in England and expected to see trains running on the line in a couple of years. Sutherland's company built forty miles of railroad that was later taken over by the Canadian Northern.

During the next twenty years, there was much talk about the line to the bay, but there was nothing encouraging until 1908, when Prime Minister Laurier, campaigning in a general election, announced to western voters that if returned to office, he would see to it that the railroad to the mouth of the Nelson River was built without delay. Laurier was returned, and there was a sod-turning ceremony in 1910, but nothing more that year. Some western people became so annoyed that they proposed that the railroad be built co-operatively: if 100,000 westerners would subscribe $100 each, they'd have half of what they needed to finish the job. The schemers were also considering developing potential water-power sites along the way to operate the railway by electricity.

No doubt the western proposal embarrassed the government. There was a revival of federal activity and a visible amount of construction from the The Pas end of the line. But when World War I came along, building was allowed to slow down, and by 1917, when the demands of the war effort were mounting, the work had stopped. Nobody complained about the war effort taking precedence, but, as many westerners had feared, Ottawa was in no hurry to resume the work at war's end. Eight years after the Armistice, government interest was still lagging and there were some official "second thoughts" about the route.

Until 1917, construction proceeded with the mouth of the Nelson River as a terminal, and a fine bridge was built across that river to carry the rails. There were also some costly improvements at the terminal—totalling $6,242,114 by March 31, 1926—including a bridge-like trestle to carry the railroad to a wharf on a man-made island. But governments can change directions, and when work was about to be accelerated on the main grade, the Minister of Railways and Canals ordered another review of the two possible terminal locations. Frederick Palmer, an eminent English engineer, was instructed to make an eleventh hour comparison of sites at the mouth of the Nelson and Churchill rivers.

Palmer didn't take long to make his decision. His report, dated August 24, 1927, stated clearly: "Churchill is undoubtedly the port to be selected." A 2.5-million-bushel terminal elevator was planned for the more distant place. Crews were sent to the Nelson to dismantle anything that could be used at Churchill, and grade construction was redirected to the more northerly terminal. The change would mean more distance and more muskeg on which to make a roadbed, but that was the decision. There at Port Churchill, across the harbour from the ancient and famous Fort Prince of Wales, the railroad was completed in September, 1929, just a month before the day of economic disaster, October 22, 1929, when 16 million shares were dumped and traded on the New York Stock Exchange and the Western world was plunged into the Great Depression.

The railroad cost about $50 million to complete. The first wheat for export was loaded on two ships belonging to the Dalgliesh Line, *Farnsworth* and *Warksworth*, in 1931. The West at last had its Hudson

Bay Railroad, but it was not without a struggle; nor did the struggle end in 1929. Resistance from the East was not new, but complacency in the West today makes an unbecoming contrast to the enthusiasm that won Canada's only rail link with the North.

Drought and Depression

Optimism was the watchword in early 1929 when the Canadian Chamber of Commerce held its annual meetings in Alberta, assembling for the first day in Edmonton and the second day in Calgary. The speeches without fail echoed confidence, and if a speaker had shown such bad judgement as to mention the Old Testament message from the Book of Proverbs (16:18), "Pride goeth before destruction, and a haughty spirit before a fall," he might have been chased out of the city.

But below the economic calm of the time, there were some undetected warning rumbles, including an overloaded world wheat market, with Argentina and Australia harvesting unusually large wheat crops, and a new wave of nationalism, with protective tariffs going up around the world, most noticeably in the United States.

Canadian wheat was selling for about $1.50 per bushel at home, and on the strength of that reasonable price remaining firm for the 1929 crop, the prairie wheat pools announced an initial payment on the season's deliveries of $1.00 per bushel. It seemed fair enough, but it was a decision the big co-ops were soon to regret.

Like a minor tremor preceding a major earthquake, there was a wild selling panic on the New York Stock Exchange a few months before the devastating jolts in October. The experts said that such panics were to be expected and that the market would recover. They were right: the markets did recover, but only briefly. They plunged lower than ever on October 17. Nor had the New York market yet seen the worst of the selling pandemonium. The next day, "Black Friday," more fortunes were swept away.

The selling panic that took place on October 24 saw more than twelve million shares change hands. It was the most disastrous day in the history of the New York Stock Exchange. Losses were reported to have reached billions of dollars. Thousands of speculators, big and small, were caught up in the trading stampede and lost much or all of their equity.[10]

The economic shock waves were felt almost instantly around the world, marking the onset of the Great Depression. In spite of the optimists that saw the return of prosperous times "just around the corner," it lasted for most of the next ten years.

Naturally, the same New York crash dealt a serious blow to the domestic and international price of wheat. One report told of wheat dropping 13 cents a bushel in one day. Actually, wheat was in for a long decline; prices dropped intermittently until December 16, 1932, when the Fort William price for the best wheat was $39^{3}/_{8}$ cents a bushel. It was the lowest price on record except the freight-adjusted price at western Canadian points, which varied from as low as $10^{1}/_{2}$ cents a bushel at remote parts of the Peace River area and $17^{1}/_{2}$ cents at Edmonton. Barley of 3CW grade was priced at 8 cents a bushel at Edmonton and 2 cents at the far parts of Peace River.

An often-told story must be related again: A Saskatchewan farmer, poor but honest, took a load of barley to his elevator at a time when it might have commanded 10 cents a bushel and he needed the few dollars it might bring for groceries. The load was weighed and dumped, and the agent began adding the usual deductions for weed seeds, high moisture content, and handling. The final figure showed the deductions totalling more than the barley would bring.

"I'm sorry, but you owe me 50 cents," the agent said. The farmer didn't have fifty cents but promised he would bring a dressed turkey to the agent next time he came to town.

The next day the honest fellow was back and presented the agent with two dressed birds. "I told you I'd settle for one turkey," said the agent.

"I know," the farmer replied, "but I brought in another load of barley."

It was doubly unfortunate for prairie farmers that drought accompanied depression. Unable to grow feed, many farmers were obliged to sell their herds, even though steers brought no more than 3 cents a pound, and a market pig, 2 cents a pound. Fresh eggs traded as low as 3 cents a dozen. Many reluctant farmers were obliged to accept relief, while rain clouds "went around" and drifting soil blackened the sky. It was difficult to be cheerful, especially when conditions seemed to grow worse. In 1937, Saskatchewan wheat yielded an average of $2^{1}/_{2}$ bushels per acre, and many farmers harvested nothing but a few loads of Russian thistles.

Some farmers moved to northern districts where the drought was not as intense. Some gave up, but most persevered, and, sure enough, rains and crops came again.

A World Grain Show in a Year of Desolation

Neither Saskatchewan nor Regina, its capital city, looked like a proper meeting place for a world-class event like an international grain show in 1933. It was an exciting idea, but if the planners had been able to foresee the weather and crop conditions of that year, they would have backed away in haste and spared themselves the embarrassment of having to make a public display of the good wheat country in a state of impoverishment. It would be too much like inviting well-to-do guests to one's home for dinner just after the creditors had seized the furniture.

The big show that was announced in 1928 was to have been held at Regina in 1932, but as the time drew near, the distressing circumstances of drought and drifting soil—to say nothing of ruinous market prices—brought calls for cancellation. Regina people were not about to surrender their claim to the first world-class event in the West, however, and they agreed to a compromise, to postpone the show for exactly twelve months. The next year was sure to be better.

But 1933 wasn't better. If anything, it was worse. The heat was more intense and the soil was no less parched. The temperature at the official opening was said to be slightly over 100 degrees Fahrenheit. At nearby Moose Jaw, the temperature was reported to have reached 106 degrees twice that week.

Despite all that, forty countries in widely scattered parts of the world accepted the opportunity to display the products of their soil. Twenty-seven hundred entries were laid out with great artistry in a big building with three acres of floor space and a two-mile indoor walkway for visitors hoping to see everything. Almost equally impressive was the number of distinguished leaders in world agriculture: Sir A. D. Hall, the chief adviser to the Ministry of Agriculture in England, for example, and Sir John Russell, director of the celebrated Rothamstead Experimental Station, who was in Regina to present a review of crop fertilizer experiments carried out over more than one hundred years at Rothamstead.

For the official opening, Robert Weir, prominent Saskatchewan farmer and minister of agriculture in R. B. Bennett's cabinet, occupied the chair, and Arthur Meighen, former prime minister and one of the best orators of his time, delivered the opening address. Then, with fitting formality, the official representatives—one national group after another—were introduced as strains from their national anthems filled the hall.

Exhibition honours were widely distributed and served to place the various crops in their proper geographical perspective. Canadian exhibitors demonstrated their supremacy in hard red spring wheat, but rice exhibits outnumbered wheat. R. D. Colquette, who covered the big exhibition for the *Country Guide*, was clearly inspired by what the Far Eastern growers had done with rice. "There are more varieties of rice in the [display] cases than all other cereals put together," he wrote. "The main competition is between Siam, India, British Guiana and the Philippine Islands. I was assured by the man in charge of the India display that there are 10,000 varieties of rice grown in his part of the Empire alone."[11]

The United States, Rhodesia, and Australia were the major winners in corn, as Siam was in rice, Canada in hard red spring wheat, and Scotland in oats. The scores of other crops would make the list read like a seed catalogue. In the class for hard red spring wheat, there were 278 entries, and when the first 15 prize winners were listed, every one was from a western Canada grower. First prize was won by Frelan Wilford, a thirty-six-year-old farmer from Stavely, Alberta, and second by Herman Trelle of Wembly in the Peace River region. Trelle, it should be noted, had already won the world wheat championship at Chicago's international show four times.

There was only an indirect connection between the World Grain Show and the International Wheat Agreement that was very much in the news at the time of the show. The agreement was expected to bring stability to the marketing of 562 million bushels of the world's wheat, of which Canada's share would be 200 million bushels. It was signed just a few weeks after the grain show, but it did not live up to expectations. It was, however, a beginning. The grain show, on the other hand, ended with a torrent of praise from its visitors. Canadians should have seen it as a truly historic event, made additionally significant by the extreme difficulties that characterized 1933.

Peace, Potash, and Petroleum

As if the years of drifting soil and depression were not enough by way of trouble from one decade, the thirties saw the beginning of the Second World War, which brought with it the usual cruel companions—slaughter, massive waste, and destruction—and a new one, a bomb with far, far more hideous destructiveness than anything known before.

When the war ended in 1945, people around the world rejoiced and wept at the same time and then settled down to deal with the postwar years. There were some surprises. Within a year after the war ended, drillers searching for oil in Saskatchewan discovered what would turn out to be the biggest or second biggest stockpile of potash in the world. Within another year, drillers struck oil at Leduc; it was the strike that ushered in the new oil era in Canada and reshaped the western economy. The years of 1946 and '47 needed nothing more to make them memorable.

Very quickly western people improved their knowledge of potash, of its limited role in industry and its world-wide importance as a crop fertilizer. Like nitrogen and phosphorus, potash is one of the essential plant food nutrients. Early settlers in eastern Canada's hardwood bush obtained much of their cash by burning wood from their big trees and leaching the ashes to recover the potash. Thus, there was added incentive for clearing land for cropping, and potash became a product for export, sometimes more profitable than conventional farming.

The first potash discovery in Saskatchewan was in the south of the province and did not excite much attention because it was presumed that the strike was nothing more than a small isolated deposit. Only a few individuals were moved to make a more serious search. The more convincing discovery was in 1946 near Unity at about 3500 feet. Real interest followed.

The great surprise was in the fact that the potash extended for almost the full width of the province, from about Unity on the west to Esterhazy on the East. It was nigh unbelievable. A widely quoted estimate of the potash salt that remained as a legacy for Saskatchewan when an ancient lake evaporated a million years ago is seven billion tons, thirteen times as much as the estimated world reserves as recently as in 1952. Canadian reserves would be sufficient to accommodate world needs for a thousand years at the 1960 rate of use.

Bringing the potassium chloride from its hiding place between half a mile and a mile underground to the surface wasn't a simple matter. Problems were many. The first recovery method was to lift the ore to the surface in a conventional manner; "solution mining" was also tried, whereby a solution was pumped down drill holes to dissolve the potassium solids, then brought to the surface in liquid form. In any case, with good management, there will still be potash under the Saskatchewan wheat fields long after the last of Canada's conventional crude oil has been withdrawn, sold, and burned.

The oil strike at Leduc in 1947 created more of a stir than the potash discovery had. That wasn't surprising because oil has always been notably newsworthy. From the first years of the Turner Valley oil field, drillers were making costly penetrations as if confident that they would find, sooner or later, the evasive prairie Eldorado. The big Imperial Oil Company persevered; it drilled 133 consecutive dry holes. For such patience and expense, the company deserved the prize, and the 134th well was the winner. Imperial Leduc No. 1 led to companion wells and new fields, and production soared.

Leduc No. 1 had further messages and lessons for Canadians. Nobody expected it to produce forever, but its retirement in June, 1975, brought sobering thoughts about nonrenewable resources. The press reported it this way: "That oil is indeed a depleting resource is demonstrated by the discovery well itself. Leduc No. 1 has been pumped dry. By the end of its economic life in 1973, the well had produced 318,000 barrels of oil. It stopped being a flowing well some years before 1973 and a pump had to be installed during its declining days. Today, capped by a black 'Christmas Tree' wellhead, it sits unproductive, 100 yards off the Devon road south of Edmonton."[12]

At the age of twenty-eight years, the "old man" of the famous Leduc field was sounding a silent warning and a rebuke to people who choose to believe their generation has better claims upon resource treasures like soil and trees and oil than those who will follow.

Notes

Chapter 1: Exploration and the Fur Trade

1. Arthur S. Morton, *A History of the Canadian West to 1870–71* (Toronto: Thomas Nelson & Sons, 1939), 51.
2. Henry Kelsey, *The Kelsey Papers* (Ottawa: Public Archives of Canada and the Public Record Office of Northern Ireland, 1929), introduction.
3. Morton, *A History of the Canadian West to 1870–71*, second edition (Toronto: University of Toronto Press, 1973), 245.
4. Ibid., 246
5. Ibid., 300.
6. J.B. Tyrrell, ed., *David Thompson's Narrative of His Explorations in Western American 1784–1812* (Toronto: The Champlain Society, 1916), 41.

Chapter 2: Red River

1. *Minutes*, February 6, 1811, Hudson's Bay Company Archives, Winnipeg.
2. Lord Selkirk to Miles Macdonell, ? 1811, Selkirk Papers, Public Archives of Canada, Ottawa.
3. Archibald MacDonald to Lord Selkirk, July 24, 1814, Red River, Selkirk Papers.
4. James Whyte (the colony surgeon) and others to Lord Selkirk, June 24, 1815, Selkirk Papers.
5. John Pritchard, who had been a North West Company wintering partner and who was in charge of Fort Souris when Sheriff Spencer had seized the huge haul of pemmican two years earlier, had since retired from the company and become a good and loyal citizen of the Selkirk settlement.
6. Alexander Ross, *The Red River Settlement* (London, 1856).
7. R. H. Clark, *Notes on the Red River Floods* (Province of Manitoba: Department of Mines and Natural Resources, 1950).
8. John Pritchard to Andrew Wedderburn, June 9, 1821, Selkirk Papers.
9. Robert Campbell, "From Highland to Fort Garry" (journal), November 6, 1832, copy in Glenbow Institute-Alberta Archives,

Calgary.
10. William Laidlaw to Lord Selkirk, July 22, 1818, Selkirk Papers.
11. Nicholas Garry, Deputy Governor, to George Simpson, February 23, 1831, London, Hudson's Bay Company Archives, Winnipeg. (With permission of the Governor and Committee of the Hudson's Bay Company.)
12. Alexander Ross, *The Red River Settlement* (London: Smith, Elder and Co., 1856; Minneapolis: Ross and Haines, 1957), 246.
13. Ibid., 244.

Chapter 3: Opening the West

1. *Hansard Parliamentary Debates* (Great Britain), no. 3, 1857, 44.
2. John Palliser, Report to the Imperial Colonial Office, April 4, 1862.
3. *Nor'-Wester*, August 28, 1860.
4. William Coldwell, diary, Provincial Archives of Manitoba, Winnipeg.
5. Robert B. Hill, *History of Manitoba* (Toronto: William Briggs, 1890), 211.
6. K. W. McNaught and Ramsay Cook, *Canada and the United States* (Toronto: Clarke, Irwin Co., 1963), 163.
7. Thomas Flanagan, *Riel and the Rebellion: 1885 Reconsidered* (Saskatoon: Western Producer Prairie Books, 1983), 3.
8. Winnipeg *Free Press*, September 16, 1876.
9. Rev. Constantine Scollan, Annual Report of Hon. David Mills, Minister of the Interior, 1877.
10. Winnipeg *Daily Free Press*, September 21, 1874.
11. Ibid., December 5, 1878.
12. Ibid., December 9, 1878.

Chapter 4: The Promised Land

1. The Dominion Lands Act, 1872, *Statues of Canada*, 35 Vic., c. 23.
2. John Macoun, *Manitoba and the Great North-West* (Guelph: World Publishing Co., 1882), 146.
3. Ibid., 213.
4. Victoria *British Colonist*, April 20, 1876.
5. Ibid., February 5, 1878.
6. James G. MacGregor, *The Klondike Rush through Edmonton* (Toronto: McClelland and Stewart, 1970), 2.
7. W. G. Hardy, *From Sea Unto Sea* (New York: Doubleday and Co., 1959), 455.
8. Grant MacEwan, *Charles Noble: Guardian of the Soil* (Saskatoon:

Western Producer Prairie Books, 1983), 75.
9. Calgary *Albertan*, editorial, October 9, 1915.

Chapter 5: Rich Land; Harsh Environment

1. L. V. Kelly, *The Range Men* (Toronto: William Briggs, 1913), 200.
2. Moose Jaw *News*, November 7, 1884.
3. *Nor'West Farmer*, October, 1884.
4. Grant MacEwan, *Blazing the Old Cattle Trails* (Saskatoon: Western Producer Prairie Books, 1962), 235.
5. George Spence, Regina *Leader-Post*, October 18, 1947.
6. R. H. Clark, *Notes on the Red River Floods*.

Chapter 6: People and Places

1. Fred Lucas, ed., *Historical Diary of Winnipeg* (Winnipeg: Cartwright and Lucas, 1923), 115.
2. Margaret McWilliams, *Manitoba Milestones* (Toronto: J. M. Dent and Sons, 1928), 158.
3. John N. Lake, "The Temperance Colonization Society and the Foundation of Saskatoon," *Narratives of Saskatoon* (Saskatoon: University of Saskatchewan Bookstore, 1927), 15.
4. *The Lethbridge News*, May 7, 1890.
5. Grant MacEwan, *Agriculture on Parade* (Toronto: Thomas Nelson and Sons, 1950), 82–87.
6. Sir Clifford Sifton, "The Immigrants Canada Wants," *Maclean's*, April 1, 1922.
7. Helen Evans Reid, *All Silent, All Damned* (Toronto, Ryerson Press, 1969), 39.
8. Calgary *Daily News*, October 6, 1908.
9. Grant MacEwan, weekly column, Calgary *Herald*, September 24, 1988.
10. Anahareo, letter to the editor, Calgary *Albertan*, May 17, 1975.
11. Dawn Grey Owl Bruce to author, June 11, 1975.
12. Anahareo, letter to the editor, Calgary *Albertan*, May 17, 1975.
13. Ken Kinkins, interview with Anahareo, *The Victorian* (Victoria), April 9, 1975.

Chapter 7: A New West

1. *Canada Year Book*, 1901 (Government Printing Bureau, 1902).
2. Ibid.
3. *Manitoba Free Press*, June 13, 1908.
4. High River *Eye Opener*, August 8, 1903.

5. Edmonton *Bulletin*, March 24, 1906.
6. Miriam Green Ellis, "Pathfinders," an address to the Canadian Women's Press Club in Edmonton, 1956.
7. J. H. Ellis, *The History of Agriculture in Manitoba, 1870–1970* (Province of Manitoba, Department of Agriculture, 1970), 243.
8. Ibid., 553.
9. Grant MacEwan, *Harvest of Bread* (Saskatoon: Western Producer Prairie Books, 1969), 98–107.
10. Toronto *Globe*, October 25, 1929.
11. R. D. Colquette, "The World's Grain Show," *The Country Guide*, Winnipeg, August, 1933.
12. Calgary *Herald*, June 17, 1975.

Index